A Volume in
Family School Community
Partnership

Promising Practices for Family
Involvement in Schools

Library of Congress Cataloging-in-Publication Data

Promising practices for family involvement in schools / edited by Diana
B. Hiatt-Michael.
   p. cm. – (Family, school, community, partnership issues ; v. 1)

Includes bibliographical references.
 ISBN 1-930608-94-2 (pbk.) – ISBN 1-930608-95-0 (hard)
 1. Education–Parent participation. 2. Home and school. I.
Hiatt-Michael, Diana B. II. Series.
 LB1048.5 .P76 2001
 371.19'2–dc21
                          2001004277

ISBN: 1-930608-94-2 (paper); 1-930608-95-0 (cloth)

Printed in the United States of America

Promising Practices for Family Involvement in Schools

Edited by

Diana B. Hiatt-Michael
Pepperdine University

INFORMATION AGE
P U B L I S H I N G

80 Mason Street
Greenwich, Connecticut 06830

This monograph is dedicated to you, the educators and practitioners, who share the authors' commitment to connecting families with their schools

CONTENTS

ACKNOWLEDGMENTS

As Editor, I extend my sincere appreciation to the dedicated scholars who contributed chapters to this monograph. Each of these scholars has a myriad of significant commitments but found the time to prepare a comprehensive chapter on a selected topic. I was honored to have the opportunity to engage in reflective dialogue with them throughout the process. I shall forever be indebted to them as they gave so much of themselves.

The contributers are listed in alphabetical order:

Don Davies, Director, Institute for Responsive Education, Boston University, MA

Mary DiCamillo, Director, The Sound Birthing Center, Santa Margarita, CA

Joyce L. Epstein, Director, Center on School, Family, and Community Partnerships, Johns Hopkins University

Vivian R. Johnson, Clinical Associate Professor, Boston University, and Senior Consultant, Institute for Responsive Education

Howard Kirschenbaum, Frontier Professor of School, Family, and Community Relations and Chair, Counseling and Human Development Program at University of Rochester

Oliver C. Moles, Jr., Education Research Analyst, Office of Educational Research and Improvement, U.S. Department of Education

Francesca K. Pomerantz, Director, ReadBoston Family Literacy Project

Beth S. Simon, Associate Research Scientist, Center on School, Family, and Community Partnerships, Johns Hopkins University

In addition to the contributers, I wish to thank my caring and enthusiastic research assistant Scott F. Gray, for his time, editing acumen, and intellectual support. Other persons who generously assisted in the online research and editing include Marilyn Angeletti, Loretta Amaro, Janet Cosman-Ross, Ciji Oakley, and Patrick Ross. I offer my gratitude to Dean John F. McManus, Provost Darryl Tippens, and President Andrew Benton who embrace scholarship endeavors at Pepperdine University and whose support made this volume possible. Lastly, my love to my husband John, who never complained about the time I devoted to this monograph, encouraged my hours at the computer, and provided caring support.

—Diana B. Hiatt-Michael
Professor of Education
Pepperdine University

LIST OF CONTRIBUTORS

Don Davies	Director, Institute for Responsive Education, Boston University, MA
Mary DiCamillo	Director, The Sound Birthing Center Santa Margarita, CA
Joyce L. Epstein	Director, Center on School, Family, and Community Partnerships, Johns Hopkins University
Diana B. Hiatt-Michael	Professor of Education, Pepperdine University
Vivian R. Johnson	Clinical Associate Professor, Boston University, and Senior Consultant, Institute for Responsive Education
Howard Kirschenbaum	Frontier Professor of School, Family, and Community Relations and Chair, Counseling and Human Development Program, University of Rochester
Oliver C. Moles, Jr.	Education Research Analyst, U.S. Department of Education
Francesca K. Pomerantz	Director, ReadBoston Family Literacy Project
Beth S. Simon	Associate Research Scientist, Center on School, Family, and Community Partnerships, Johns Hopkins University

INTRODUCTION

Diana B. Hiatt-Michael

Parent involvement as one of the eight National Education Goals has brought heightened awareness to the importance of connecting educational institutions and their communities. The eighth goal supports "school partnerships that will increase parent involvement and participation in promoting the social, emotional, and academic growth of children." Public and private educational institutions should consider the larger social context of family and community since this context affects productivity as defined by student outcomes. The purpose of this series is to provide practitioners and researchers a forum for securing the most current knowledge pertinent to family, school, and community partnership issues. Family, school, and community partnerships involve persons across educational and relational groups, including administrators, parents and family members, students, community groups, teacher training institutions, policymakers, and businesses.

This series will produce one issue annually and focus on selected themes each year. Each monograph will highlight the most comprehensive and robust theory and practice. The Executive Board and membership of the Family, School, Community Partnership Special Interest Group of the American Educational Research Association serves as the sponsor of this series. This group will determine the themes and topics for each monograph.

The theme for this first monograph is "Promising Practices for Family Involvement in Schools." This volume will address major frameworks for understanding family involvement and government support of family involvement projects in the initial chapters. The following six chapters present a theoretical base for understanding school, family, and community partnerships and research supporting promising practices. Included within each chapter are examples of research in action, focusing on specific interactive activities or programs designed to bring families and schools together. Such promising practices are organized into chapters dealing with two-way home-school communication, family literacy projects, school-site parent centers, parent- school collaborative governance, and family-school education programs spanning infancy through young adulthood. The monograph concludes with a chapter on teacher preparation for work with family, school, and community partnership issues.

Some authors selected for this monograph are internationally recognized for outstanding research in this area, and others are promising newcomers to the field. Don Davies, a kindly guru, has spearheaded parent involvement for many decades at the Institute for Responsive Education at Boston University. Joyce Epstein, with great warmth and persuasiveness, has brought together research and schools into the National Network of Partnership Schools in the Center on School, Family, and Community Partnerships at Johns Hopkins University. Ollie Moles nudges and promotes family partnership issues and research at the federal level within the US Department of Educational Research. Recognized as the authority on parent centers, Vivian Johnson, Clinical Associate Professor at Boston University, is affiliated with the Institute for Responsive Education. Howard Kirschenbaum, Professor at the University of Rochester, has worked extensively with the Rochester City School District on family, school community partnership issues and created a model course to prepare teachers to work with families. Diana Hiatt-Michael has fervently participated, taught, and devoted research to family involvement within public schools and later worked with teacher and administrator preparation as a Professor of Education at Pepperdine University. Mary DiCamillo, Francesca Pomerantz, and Beth Simon are recent doctoral graduates. Mary is active in innovative family-oriented prenatal and early childhood education research and practice. Francesca taught and conducted research in a family literacy program and currently directs the ReadBoston Family Literacy Project. Beth conducts research at the Center on School, Family, and Community Partnerships at Johns Hopkins University.

Besides their research expertise, each author brings a unique background as classroom teacher, parent, and community social advocate to their writing. Individually, most of us have spent our early professional years within the classroom, acquiring the value of connecting home with school for the benefit of the children. As parents and grandparents, we have advocated for parental interests within the school. As community advocates, we strive for collaborative communication across groups who serve children and their families. We invite you to share our passion for working with families and community groups within our schools.

CHAPTER 1

SCHOOL, FAMILY, AND COMMUNITY PARTNERSHIPS

Linking Theory to Practice

Beth S. Simon and Joyce L. Epstein

INTRODUCTION

Across the country, elementary, middle, and high schools, school districts, and state departments of education are beginning to integrate school, family, and community partnerships into comprehensive school reform (OERI, 1998; NWREL, 2001). There is a growing recognition that all aspects of school improvement—challenging curricula, instruction for active learning, rigorous assessments, and effective school management and classroom organization—are more likely to succeed if families and communities are effectively involved.

Research is accumulating information on specific ways that family and community involvement can boost and sustain student achievement, report card grades, good attendance, homework completion, positive attitudes, good behavior, and other indicators of success in school. Well-informed discourse on partnerships, however, requires a clear understanding of how educators, parents, and others may work well together to support student learning and development. This chapter provides readers with a theoretical basis for organizing and integrating knowledge on school, family, and com-

1

munity partnerships and a framework to help researchers and educators study, discuss, and implement partnership activities.

EXTENDING "PARENT INVOLVEMENT" TO "PARTNERSHIPS"

Although researchers analyze and practitioners implement parent involvement activities, there is still some confusion about what, precisely, "parent involvement" means. Does it refer to how parents are involved at home when they check children's homework, review report cards, or talk with teens about applying to college? Is it how parents are involved at school when they volunteer as chaperones for school dances, tutor students in spelling skills, or attend PTA/PTO meetings? Parent involvement, we believe, is more complex and important than any single list of practices can capture.

The term "parent involvement" is too narrow and limited a label for the work that educators, parents, and community partners must do together. Instead, we refer to "school, family, and community partnerships" to signify the broader collaborations that support children as students. Partnerships refer to the overlapping influences and shared responsibilities of families, schools, and communities for the education and development of children (Epstein, 1994, 1995). These three contexts are important influences in every child's life. To clarify how the home, school, and community interact, we turn to the theoretical model of the overlapping spheres of influence.

THEORETICAL PERSPECTIVES ON PARTNERSHIPS

Overlapping Spheres of Influence

A theoretical model of overlapping spheres of influence (Epstein, 1987, 2001) emphasizes that youngsters are best supported when families and schools have shared goals and when they work collaboratively. In addition, this model extends previous theories by including the community as an important arena of child and adolescent learning and development. Schools that base their work on the model of overlapping spheres of influence encourage families and communities to collaborate in various ways to support student learning. Educators holding this view might say, "I can do my job best if I work with families and communities toward shared goals for student success."

Figure 1 depicts the *external* model of overlapping spheres to illustrate the major contexts of students' lives—families, schools, and communities.

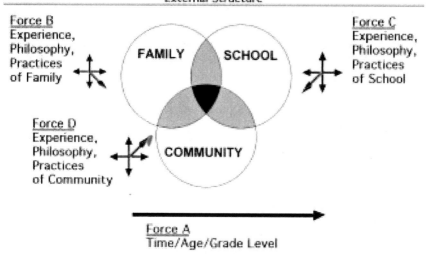

Figure 1.   Theoretical Model (from Epstein, Coates, Salinas, Sanders, & Simon, 1997)

The model shows that some family activities and some community activities are conducted independently, in the non-overlapping areas. Not all school-based activities necessarily involve families or the community. Some activities, however, are conducted jointly by partners in two or more contexts. The shaded areas in the model represent the spaces where, for example, families and schools, or schools, families, and communities *share* responsibilities for activities that support students' development and education. The overlapping spheres of schools, families, and communities may be pushed together (more overlap and more joint activities) or pulled apart (less overlap and fewer shared activities).

How many activities are shared among schools, families, and communities depend greatly on the perspectives and actions of educators, parents, and others in the community. These conditions change over time. For example, when families and educators work toward similar goals for students, the two spheres of home and school are pushed together. When schools and families avoid contact and do not work together, the spheres are pulled apart. Traditionally, as students get older, the spheres of influence are more often pulled apart if parents feel less able to support their children, and if schools assume that parents are less influential or less interested in supporting their adolescents.

The theory of overlapping spheres of influence also includes an *internal* model that identifies interpersonal interactions among parents, children, educators, and members of the community (Epstein, 1987, 2001). These exchanges may occur at the *institutional* level (e.g., when schools invite all families or community groups to an event) and at the *individual* level (e.g., when a teacher and parent confer about one student's work). The internal structure sets the student at the center of the model as the main actor in learning and as the reason why parents and educators communicate.

Of course, any exchanges and activities may be well or poorly designed and implemented, and yield positive or negative results. If successful, however, the interactions and social ties developed among partners in education will generate "social capital" that may be used to benefit students, families, schools, and the community (Coleman, 1988; Lin, 2000). For example, parents may meet and interact with other parents and with other helpful adults to obtain information, ideas, and other resources about education, which then guides their involvement at school and at home (Sheldon, in press). When positive connections occur across contexts, more students are likely to be recipients of common messages and high expectations from significant adults in their lives about the importance of school, good attendance, doing homework, and good behavior. These connections are likely to result in "family-like schools" where educators welcome parents and community partners, and treat each student as an individual; and "school-like families," where parents guide their children to fulfill their roles and responsibilities as students (Epstein, 2001).

Contrasting Perspective: Separate Influences of Home and School

Unlike the overlapping influences discussed above, another theoretical perspective focuses on the *separate* influences of families and schools in children's lives. According to this perspective, families and schools are most efficient and effective when each organization has a unique mission, and there are clear boundaries between organizational roles and responsibilities (Parsons, 1959; Waller, 1932; Weber, 1947). Teachers and school administrators with this view tend to avoid contact with families and communicate only when students are having problems. These schools tend to be less welcoming places where educators do not reach out to families, and few families actively support the school. Educators holding this view might say, "I can do my job best if parents do their job and just stay out of my way."

The *separate* and *overlapping* spheres of influence are two very different theoretical perspectives. Which one is correct? Do schools and families have only separate influences on students? Do educators do their best when families stay out of their way? Or, do students learn and develop within multiple contexts? Do schools, families, and communities overlap in many ways that support student success? Research indicates that the separate spheres of influence cannot explain the real-life social and educational development of youth (Becker and Epstein, 1982; Epstein, 1986). Instead, the overlapping spheres of influence model recognizes the simultaneous influence of schools, families, and communities in some aspects of students' lives, and may better reflect how children and adolescents develop. Studies indicate that schools, families, and communities can partner in many ways to support student success (Catsambis, 1998; Desimone, 1999; Epstein & Dauber, 1991; Ho & Willms, 1996; Lee, 1994; Schneider & Coleman, 1993; Simon, 2000; Useem, 1992; Van Voorhis, 2000).

SIX TYPES OF INVOLVEMENT

In practice, the shared interests, responsibilities, and investments of schools, families, and communities are reflected in activities that support student development and success. Partnership activities take a variety of forms to match the particular needs, goals, and interests of students and families, and to use the resources of the community. Because there are so many possible partnership activities, we will not try to list them all. Instead, we focus on a framework of six types of involvement, which organizes partnership practices. This framework is helpful not only for discussing and studying partnerships, but also for guiding educators, parents, and others to develop comprehensive partnership programs.

Based on results of research conducted in preschool, elementary, middle, and high schools, Epstein (1995) developed a framework of six types of involvement to organize how researchers and educators think about and implement partnership activities. The six types of involvement, Type 1—Parenting; Type 2—Communicating; Type 3—Volunteering; Type 4—Learning at Home; Type 5—Decision Making; and Type 6—Collaborating With the Community, represent six categories of partnerships that support student development and academic success. The six types are not a hierarchy where one type is more or less important. Rather, all six types are essential for strong, diverse, and balanced partnership programs that enable all families to find ways to be productively involved at school and in their children's education at home and in the community.

This comprehensive framework of six types of involvement extends beyond research, for use in policy and practice. For example, the framework was adopted by the National Parent Teacher Association (National PTA, 1998) as the organization's standards for family involvement. The National Education Association (Dianda & McLaren, 1996) and the American Federation of Teachers also use this framework in their materials and training. In addition, during the 2000–2001 school year, more than 1400 schools, 140 school districts, and 19 state departments of education used the framework of six types of involvement to begin developing comprehensive partnership programs as part of their membership in the ongoing and growing National Network of Partnership Schools at Johns Hopkins University. Each school in the Network organizes an Action Team for Partnerships (ATP) with teachers, a school administrator, parents, and community members. The ATPs use the framework of six types of involvement to write a plan with partnership activities that involve families and communities to help meet important school improvement goals (Epstein, 2001; Epstein et al., 1997).

In this chapter, we review the six types of involvement (sometimes called the "six keys to successful partnerships"), and discuss a few examples of partnership activities for each type. We also review some important challenges that schools must meet for each type of involvement in order to create a truly successful partnership program. Then, we point out some expected results for students, families, and teachers when key challenges are met. To illustrate how the framework is used in practice, we share stories about creative and successful ways that elementary, middle, and high schools in the National Network of Partnership Schools are implementing activities and meeting challenges for each of the six types of involvement. These stories are drawn from *Promising Partnership Practices,* an annual collection of involvement activities submitted by and distributed to National Network members (Salinas & Jansorn, 2000).

Type 1—Parenting

Families work hard to raise happy, healthy, well-adjusted children who come to school every day ready to learn. This, we know, is no simple task for any family. Programs of school, family, and community partnerships can support families by providing ongoing information and guidance on parenting skills and setting home conditions that support children's learning and behavior at every age and grade level. We refer to partnership practices that support the basic responsibilities of families as Type 1—Parenting activities. They include workshops for families on nutrition, discipline, drug abuse prevention, and other health and safety topics. In addition, schools may host support groups where families share parenting tips for getting children to bed on time, helping teens cope with peer pressure, or other child and adolescent development issues. Preschools, elementary, and secondary schools may host health clinics to help families meet immunization requirements for student enrollment. Through teachers' home visits or attendance at neighborhood meetings, or parent surveys about families' goals for children, educators can gather information to better understand students and families. The accompanying box lists a few of the many creative and successful parenting practices that support families and help teachers understand families.

TYPE 1—PARENTING
Assist families with parenting skills and setting home conditions to support children as students. Also, assist schools to understand families.

✓ Workshops on parenting and child and adolescent development
✓ Family support programs like clothing swap shops, parent-to-parent groups
✓ Home visiting programs

Source: From Epstein, Coates, Salinas, Sanders, and Simon (1997).

As discussed above, workshops are a popular Type 1—Parenting activity. Successful workshops, however, require excellent planning such as scheduling sessions with families' needs in mind. For example, planners must take into consideration how many parents are employed during the day or evening; or if childcare or transportation is needed for parents to attend a workshop. With these issues in mind, organizers might schedule some activities in the evening hours or on weekends, provide onsite childcare during the workshop, or host workshops in the community instead of at the school building to be closer to where families live.

Meeting Challenges

Even with excellent planning, however, it is unlikely that all families will attend every workshop at school. Although frustrating for organizers, only a small percentage of families who could benefit from attending workshops actually participate. Consider, then, that "workshops" refer not only to meetings on particular topics, but also to the content of a topic that may be viewed, heard, or read at convenient times and varied locations. By redefining workshops, schools can meet an important challenge for Type 1—Parenting activities: Get the information to all families, including those who cannot come to workshops (Epstein, 2001; Epstein et al., 1997). Schools may videotape a workshop and lend the recording to families who can view the workshop at home or in the school's media center. An article in the school newsletter or a special memo may summarize the workshop's content. Schools with family resource centers may provide copies of brochures or handouts that were distributed at the workshop. Schools with

Web sites may also post a summary of the workshop and list links to additional, relevant information available on the Internet.

Expected Results

When schools and families meet challenges for effective Type 1—Parenting practices, students may gain greater awareness of their families' care and supervision, and learn valuable lessons about their families' values and beliefs in the importance of education. For example, if workshop information on the importance of student attendance is widely shared in useful forms, students' attendance may improve (Epstein & Sheldon, in press). Parents may gain confidence in parenting skills as they become knowledgeable about child and adolescent development from information shared by other parents, and from school and community experts. As a result, parents may modify the home environment to better support their children and teenage learners. Students' time may be better balanced if parents guide and supervise the allocation of time to chores, homework, after-school jobs, and other extracurricular activities. With good Type 1—Parenting practices, teachers may gain a better understanding of students and their families, and may see why teachers are important partners in helping families better understand children and adolescents (Epstein, 2001; Epstein et al., 1997).

Spotlight on Type 1—Parenting

Shaker Heights High School, in Shaker Heights, Ohio, established a parent support group to address families' concerns about raising adolescents. Recognizing that the informal ways that parents get to know one another tend to decrease over the years, the school organized the support group to facilitate communication among parents of high school freshmen. A teacher and two community members facilitated the sessions, held at 8:00 p.m. so that parents could first get teens settled into evening activities. Topics discussed included: where to draw the line between respecting a teen's privacy and the parent's "right to know"; how to handle a spouse who insists on participation in sports for a teen who is not interested; how to open dialogue when a teen refuses to communicate; and how to handle stress when teens make bad choices. Parents who participated agreed to attend sessions for four weeks so that the group could build rapport and trust.

Source: Adapted from Promising Partnership Practices—1999, National Network of Partnership Schools at Johns Hopkins University.

Type 2—Communicating

Schools have a responsibility to share information with all families about students' progress; academic programs; classroom, school, and district policies; and school activities and events. Parents at all grade levels are eager for these specific kinds of information in order to better support their children and adolescents as students (Dauber & Epstein, 1993; Epstein, 1986; Sanders, Epstein, & Connors-Tadros, 1999). Type 2—Communicating practices include report cards or progress reports, parent-teacher-student conferences, newsletters with information about school policies and academic programs, voice mail systems for teachers to leave messages about homework, and Web sites that list class assignments, school events, lunch menus, and other important dates and information. Communications often contain information about students' problems in school, but may also include messages home about students' special achievements and accomplishments. Several high schools in the National Network recognized that school-to-home communications tended to focus on negative issues. In response, they established "good news" postcards for teachers to easily send messages home about students' positive achievements. This low-cost communication helped parents look forward to hearing from the school and helped teachers focus on students' positive behaviors and academic advances. The accompanying box lists a few of the many communicating practices that encourage connections between educators and families.

TYPE 2—COMMUNICATING
Conduct effective communications from school-to-home and from home-to-school about school programs and student progress.

✓ Conferences with every parent at least once a year with follow-ups as needed
✓ Folders of student work sent home regularly for parent review and comments
✓ Effective newsletters including information about school events, student activities, and parents' questions, reactions, and suggestions
✓ Clear information on all school policies, academic programs, and transitions

Source: From Epstein et al. (1997).

Simply sending home newsletters, report cards, and other communications does not mean that schools have communicated with families in a meaningful way. Families may not understand or even receive the information sent by the school. For example, in some schools, newsletters, notices, permission slips, and other messages may need to be translated into various languages to reach all families. For families with limited reading skills, information may need to be available on a recorded message that parents may access by phone.

Students often serve as messengers to transport flyers or newsletters home. However, not all information journeys successfully from teachers' desks to parents' hands. In one middle school, for example, only about a third of the newsletters made it home (Epstein & Herrick, 1991) before the school learned of this statistic and took action to improve delivery. How, then, can schools ensure that clear and understandable communications reach all families?

Meeting Challenges

One Type 2—Communicating challenge that schools must meet is to develop two-way channels of communication from school to home and from home to school (Epstein, 2001; Epstein et al., 1997). Two-way channels allow for an easy exchange of information, but also check whether parents receive and understand messages that are sent home. Channels may include a "tear-off" section of a newsletter or the bottom half of notices where parents can sign their names and jot down any questions or comments they may have. Alternatively, a school may have a Web site where parents can submit questions or comments to school personnel at any time. Schools may also use notebooks or homework agendas that children deliver between teachers and parents on a regular schedule. There are many easy and inexpensive ways for parents and teachers to communicate regularly about school programs and children's progress, keep each other up-to-date on issues or concerns, and respond to students' needs and progress.

Expected Results

When schools meet challenges for successful Type 2—Communicating activities, students and parents learn more about school activities and programs. Parents are better able to respond to student problems when notified regularly about student progress. Parents may help prevent student problems if they are well informed and can help their students make decisions about school activities, courses, and programs (Epstein, 2001; Epstein et al., 1997). In addition, when teachers inform parents about students' special or positive accomplishments, families can celebrate. Students, too, become more aware of their own progress and of what they need to do to improve or maintain grades, attendance, or behavior. Teachers improve their communication skills as they meet challenges to reach all families. With successful two-way communications, they may also learn how eager families are to remain knowledgeable partners in their children's education.

Spotlight on Type 2—Communicating

Fayetteville Elementary School, in Fayetteville, New York, recognized that although teachers sent home lots of papers for parents, there was no method for parents to communicate easily back to the school. When teachers did receive messages, they had to sift through a pile of absences and tardy excuses to get to notes or questions from parents about students' achievement, or notes of personal information about things going on in children's lives. The school developed a standard notepad, which featured a logo at the top of the page indicating two-way communication. The brightly colored notes were distributed to all parents and teachers and were well received. The school reports more effective two-way communications from home-to-school and from school-to-home.

Source: Adapted from Promising Partnership Practices—2000, National Network of Partnership Schools at Johns Hopkins University.

Type 3—Volunteering

Families support teachers, students, and the school community in many ways. They may assist individual teachers in classrooms, work one-on-one with students as tutors or mentors, chaperone field trips, serve food at the school's annual picnic, monitor the playground or cafeteria, or help with administrative tasks, such as notifying parents about student absences. Families also support the school by attending student performances, games, and assemblies. We refer to these kinds of involvement as Type 3—Volunteering activities. By providing direct assistance to teachers, school staff, and students, or by volunteering as an audience member to support students' activities and accomplishments, families contribute their time, talents, and resources. To encourage and guide families' volunteer efforts, schools may recruit and train families to volunteer in and out of the classroom. They may also survey families to identify the resources and interests of potential volunteers. Schools may set aside space for a "family room" for volunteers to assist in various activities that may be conducted outside of the classroom. For example, families may volunteer to join a "telephone tree" to call or contact all families with school-related information. The accompanying box, presents a few of the many volunteering activities that may be conducted at any grade level.

TYPE 3—VOLUNTEERING
Organize volunteers and audiences to support the school and students. Provide volunteer opportunities in various locations and at various times.

✓ Annual survey to identify interests, talents, and availability of volunteers
✓ Parent room/family center for volunteer work and resources for families
✓ Class parents, telephone trees, and other ways to share information with families
✓ Parent patrols to increase school safety

Source: From Epstein et al. (1997).

Schools can do a lot to encourage volunteering, but some schools inadvertently discourage many families from contributing their time and talents. For example, once-eager volunteers may "burn out" if the pool of helpers is too small and if the same parents are asked repeatedly to volunteer. To increase the number of volunteers and retain them from year to year, schools must recruit widely from all families, train volunteers to become confident and meaningful helpers, and carefully match volunteers' interests and talents with schools' needs. A study of more than 11,000 high school students and their parents found that 43% of parents said the school never contacted them about doing volunteer work. Not surprisingly, 72% of their teens indicated that their parents never volunteered at the school. However, when schools *did* reach out and ask parents to volunteer for the school, parents were much more likely to volunteer, particularly as members of audiences to support school events (Simon, 2000). Still, even those schools with organized systems of recruiting, training, and matching volunteers to school goals and student needs, may still exclude many potential volunteers by limiting how they define volunteer work.

Meeting Challenges

For successful volunteering programs, schools must meet a major Type 3—Volunteering challenge: provide options for volunteering not only at the school during the school day, but also in varied locations at varied times (Epstein, 2001; Epstein et al., 1997). Many families, including employed parents, cannot come to the school building during the school day. Other families may not feel comfortable volunteering at school or in the classroom. Families can volunteer, however, in a myriad of ways that support school goals and student learning at any place at any time. A parent who has access to a computer at work, for example, might volunteer to type the school's newsletter or flyers, or translate notices to another language during a lunch hour. Volunteers also can work from home to make decorations for school activities; care for classroom pets on the weekends; record books on tape so that students can read along and practice language skills; and engage in other useful activities.

Expected Results

Well-functioning partnership programs may use volunteers to help students improve specific skills and help students communicate better with adults who volunteer at school. Parents learn that they are welcome at the school, and gain self-confidence about working with teachers and students. Additionally, parent volunteers gain a better understanding of the teachers' job, just as teachers learn more about parents' talents. Some volunteers also may assist in ways that enable teachers to spend more time with individual students (Epstein, 2001; Epstein et al., 1997).

Spotlight on Type 3—Volunteering

Williamston Middle and High Schools in Williamston, Michigan recognized that all families have talents to share and contributions to make to the school community. The Action Team for Partnerships developed a survey for parents to report their interests, talents, and availability in particular volunteering activities, including those they could conduct at home. The data were presented in a "Parent Resource Directory." When teachers or staff need volunteers to help with a specific activity or event, they use the directory to find the parents who are the best match for the task at hand. The schools reported an "explosion" of parent help and involvement in the secondary schools where, previously, parent volunteers had been infrequently tapped.

Source: Adapted from Promising Partnership Practices—1998, National Network of Partnership Schools at Johns Hopkins University.

Type 4—Learning At Home

Of all partnership activities, parents are most eager to find out what they can do at home each year to help their children do better in school. Many families are not sure how or when to help with homework or how to assist their children with study skills. At the high school level, in particular, the increasingly complex curriculum may intimidate parents from working with teens at home on schoolwork. Students in middle and high school may not ask for help or engage parents in conversations about schoolwork unless their teachers encourage or require such interactions. Still, reports from more than 11,000 parents revealed that when schools sent home information about how to help teens at home with specific skills, more parents were likely to interact with their teens on homework, regardless of their own educational backgrounds (Simon, 2000). Schools may conduct a variety of Type 4—Learning at Home activities to provide families with information and strategies on supporting students' learning. For example, schools may host family fun and learning nights where teachers, families, and students read together, conduct science experiments, and engage in other educational activities. Other schools may leave their libraries open in the evening hours one or two nights a week so that families can select books to read at home with their children. Schools also may encourage families to discuss school programs and academic-related decisions with their children. The accompanying box summarizes some of the ways that schools engage families in learning at home activities.

TYPE 4—LEARNING AT HOME
Involve families with their children on homework
and in other curriculum-related activities and decisions.

✓ Information on homework policies and monitoring and discussing schoolwork at home
✓ Information on how to assist students with skills that they need to improve
✓ Regular schedule of interactive homework
✓ Summer learning packets or activities
✓ Involve families in students' academic goal setting and planning for college or work

Source: From Epstein et al. (1997).

Students and their families should not spend their evenings locking horns over homework. When parents feel pressure to teach a school subject instead of giving encouragement to support student learning, homework may become synonymous with stress or conflict. Teachers are not responsible for instructing every parent of every child in their classrooms how to *teach* every subject. Instead, teachers may encourage and guide families to *support* their students' learning by reacting to, monitoring, praising, and guiding homework, and by discussing schoolwork and ideas at home. Because parents vary greatly in their own educational background, experience, and expertise, parents should not be expected to know how to teach every topic covered in school.

Meeting Challenges

A key Type 4—Learning at Home challenge is to provide positive ways that families can support students' learning without requiring parents to teach school skills. One way to develop productive and rewarding collaborations between students and their families is through carefully designed interactive homework. Interactive homework assignments are tied to lessons taught in class and completed by students with a family partner's participation. Excellent interactive homework activities do not expect parents to teach anything. Instead, students might interview or read something they wrote to a family partner, or conduct simple science experiments with a family partner as an assistant. A recent study investigated how middle school students and their parents conducted interactive science homework. Teachers in this study used the Teachers Involve Parents in Schoolwork (TIPS) interactive homework process (Epstein, 2001; Epstein, Salinas, & Jackson, 1995), and asked family partners to monitor and react with students about science experiments. The data showed that parents and students not only liked the interactive homework more than regular homework, but that completing these assignments with a family partner boosted students' science grades over time (Van Voorhis, 2000). Similar results were reported in a study of TIPS interactive homework in language arts (Epstein, Simon, & Salinas, 1997).

Expected Results

Successful Type 4—Learning at Home activities may lead to greater homework completion, better grades, and higher test scores. Students may gain more positive attitudes toward school and schoolwork when parents participate in discussions about students' work and important school decisions that affect students' programs, courses, and learning (Van Voorhis, 2000). Also, students may gain confidence in their academic abilities. With good information on the curriculum and academic tasks and decisions, parents may gain an understanding of how to best support their children and adolescents as learners and how to guide students' future plans for college or careers. Parents also may learn more about what their children and teachers do in various subjects from week to week or month to month (Balli, Demo, & Wedman, 1998). By designing interactive homework and two-way communications with students and families about the curriculum, teachers learn more about how to support the goals of both students and parents for good work and good grades.

Spotlight on Type 4—Learning at Home

Teachers at Woodridge Primary School in Cuyahoga, Ohio make learning interactive and fun for children and parents. They host a Parent Club for families to learn how to work more effectively with children in learning-at-home activities. For each Parent Club meeting, teachers come prepared to demonstrate one learning-at-home activity that is directly linked to class lessons and learning objectives. With supplies provided, parents construct a similar activity and are taught how to use it at home with their children. For example, a first grade team worked on three take-home projects related to the math topic children were learning in class—money. Parents made a magnetic money board, learned rules, created a game board, and turned an empty box into activities that help children learn how to count money. Giving children a hands-on activity to learn about money made a lot of "cents" at Woodridge!

Source: Adapted from Promising Partnership Practices—1999, National Network of Partnership Schools at Johns Hopkins University.

Type 5—Decision Making

It is unreasonable for schools to involve families in every decision that teachers, administrators, and school staff make about the school. At the same time, there are many choices that should be made with families as partners. We refer to Type 5—Decision Making as a collection of activities that include families as participants in school decisions, and that invite all parents' voices to be heard for their input, ideas, reactions, and improvements to school decisions. Parents may be active partners on school councils, committees, and other decision-making groups. Families may work with the school staff through PTA/PTO and other participation, such as curriculum, safety, and personnel committees. Families, teachers, administrators, and community members work together as partners on committees, such as the Action Team for Partnerships, which plans an annual program of partnership using the six types of involvement. The accompanying box lists a few of the ways that families may serve in decision-making capacities.

TYPE 5—DECISION MAKING
Include families as participants in school decisions,
and develop parent leaders and representatives.

✓ Active PTA/PTO or other parent organizations, advisory councils, or committees for parent leadership and participation
✓ Action Team for Partnerships to develop the school's partnership program with practices for six types of involvement
✓ Information on school or local elections for school representatives

Source: From Epstein et al. (1997).

In most schools, only a small group of parents actively pursues leadership roles in the PTA/PTO, school improvement teams, and other decision-making committees. The small number of parent leaders may not reflect the school's larger parent population, including parents who do not want leadership roles or who are unable to attend committee meetings. Just having parents in a decision-making body, then, does not ensure that all families at the school are represented.

Meeting Challenges

Schools must meet important challenges for Type 5—Decision Making, such as including family and community leaders from all racial, ethnic, socioeconomic, and neighborhood groups represented in the school, and training leaders to be effective representatives of other families. For example, a school in California included a student body that was 80% Latino and 20% Anglo students. Just about all parent representatives and committee members, however, were from Anglo families until a new principal created neighborhood representatives, and other opportunities to improve the representation of all families (Epstein, 1994). Schools have the responsibility of recruiting and training parents who vary in their opinions and concerns, and who reflect, gather ideas from, and distribute information to parents whom they represent in their neighborhood, grade level, or cultural or other groups.

Expected Results

When students' and families' voices are well-represented in school decisions, students recognize that their interests are being monitored and protected. When students' families become part of the decision making process, students may receive more consistent messages about academic expectations from their parents and the school. Parents may gain a sense of ownership of the school as they contribute ideas and reactions to policies that affect their children's education (Epstein, 2001; Epstein et al., 1997). Parents also form working relationships with other involved families, community members, and school staff. Teachers may recognize the legitimacy of parents' views as they share in decision-making activities. Teachers and administrators also may make better informed choices and decisions the more they learn of parental perspectives and preferences.

Spotlight on Type 5—Decision Making

Aniwa Elementary School in Aniwa, Wisconsin, designed a plan to encourage families' attendance at meetings of a new, district-required school leadership team. Meeting planners had a tough task because parents' attendance was very low at PTO meetings, another Type 5—Decision Making activity. Taking into consideration the high rate of attendance at school potluck dinners, the leadership team meeting planners decided to include a potluck dinner for whole families on the agenda for the leadership meetings. Compared to families' attendance at PTO meetings when no food was shared, families' attendance at the new leadership meetings skyrocketed! After enjoying a meal with others in the school community, parents got down to business, while the children went to the gym for supervised play. The parents talked about district and school goals, brainstormed ways to improve children's scores on statewide reading tests, and listened to and talked about a video on age-appropriate learning activities at home. With some creative planning, Aniwa Elementary involved many parents—not just a few—in school decisions.

Source: Adapted from Promising Partnership Practices—2000, National Network of Partnership Schools at Johns Hopkins University.

Type 6—Collaborating With the Community

Local businesses and community groups, agencies, and individuals may provide many kinds of support and services to schools, students, and their families. Schools, too, can give back to their communities by conducting various service activities. We refer to these connections as Type 6—Collaborating With the Community practices. Activities involve reciprocal support, shared information, and useful programs and services among business and community representatives, families, students, and educators (Sanders, in press). Families may receive information on community-based health, cultural, and social support programs. Schools may establish a community service-hub where students and families come for "one-stop shopping" for counseling, job training, education, and parenting information provided by resources in the community. Families, students, and the schools also may contribute to the community in environmental protection programs, such as recycling efforts. Students and families may conduct programs for community members or provide other services, such as student-senior citizen buddy or coaching programs. Also, businesses may choose to donate time, money, or employee volunteer hours to support the high school. The accompanying box summarizes a few of the many collaborations with community activities.

TYPE 6—COLLABORATING WITH THE COMMUNITY
Coordinate resources and services from the community for families, students, and the school, and provide services to the community.

✓ Information for students and families on community, health, cultural, recreational, social support, and other programs or services
✓ Service to the community by students, families, and schools
✓ School-business partnerships

Source: From Epstein et al. (1997).

Importantly, "community" refers not only the neighborhoods immediately surrounding the school building, but also to other partners in the areas where students live, where parents work, where families worship, and where students have part-time jobs and later employment (Epstein, 2001; Epstein et al., 1997). Schools in the National Network of Partnership Schools are developing partnerships with recreational and cultural institutions (e.g., zoos, museums, libraries, and recreation centers); military and government institutions (e.g., fire departments, police departments, chambers of commerce, city councils, and other local and state governmental agencies and departments); faith organizations (e.g., churches, mosques, synagogues, and other religious organizations and charities); national service and volunteer organizations (e.g., YMCA, United Way, Urban League, Lions Club); businesses and corporations; health care organizations; and many other groups (Sanders, in press). By reaching out to a larger network of community partners, schools can better match resources from the community to needs of students, families, and the school.

Meeting Challenges

Schools must not only take the first step of connecting with community partners to help reach school goals, but also must meet an important Type 6—Collaborating With the Community challenge: ensuring that all families and all students have access to information and resources from community partners. Through workshops, information fairs, newsletters, telephone hotlines, schools' Web sites, and other avenues, schools can link families and students to the resources that are available from individuals and organizations in the community. By emphasizing equity in access to community programs and services, schools can connect many families with resources they need to support their children's success in and out of school.

Expected Results

When challenges for Type 6—Collaborating With the Community are successfully met, students may gain a sense of community and connectedness to the larger world beyond their school and family. Students may also benefit from positive relationships with diverse adults from the community. Additionally, students may improve selected skills and gain new talents through extracurricular activities conducted in business or service organization partnerships. Parents benefit from a range of community resources and from networks formed with other families in the community. Students and parents also may make contributions to their own communities through various service activities. Teachers, too, learn more about the community resources that may enrich or extend their curricula.

Spotlight on Type 6—Collaborating With the Community

Bentalou Elementary School in Baltimore, Maryland teamed up with state agencies to create a "Classroom Without Walls." The classroom was really a hiking trail where students translated school lessons about landscaping into real-life gardening experiences. With assistance from parents and others, students surveyed the land, marked off boundaries for the garden, chose native plants, prepared the ground for planting, and watered the garden. The activities encouraged students and parents to preserve nature, and showed them how their actions had a larger impact on the surrounding environment. The project's curriculum linked to science, social studies, reading, and math activities that students were learning in school, including skills tied to the statewide performance tests. When Bentalou students raise their hands, you can expect to find a few green thumbs!

Source: Adapted from Promising Partnership Practices—2000, National Network of Partnership Schools at Johns Hopkins University.

CONCLUSION

In this chapter, we explained how school, family, and community partnerships refer to the shared interests and responsibilities for students' learning and development. We reviewed the theory of overlapping spheres of influence to explain how students are at the center of this model, and how the interactions of teachers, administrators, parents, and community partners can be increased or decreased by design. Finally, we outlined a framework of six types of involvement that helps researchers frame new questions on the nature and effects of partnerships, and helps educators organize their thinking, plans, practices, and purposes of school, family, and community connections. The development of these theoretical perspectives is the result of an important evolution of views on and practices of partnership.

Historically, there have been dramatic changes in beliefs and practices of family and community involvement in education in the United States. In colonial times, families, churches, and community leaders controlled school personnel and programs. There was nearly complete "overlap" of home, school, and community influence on children's learning. Later, changing social and economic conditions led to a strong emphasis on the educational leadership of school professionals, separate and distinct from the contributions of families and communities. More recently, due to new and greater demands on schools stemming from a global, competitive economy that requires all students to have strong skills and marketable talents, educators are recognizing the need for good partnerships and shared responsibilities with families, businesses, and other community groups (Epstein & Sanders, in press). As demonstrated by the reports from members of the National Network of Partnership Schools that were spotlighted in this chapter, elementary, middle, and high schools across the country are, indeed, working to develop and implement partnership activities to meet specific goals for student success in the 21st century.

The theory and framework provide a foundation for studying and thinking about school, family, and community connections, and also serve as a basis for understanding how partnerships work in practice. This foundation should help readers integrate the topics and discussions that follow in this volume.

ACKNOWLEDGMENTS

This research was supported by grants from the U.S. Department of Education, Office of Educational Research and Improvement, OERI, to the Center for Research on the Education of Students Placed at Risk (CRESPAR), and from Disney Learning Partnership to the Center on School, Family, and Community Partnerships at Johns Hopkins University. The opinions expressed are the authors' and do not represent the policies or positions of the funding sources. For more information, contact either author by e-mail at: bsimon@csos.jhu.edu or jepstein@csos.jhu.edu. Or, visit the National Network of Partnership Schools' Web site at www.partnershipschools.org.

REFERENCES

Balli, S.J., Demo, D.H., & Wedman, J.F. (1998). Family involvement with children's homework: An intervention in the middle grades. *Family Relations, 47,* 149–157.

Becker, H.J., & Epstein, J.L. (1982). Parent involvement: A study of teacher practices. *The Elementary School Journal, 83,* 85–102.

Catsambis, S. (1998). *Expanding the knowledge of parental involvement in secondary education: Effects on high school academic success* (Report 27). Baltimore, MD: Center for Research on the Education of Students Placed at Risk, Johns Hopkins University.

Coleman, J.S. (1988). Social capital in the creation of human capital. *American Journal of Sociology, 94,* 95–120.

Dauber, S.L., & Epstein, J.L. (1993). Parents' attitudes and practices of involvement in inner-city elementary and middle schools. In N. Chavkin (Ed.), *Families and schools in a pluralistic society* (pp. 53–71). Albany: State University of New York Press.

Desimone, L. (1999). Linking parent involvement with student achievement: Do race and income matter? *Journal of Educational Research, 93,* 11–30.

Dianda, M., & McLaren, A. (1996). *Building partnerships for student learning.* National Education Association.

Epstein, J.L. (1986). Parents' reactions to teacher practices of parent involvement. *Elementary School Journal, 86,* 277–294.

Epstein, J.L. (1987). Toward a theory of family-school connections: Teacher practices and parent involvement. In K. Hurrelmann, F. Kaufmann, & F. Losel (Eds.), *Social intervention: Potential and constraints* (pp. 121–136). New York: DeGruyter.

Epstein, J.L. (1994). Theory to practice: School and family partnerships lead to school improvement and student success. In C.L. Fagnano & B.Z. Werber (Eds.), *School, family, and community interaction: A view from the firing lines* (pp. 39–52). Boulder, CO: Westview Press.

Epstein, J.L. (1995). School/family/community partnerships: Caring for the children we share. *Phi Delta Kappan, 76,* 701–712.

Epstein, J.L. (1996). Perspectives and previews on research and policy for school, family, and community partnerships. In A. Booth & J.F. Dunn (Eds.), *Family-school links: How do they affect educational outcomes?* (pp. 209–246). Mahwah, NJ: Lawrence Erlbaum Associates, Inc.

Epstein, J.L. (2001). *School, Family, and Community Partnerships: Preparing educators and improving schools.* Boulder, CO: Westview.

Epstein, J.L., Coates, L., Salinas, K.C., Sanders, M.G., & Simon, B.S. (1997). *School, family, and community partnerships: Your handbook for action.* Thousand Oaks: CA: Corwin Press, Inc.

Epstein, J.L., & Connors, L.J. (1994). *Trust fund: School, family, and community partnerships in high schools* (Report 24). Baltimore, MD: Center on Families, Communities, Schools and Children's Learning, Johns Hopkins University.

Epstein, J.L., & Dauber, S.L. (1991). School programs and teacher practices of parent involvement in inner-city elementary and middle schools. *Elementary School Journal, 91,* 289–303.

Epstein, J.L., & Herrick, S.C. (1991). *Improving school and family partnerships in urban middle grades schools: Orientation days and school newsletters* (Report 20). Baltimore, MD: The Johns Hopkins University Center for Research on Effective Schooling for Disadvantaged Students.

Epstein, J.L., Salinas, K.C., & Jackson, V.E. (1995). *Manual for teachers and prototype activities: Teachers involve parents in schoolwork (TIPS) language arts, science/health, and math interactive homework in the middle grades.* Baltimore, MD: Center on School, Family, and Community Partnerships, Johns Hopkins University.

Epstein, J.L., & Sanders, M.G. (in press). Family, school, and community partnerships. In M.H. Bornstein (Ed.), *Handbook of Parenting.* Mahwah, NJ: Lawrence Erlbaum Associates.

Epstein, J.L., & Sheldon, S.B. (in press). Improving student attendance: Effects of family and community involvement. *Journal of Educational Research.*

Epstein, J.L., Simon, B.S., & Salinas, K.C. (1997). Involving parents in homework in the middle grades. *Research Bulletin, No. 18.* Bloomington, IN: Phi Delta Kappa/Center for Evaluation, Development, and Research.

Ho, E.C., & Willms, J.D. (1996). Effects of parental involvement on eighth-grade achievement. *Sociology of Education, 69,* 126–141.

Lee, S. (1994). *Family-school connections and students' education: Continuity and change of family involvement from the middle grades to high school.* Unpublished doctoral dissertation. Johns Hopkins University, Baltimore, MD.

Lin, N. (2000). *Social capital: Theory of structure and action.* Cambridge: Cambridge University Press.

National Parent Teacher Association. (1998). *National standards for parent/family involvement programs.*

NWREL. (2001). *Comprehensive school reform demonstration program.* Portland, OR: Northwest Regional Educational Laboratory Web site: www.nwrel.org.

Office of Educational Research and Improvement. (1998). *Tools for schools.* Washington DC: U.S. Department of Education/OERI.

Parsons, T. (1959). The school class as a social system: Some of its functions in American society. *Harvard Educational Review, 29,* 297–318.

Salinas, K.C., & Jansorn, N.R. (Eds.). (2000). *Promising partnership practices.* Baltimore, MD: National Network of Partnership Schools, Johns Hopkins University. (See collections for 1998, 1999, and 2000 at www.partnershipschools.org.)

Sanders, M.G. (in press). A study of the role of "community" in comprehensive school, family, and community partnership programs. *Elementary School Journal.*

Sanders, M.G., Epstein, J.L., & Connors-Tadros, L. (1999). *Family partnerships with high schools: The parents' perspective* (Report 32). Baltimore, MD: Center for Research on the Education of Students Placed At Risk, Johns Hopkins University.

Schneider, B., & Coleman, J.S. (Eds.), (1993). *Parents, their children, and schools.* Boulder, CO: Westview Press, Inc.

Sheldon, S.B. (in press). Beyond Beliefs: Parents' social networks and beliefs and predictors of parent involvement. *Elementary School Journal.*

Simon, B.S. (2000). *Predictors of high school and family partnerships and the influence of partnerships on student success.* Unpublished doctoral dissertation, Johns Hopkins University, Baltimore, MD.

Useem, E.L. (1992). Middle school and math groups: Parents' involvement in children's placement. *Sociology of Education, 65,* 263–279.

Van Voorhis, F.L. (2000). *The effects of TIPS interactive and non-interactive homework on science achievement and family involvement of middle grades students.* Unpublished doctoral dissertation, University of Florida, Gainsville.

Waller, W. (1932). *The sociology of teaching.* New York: Wiley.

Weber, M. (1947). *The theory of social and economic organization.* New York: Oxford University Press.

CHAPTER 2

FAMILY INVOLVEMENT IN FEDERAL EDUCATION PROGRAMS

Oliver C. Moles, Jr.

INTRODUCTION

The federal government entered the arena of public education in 1965 as a response to the social action of the times. To equalize opportunities for underachieving groups, the Elementary and Secondary Education Act and Head Start authorized federal monies to fund public education and child development programs. These programs fostered the emergence of major changes within public education. One of these changes focused on parent involvement in educational programs.

This chapter reviews programs funded by the U.S. Department of Education that include provisions for parent involvement in K-12 schooling. For the purposes of this article, *parents* are defined broadly to include all family members who have responsibilities for the care and upbringing of children and youth, including stepparents, grandparents, and older siblings. *Family involvement* and *parent involvement* are used interchangeably to denote activities of all these possible resources in contemporary families.

Family involvement may take various forms both inside the family, such as support of children's home learning activities, and between family members and schools, such as communicating back and forth, attending parent education workshops, or serving on school governance boards. Several aspects of each major Department program with a family involvement component will be discussed: the legislation regarding parents, the nature and scope of the mandated parent involvement activities, and any recent evaluations of these aspects of the program. All major legislated programs will be discussed plus the Department's Partnership for Family Involvement in Education.

Most of the federal programs try to overcome various conditions affecting why children may not be achieving well. Manifestations of poverty play a large role. The families of such students tend to be economically and educationally disadvantaged as well. In general, there has been more legislative attention to the educational roles of families and developing partnerships with them in the 1990s than in earlier times, as the following information will reveal.

TITLE I

Title I, Part A is the first section of the Elementary and Secondary Education Act (ESEA), as amended by the Improving America's Schools Act (IASA) of 1994 (Public Law 103-382). It is perhaps the most prominent program in the Department designed to assist low achieving students. As of 2001, ESEA awaits a new reauthorization that could change its provisions. For the fiscal year 2001, 9.5 billion dollars were appropriated by the Congress for Title I, Part A, programs. They serve more than 10 million students.

The overall goal of Title I, Part A (henceforth Title I) is to improve the teaching and learning of children in high poverty schools so that they can meet challenging academic content and performance standards. To achieve this goal, schools decide how to spend their Title I monies. Schools with 50% or more poverty can combine their Title I funds with other resources to support comprehensive reform through school wide programs. There were no parent involvement requirements at the beginning of Title I. Later, states and localities were encouraged to promote parent and community involvement. In 1971 they were required to consult with parents on the development and operation of programs and to establish parent advisory councils. In 1974, such councils were required in all schools with 40 or more Title I students; however, in 1981 the parent advisory functions were greatly reduced with a revision of the law from Title I to Chapter 1. But, in the law's 1988 amendments, local education agencies were again required to involve parents in program planning and implementation, and also to give parents information in their own language, and to evaluate parent programs. Districts and schools were encouraged to develop parent advisory councils, resource centers, liaison staff, and resources for home learning (D'Agostino et al., 2001).

The provisions of the 1994 IASA continue the 1988 amendments and add several new provisions for parent involvement (see Sec. 1118 of PL 103-382). School districts that receive more than $500,000 per year in these funds must reserve at least 1% for parent involvement activities. Each school must also develop a school-parent compact jointly with parents that describes the school's responsibilities to provide high quality curriculum and instruction, parents' responsibilities to support their children's learning at home, and the ongoing school-home communication necessary for achieving high standards.

Title I also requires that schools develop with parents a written parent involvement plan and make it available to parents of participating children. The plan must include the involvement of parents in policies at the school level, shared responsibility for high student performance, and building further capacity for involvement. For example, schools must hold an annual meeting for Title I parents to explain the program and provide profiles on school progress toward meeting the State performance standards. In addition, schools and districts must provide materials and training including literacy training to help parents improve their children's achievement, and training for school staffs on how to reach out and work with parents as equal partners.

An extensive study of the Title I (then Chapter 1) national program in the early 1990s, known as the Prospects Study, included much information on parent involvement. Analysts found no connection between student achievement and school-based parent involvement such as volunteering or serving on school governance boards, or between student achievement and Title I school activities to involve parents. But parents reported more home-based involvement when schools offered home learning materials, open communication with parents, learning compacts and other aspects of a comprehensive program. Since stronger home-based learning is linked to Title I student reading achievement, the authors conclude that Title I may influence achievement indirectly by helping parents to become better home educators and that comprehensive programs are needed if parents are to be more involved in their children's home learning (D'Agostino et al., 2001).

Building comprehensive programs to involve parents faces serious obstacles. Representatives of the National Coalition of Title I/Chapter 1 Parents have reported that many school staffs and parents across the country are unfamiliar with the parent involvement provisions of Title I and do not know about the resources that Title I and other programs provide to support parent involvement. On the other hand, 64% of Title I principals in a national survey reported that they obtained input from parents in developing their parent involvement activities and even more (78%) said they had an advisory group or policy council that included parents. In addition, almost two-thirds of the 36 states responding to a survey reported that they have developed guidelines to support schools and districts and most provide technical assistance to schools in implementing the Title I parent involvement provisions (U.S. Department of Education, 1997b). As more time has elapsed since the last reauthorization, there may well be more local compliance, although full awareness and action on the parent involvement provisions at the school level is probably still far from universal.

A number of barriers to parent involvement have been reported by principals in Title I schools, according to a recent report to Congress (U.S. Department of Education, 1997b). Lack of time by parents and school staff heads the list, followed closely by lack of staff training to work with parents and lack of parent education to help with homework. In the highest poverty Title I schools, principals report less parent attendance at regular parent-teacher conferences and special school events than in the lowest poverty Title I schools.

Title I principals report far fewer parents attending parent-teacher conferences and special school events in middle than elementary schools. As all children progress to the upper grades, fewer parents report personal contacts initiated by the schools. Fewer parents in the upper grades also are satisfied with the communication from schools regarding how well their child is doing, available community services, opportunities to volunteer and other topics (U.S. Department of Education, 1997b).

In conjunction with the report to Congress, twenty Title I schools with successful approaches to involving families were studied. A number of ways to overcome barriers to family involvement were identified: overcoming time and resource constraints, providing information and training to parents and school staff, restructuring schools to support families better, bridging school-family differences, and tapping external supports for partnerships. This information has been disseminated widely in an Idea Book (U.S. Department of Education, 1997a) and in workshops held in many locations.

There has been little study of school-parent compacts. By 1998, compacts were used in 75% of Title I schools, and most schools with them said that parent involvement was enhanced by the compacts (D'Agostino et al., 2001). The development and implementation of new and promising compacts were analyzed in five Title I schools. All of these schools viewed the written compact as part of their larger parent involvement efforts. Still, stakeholders said it was difficult to maintain active support for the compacts after their initial introduction. Compact-related discussions and activities became less visible over time making the compact's impact sometimes questionable (Funkhouser, Stief, & Allen, 1998). Thus, serious obstacles limit full use of Title I services by parents, and there is much yet to learn about the effects of the current Title I provisions for parent involvement in their children's education. New studies of the Title I program should help to fill this gap.

MIGRANT EDUCATION

When schools serve migrant and other highly mobile students, developing effective partnerships with parents can be a challenge. Such parents tend to stay in a school or district too short a time to become involved in school planning and committees. Their mobility also makes it hard for them and for school staffs to develop relationships with each other.

A program of educational services for the children of migratory workers has been a part of Title I of the ESEA since 1966. Federal funds go to state education agencies that typically provide sub-grants to local education agencies to provide supplemental education and support services. Services are to be integrated with Title I grants and other related programs. More than 80% of the some 580,000 migrant students are Hispanic, and about half are English language learners (Weiner, Leighton, & Funkhouser, 2000).

Under the current ESEA school districts receiving migrant education program funds must provide the same level of parent consultation as is required by Title I. Programs also provide for advocacy and outreach activities for migratory children and their families including helping them gain access to other education, health, nutrition and social services. Except for school-wide Title I programs with many migrant students, schools tend to implement parent involvement activities without regard to whether parents are migrants.

The Congress mandated a study of migrant student participation in school-wide Title I programs. These approximately 2770 schools served about 28% of the children eligible for migrant education programs. Parent involvement received considerable attention in the report of this study (Siler et al., 1999). The nationally sampled schools with school-wide programs in this study were not likely to target migrant parents as a group. However, the schools surveyed considered parent involvement important, and they tried a range of means from formal committees to social events to encourage parents to become active in their children's education and to feel welcome in the schools. For migrant parents, the most common means cited by principals was providing conferences, assemblies, and fairs, closely followed by personal contacts.

About 75% of the surveyed schools had parent liaisons or social workers charged with maintaining ongoing contacts with all parents. In half of the schools teachers made home visits to parents. Rural schools and those with more than 70 migrant students were most likely to have staff contacts with migrant parents. About half of the schools surveyed indicated that parents of migrant students were actively involved in developing their school-wide plans. More than 80% of the schools reported that activities for parents were introduced or strengthened due to implementing their school-wide program. Schools that introduced or strengthened parent activities when they implemented school-wide Title I programs tended to have migrant parents and/or staff involved in developing the school-wide plan and larger numbers of migrant students (Siler et al., 1999). This study suggests that the federal requirements for migrant parent outreach and advice were fulfilled by half or more of the sampled schools with school-wide Title I programs, especially if they had large numbers of migrant students. Establishing a school-wide program seems to have stimulated parent involvement activities in a large majority of these schools.

PARENT INFORMATION AND RESOURCE CENTERS

The Goals 2000: Educate America Act of 1994 established a program of state Parent Information and Resource Centers. Their purpose broadly is to increase parents' knowledge of child-rearing activities, to strengthen partnerships between parents and professionals, and to promote the development of assisted children. Training and support is given to parents of children from birth through high school and to persons and organizations that work with them. At least half the funds must go to areas with many low-income families. Part of the funds must also be used to operate the Home Instruction Program for Preschool Youngsters (HIPPY) or the Parents as Teachers program (Public Law 103-227).

The Parents as Teachers program has grown to national proportions from its start in Missouri. It provides regular home visits by certified parent educators, group meetings among parents, developmental screenings, and links with other community services for parents of 0–3 year olds. A series of evaluation studies has shown higher intellectual and social skills and school achievement among program children than among comparison groups, and parents were also more involved with their children's schools (Parents as Teachers National Center, 1998).

HIPPY is an early learning program for 4–5 year olds of parents with limited formal education. It includes bimonthly home visits by paraprofessionals and bimonthly group meetings led by a professional coordinator. HIPPY focuses on parent and child learning experiences, providing resource materials to parents, and other activities to help parents improve learning at home. While earlier studies have been promising, a comprehensive American evaluation found positive results for parent and child behaviors associated with school success in one cohort of children but not in a second one (Baker & Piotrkowski, 1996).

There is now a Parent Information and Resource Center in every state. Since the centers began in 1995, a large number of parents and families have been served.

More than 2.5 million families have received direct services as have 43,000 school personnel since the inception of the program (McFarland, 2000). In order to increase the flow of information, the centers use strategies from disseminating flyers and newsletters to presentations at public events, in care centers, and in Head Start and local school classes. Many centers cosponsor training with state and national affiliates and organizations. The most frequently offered services to increase parents' knowledge of educational issues are (in order) brochures and pamphlets, parent and school personnel workshops, referral services, web sites, audio/video tapes, and parent support groups (McFarland, 2000).

While no systematic study of center effects has been done, much information on individual program activities has been provided by the centers. The national technical assistance organization for the centers concludes that parents are being equipped to be more involved in various aspects of their children's education and that schools and agencies are assisting families more due to the centers' work (McFarland, 2000).

BILINGUAL EDUCATION

Title VII of the amended ESEA authorizes programs that serve children with limited English proficiency (LEP). The purpose of these programs, which are administered by the Office of Bilingual Education and Minority Language Affairs (OBEMLA), is to support State and local education agency efforts to develop the English language skills and academic achievement of LEP children. Funds may be used for parent outreach and training activities to help parents become more actively involved in their children's education. Local education agencies are required to inform parents about the program and why their children were selected. Parents may decline to enroll their children in the program if they wish. There are almost 700 local projects at present.

The Bilingual Education Act of 1968 is the origin of this program. A number of family English literacy projects have been supported by OBEMLA in past years. These projects were designed to help LEP adults and out-of-school youth become competent in the English language and to provide instruction on how parents and other family members can facilitate the achievement of their children. One such program at Florida International University demonstrated a completion rate much higher than comparable adult education programs, and strong increases in English literacy skills, parent involvement in schools and children's academic performance (Garcia, 1993).

There are no national data on the parent involvement aspects of these bilingual education programs. However, information from abstracts of several local projects gives an indication of the range of parent activities. A Los Angeles County elementary school with a largely Hispanic student body uses parents as tutors in phonemic awareness, language development and reading strategies in after school and extended school year programs. A Dallas, Texas elementary school offers classes in English as a second language to Hispanic parents. A full time parent liaison helps parents become comfortable with American schools and encourages their participation in school activities. In coordination with Even Start (see below), this school provides parenting activities, home visits, and instruction on helping students with schoolwork. A New York City high school with many Asian immigrant students provides English literacy and parenting classes on Saturdays and other services to parents. Thus parent outreach and training comes in a variety of forms in the OBEMLA programs.

EVEN START

The Even Start Family Literacy Program provides low-income families with a unified program that integrates early childhood education, adult literacy training intended to lead to economic self-sufficiency, parenting education, and interactive literacy activities between children and their parents. Parenting education is to help parents become better primary teachers of their children and full partners in their education. The children range from birth through seven years of age. Each family must also include a parent who is eligible for adult basic education.

Even Start was first authorized in 1988 and is Part B of Title I of the Elementary and Secondary Education Act of 1965 (ESEA). Even Start now has 1400 projects in all 50 states and served 36,000 families in 1999–2000. It draws families that are the most disadvantaged in income and literacy levels; in 1998–99, 85% of adults had not finished high school when they enrolled in Even Start (St. Pierre et al., 2001). Programs must include home-based instructional services for each family, recruitment and screening procedures, flexible service delivery, and support services such as child care and transportation, as well as research-based instructional programs that promote adult literacy, train parents to support the educational growth of their children, and prepare for children's success in school.

An independent evaluation of each local Even Start program is required. A study of these local evaluations for 1996–97 showed a consistent pattern of gains on measures of child and adult development. However, only 10% of these studies used comparison groups. While the studies concentrated on effects on participants, they did not provide much information to help improve the local programs (St. Pierre, Ricciuti, & Creps, 2000).

A review of all completed national evaluations of Even Start showed that adults increased their literacy level and educational attainment after being in the program, but so did control groups. On children's development, those in Even Start increased their language development and reading readiness skills, but control group children either gained similar amounts or caught up in the next year when they entered preschool or kindergarten. On parenting skills, Even Start families gained on measures of cognitive stimulation and emotional support provided to children more than would be expected without Even Start. However, in the In-Depth Study the control group made similar gains in these areas. Only for kinds of reading material in the home, which is a targeted activity, did Even Start families gain more than the controls. These results may be due to a weakening of the earlier literacy-based parenting education focus (St. Pierre et al., 1998). A third national Even Start evaluation is in the field and some impact findings will be available in 2002. This evaluation could show stronger benefits since Even Start has been serving fewer families with more intensive services in recent years.

SPECIAL EDUCATION

Special education is a form of instruction designed for the unique needs of children with disabilities. There is no cost to the parents. Special education can be conducted in the classroom, the home, a hospital or institution, or other settings. Each year more than 5 million children 6–21 years of age receive special education and related services in the United States (NICHCY, 1999).

The number of children with disabilities receiving special education and related services has grown steadily since the Education for All Handicapped Children Act was passed in 1975. According to its successor, the Individuals with Disabilities Education Act (IDEA) of 1990, the disability must affect the child's educational performance for special educational services to be required. There are 13 categories of disability. The most common types among students aged 6–21 are specific learning disabilities (51%), speech and language impairments (19%), mental retardation (11%), and emotional disturbance (8%) (U.S. Department of Education, 2000).

If parents think their child has a disability, they can ask the school for an evaluation. They can also contact one of the 94 Parent Training and Information centers across the country to learn more about special education, their rights and responsibilities, and the law. In addition, there are 13 Community Parent Resource Centers that help meet the needs of racially and ethnically diverse communities. For eligible children, an Individualized Education Program (IEP) is drawn up to set learning goals and to identify the services to be provided for the child. Parents have the right to be involved in developing their child's IEP and to consent or refuse decisions about their child's initial placement (NICHCY, 1999). In fact, the IDEA challenges schools to focus on the family as the unit of service instead of the child.

The IDEA amendments of 1997 expanded opportunities for parents and school staffs to work in partnership at the state and local level. A new federal continuous monitoring process that reviews state activities solicits input from state-specific steering committees of parents, agencies and other stakeholders. The monitoring process has found these kinds of promising practices: joint training that includes parent groups, training materials developed with parents, and mediation to resolve conflicts where parents report that they are valued as partners in the mediation. (States must now create such a mediation system.) Parents are supposed to be part of the group that reviews evaluation data to decide whether a child has a disability, although this does not occur in all states. However, in a number of states parents and communities provide strong support for the education of their children, and schools actively involve parents in meetings about their child's special education (U.S. Department of Education, 2000).

INDIAN EDUCATION

Title IX of the Elementary and Secondary Education Act of 1965 as amended supports local and State educational agencies and Indian tribes and organizations among other entities to improve the teaching and learning of American Indian and Alaska native children and adults and to meet their special educational and culturally-related academic needs. There are more than 1100 grantees. The Title IX program encourages all Indian students to achieve to the same high standards expected of all students and promotes comprehensive planning by local school districts to meet the needs of Indian children.

Title IX requires that the local education agency (LEA) develop their Indian education program in consultation with a committee of parents of Indian children and where appropriate secondary school students. The LEA must also assess the progress of the children in its schools and provide the results of that assessment to the parent committee (Public Law 103-382). The LEA must also operate and evaluate the program with parents of the children being served.

Provisions for parent involvement were incorporated as early as the Indian Education Act of 1972. In 1993 the Office of Indian Education showcased effective programs. Each of these programs promoted native culture and language. One criterion for selection was parent/community involvement throughout the school year. One program used a home-school coordinator to monitor school attendance and visit homes to work with parents to improve attendance and reduce student dropouts. Several celebrated student successes with community activities and held naming ceremonies for students that build bonds with families and the community (U.S. Department of Education, 1993).

Now every grantee except Bureau of Indian Affairs funded schools is required to have a parent committee. There are no studies of the current parent involvement requirements, but performance reports are being collected on various aspects of the overall program for future analyses (Brayboy, personal communication).

THE PARTNERSHIP FOR FAMILY INVOLVEMENT IN EDUCATION

The U.S. Department of Education is engaged in a Partnership for Family Involvement in Education with more than 7000 family and education, community, business and religious organizations with many at the national level. Begun in 1994, the Partnership aims to increase opportunities for family involvement in their children's education at home and at school, and to further children's learning and achievement. It holds forums and conferences, provides partners with partnership building tools, and uses local best practices and research findings to mobilize interest and activity (U.S. Department of Education, 2001).

An extensive white paper called *Strong Families, Strong Schools* (U.S. Department of Education, 1994) presents the rationale for the Partnership. It draws on research and promising practices to show how families, schools and other organizations can collaborate and contribute to children's learning. Each year America Goes Back to School activity kits have highlighted promising approaches and local activities for all partners. These kits were distributed to all public schools in earlier years. The Partnership has also developed materials for preparing teachers to work with families (Shartrand et al., 1997), employer booklets, and a report with strategies to improve the participation of fathers in children's learning (U.S. Department of Education and U.S. Department of Health and Human Services, 2000).

A key aspect of the Partnership is to help schools involve all parents in their children's education. To this end, the Partnership has produced a booklet of accumulated knowledge and fresh ideas on school outreach strategies called *Reaching All Families* (Moles, 1996) and mailed it to every public school in the country. The monthly bulletin of the Department *Community Update* features local and national partnership activities of schools and other organizations. A detailed web site (www.pfie.ed.gov) also displays various publications and activities of the Partnership.

Several customer satisfaction surveys have been conducted with members of the Partnership. During 1999 samples of the employer and family-school partners were queried. Most respondents in both groups felt their membership had been valuable and most often joined out of a commitment to education and to discover new ways to promote learning. Overall, the surveyed family-school partners judged most of the materials produced by the Partnership to be helpful, though focus groups were less positive. The resources deemed helpful most often by family-school partners were the web site, Goals 2000 materials, the satellite town meetings, and the Department's 1-800 helpline (Westat, 2000). Similar surveys of the religious groups and community organizations that are partners were conducted in 2000. A majority of respondents joined the Partnership for the same reason as the other kinds of partners mentioned (U.S. Department of Education, 2001b).

CONCLUSION

It is clear that the legislation for various programs of the U.S. Department of Education devotes considerable attention to the supporting role of families. This often takes the form of involving parents in the planning and review of programs. The family involvement theme also appears in provisions for outreach and training to help families strengthen their home learning environments and provisions to coordinate their efforts better with the schools. Some evidence presented suggests that comprehensive programs to help parents support their children's home learning are more beneficial to school achievement than other forms of parent involvement (D'Agostino et al., 2001). The Partnership for Family Involvement in Education can help provide the background information and strategies to make this happen.

There is much information from individual local projects about their family involvement activities, and most programs have overall program statistics. Lacking in most cases, however, are strong evaluations of the benefits of the programs. When strong evaluation designs are employed, as in comparing Even Start participants to other similar children and families over time, program benefits may become less clear than would otherwise be supposed. Despite that possibility, strong evaluations are important to provide convincing information on which to base program changes and improvements.

Barriers to parent and family participation are a potential problem in all service programs however they are funded. Barriers may reside in the lives of families and also in programs themselves and the ways they communicate with families. Approaches to overcome various barriers have been identified for Title I schools (U.S. Department of Education, 1997a). This line of study deserves to be expanded for other programs. The resources that families can bring to the education of their children need to be strengthened and utilized to the fullest if the nation is to see that all its children achieve to high standards.

For more information on these programs of the U.S. Department of Education, one may consult the Department web site at www.ed.gov or call 1-800-USA-LEARN. The Partnership for Family Involvement in Education has its own web site at http://pfie.ed.gov.

ACKNOWLEDGMENTS

I wish to express my gratitude to the following persons from the U.S. Department of Education for their very helpful comments on this paper: Lonna Jones, Patricia McKee, Tracy Rimdzius, Thomas Skelly, Steve Winnick, and Lorraine Wise.

REFERENCES

Baker, A., & Piotrkowski, C. (1996). *Parents and children through the school years: The effects of the Home Instruction Program for Preschool Youngsters.* New York: National Council of Jewish Women Center for the Child.

Brayboy, M. (2000). Office of Indian Education, U.S. Department of Education. Personal communication.

D'Agostino, J., Hedges, L., Wong, K., & Borman, G. (2001). Title I parent-involvement programs: Effects on parenting practices and student achievement. In G. Borman, S. Stringfield, & R. Slavin (Eds.), *Title I: Compensatory education at the crossroads.* Mahway, NJ: Lawrence Erlbaum.

Funkhouser, J., Stief, E., & Allen, S. (1998). *Title I school-parent compacts: Supporting partnerships to improve learning.* Washington, DC: Policy Studies Associates, Inc.

Garcia, D. (1993). *Family English literacy project: PEP submission.* Miami, FL: Florida International University, College of Education, Family English literacy program.

McFarland & Associates, Inc. (2000). *Parental Information and Resource Centers' annual report.* Silver Spring, MD: Author.

Moles, O. (1996). *Reaching all families: Creating family-friendly schools.* Washington, DC: U.S. Department of Education, Office of Educational Research and Improvement.

NICHCY. (1999). *Questions often asked by parents about special education services* (4th ed.). Washington, DC: National Information Center for Children and Youth with Disabilities.

Parents as Teachers National Center. (1998). *Evaluations of parents as teachers.* St. Louis, MO: Author.

Public Law 103–227. (1994). *Goals 2000: Educate America Act.* Washington, DC: Government Printing Office.

Public Law 103–382. (1994). *The Improving America's Schools Act of 1994.* Washington, DC: Government Printing Office.

Shartrand, A., Weiss, H., Kreider, H., & Lopez, M. (1997). *New skills for new schools: Preparing teachers in family involvement.* Cambridge, MA: Harvard Family Research Project, Harvard Graduate School of Education.

Siler, A., Stolzberg, S., von Glatz, A., & Strang, W. (1999). *Report of the Congressionally mandated study of migrant student participation in schoolwide programs.* Rockville, MD: Westat, Inc.

St. Pierre, R., Gamse, B., Alamprese, J., Rimdzius, T., & Tao, F. (1998). *Even Start: Evidence from the past and a look to the future.* Washington, DC: U.S. Department of Education, Planning and Evaluation Service.

St. Pierre, R., Ricciutti, A., & Creps, C. (2000). *Synthesis of local and state Even Start evaluations.* Washington, DC: U.S. Department of Education, Planning and Evaluation Service.

St. Pierre, R., Ricciuti, A., Tao, F., Creps, C., Kumagawa, T., & Ross, W. (2001). *Third national Even Start evaluation: Interim report on 1997–1998 and 1998–1999 data.* Washington, DC: U.S. Department of Education, Planning and Evaluation Service

U.S. Department of Education. (1993). *Effective showcase projects Office of Indian Education.* Washington, DC: Author.

U.S. Department of Education. (1994). *Strong families, strong schools: Building community partnerships for learning.* Washington, DC: Author

U.S. Department of Education. (1997a). *Family involvement in children's education: Successful local approaches.* Washington, DC: U.S. Department of Education, Office of Educational Research and Improvement.

U.S. Department of Education. (1997b). *Overcoming barriers to family involvement in Title I schools: Report to Congress.* Washington, DC: U.S. Department of Education, Office of Educational Research and Improvement.

U.S. Department of Education. (2000). *To assure the free appropriate public education of all children with disabilities: Twenty-second annual report to Congress on the implementation of the Individuals with Disabilities Education Act.* Washington, DC: Author

U.S. Department of Education. (2001a). *The Partnership for Family Involvement in Education: Who we are and what we do.* Washington, DC: Author.

U.S. Department of Education (2001b). *The Partnership for Family Involvement in Education: 2000 survey of religious and community partners.* Washington, DC: Author.

U.S. Department of Education and U.S. Department of Health and Human Services. (2000). *A call to commitment: Fathers' involvement in children's learning.* Washington, DC: Author.

Weiner, l., Leighton, M., & Funkhouser, J. (2000). *Helping Hispanic students reach high academic standards: An idea book.* Washington, DC: U.S. Department of Education.

Westat. (2000). *Partnership for family involvement in education: Customer satisfaction study* (Final report). Rockville, MD: Author.

CHAPTER 3

HOME-SCHOOL COMMUNICATION

Diana B. Hiatt-Michael

INTRODUCTION

"How I dread this conference with Jose's mom. She takes offense at every suggestion I make." Although both teachers and parents may deeply care about the child, teachers and parents may fear communicating their concerns to each other. Open and regular home-school, two-way communication will replace these fears with knowledge, confidence, and caring to work with each other. Educators and homes have many diverse options to implement this two-way communication and create a collaborative climate between home and school.

Establishing two-way communication between families and the school becomes a critical aspect of school life, according to Simon and Epstein (this volume, Ch. 1) because the child is the focus of the educational enterprise. However, educators play the initial role to reach out and connect with families in order to create and maintain this two-way communication. The better the communication between the home and school, the less stress the child experiences as he navigates between these two cultures.

COMMUNICATION BEGINS AT THE SCHOOL DOOR

Communication friendly schools set the tone at the front door. Warm colors, a cozy place to sit down, student work displayed, and friendly staff make coming to school a pleasant experience. In Lawndale, California, each school devoted a small sum of discretionary funds to purchase a new couch, chairs and tables that created a home-like atmosphere in the reception area. The coffee and end tables display parent-related materials. This inviting ambiance encourages parents to sit, converse, and complete school forms in this area.

Parents and children highlight the importance of the teacher being at the classroom door, smiling and sharing a welcome. This begins the school day on a positive note. The teacher's smile and pleasant words when the child arrives at school reassures both child and parent that the teacher will care for the child while the parent is gone. Personal communication between teachers and family members before and after school provides opportunities to share information or concerns in a casual atmosphere.

An open door policy for families entering the school and setting appointments with teachers removes barriers that often separate schools and families. Part of that open door policy is installing telephones in every classroom. An example of an open door policy is to publish a time period in which all teachers are available for a walk-in session, such as 30 minutes at the beginning of school, on one day per week. Parents at the Rodney B. Cox Elementary School in Dade County, Florida, report that the Open Door policy has promoted a sense of acceptance and warmth between staff and parents.

Because creating positive home-school communication requires a full school commitment, every individual within the school serves as a conduit for information and feeling tone. "Breakfast with the Principal" is a monthly practice at Robert L. Campbell PAU in Bellflower, California. Once per month from 7:30–9:30 a.m. on an open door basis, the principal hosts a breakfast for family members. He invites active members of the PTO to participate and encourages open communication. Parents who attend discuss personal as well as school concerns. Frequently, during these breakfast sessions, the principal connects parents to social agencies that can serve their needs such as homelessness, health problems, drug abuse, or child abuse. He regards these sessions as positive experiences for all participants: families, their children, school staff, and the community.

Frances Starms Early Childhood Center in urban Milwaukee selects staff who are open, warm, and caring toward families from the receptionist, to the parent who serves as the Family Center liaison and the building custodians. The school dedicated a large vibrant front room for a family center, filled with books and toys to lend families, parent materials, and comfortable furniture for parent meetings. This room bustles with parent activity.

For schools with limited or non-English speaking parents, Nicolau and Ramos (1993) reviewed 42 projects and suggested that staffing the reception area with persons who speak the native language of the families promotes parent involvement. Some parents, not literate in their native language or English, require a native-speaking staff member to help them complete necessary forms and understand critical school policies.

REACHING OUT

The most powerful form of communication is personal. The teacher and school need to reach out to parents if they expect family involvement (Decker & Majerczyk, 2000; Johnstone, 1997). Hoover-Dempsey (1995) urges schools to send a steady flow of invitations. The more opportunities there are for personal messages and contact, the stronger will be the bonds that link home and school. A review of national data indicated that reaching out to parents by the school affected parent attendance and volunteering more than other variables, such as gender, race, ethnicity, and socioeconomic status (Simon, 2001). This holds true especially for Hispanic parents who are more sensitive to nonverbal indicators of feelings (Espinosa, 1995). Though expected communication is two-way in American mainstream culture, in the Hispanic as well as Asian cultures, parents often wait for the school to initiate the request.

Pen Greene Centre, established in 1983 in the United Kingdom, was created on the basis that schools must reach out to parents (Whalley, 2001). The Centre, working on the assumption that all people are self-directed and all participants care about the welfare of the child, opened its doors to new parents with the vision of a community educational enterprise. When the child begins school, the child's teacher asks that a member of the family spend the first days or weeks within the classroom. During the direct daily exchanges, the family member learns first-hand the child's school life and shares with the teacher any information regarding the child's past or home experiences. As central to their endeavor, the Centre connects families to social agencies and services throughout the community.

The "Met," Metropolitan Regional Career and Technical Center in Providence, Rhode Island, a school with an ethnically diverse student population, focuses on Full Family Engagement, whose title represents the school's concern about total family life, not simply the child's life at school (personal communication, 2001). The school advertises that it enrolls families, not simply the child. The school belongs to the Family, School, and Community Partnership network and is a member of the Essential Schools.

At the Met, staff pair veteran families with new families so that the veteran parents help the new family meet and get acquainted with the school's network of families. The veteran family initiates invitations to the new families and attends activities with them in order to make the new families feel comfortable. Met staff continues their promotion of home-school connections throughout the school year, building upon these initial activities. Parents participate in planning the learning goals with their child and a teacher-advisor, attend thrice-yearly team meetings, and keep in touch with the school via telephone or e-mail (Cushman, 1998). The year ends with most parents present at the child's culminating exhibition, in which the student demonstrates the year's academic achievements.

Reaching out to the home early in the school year is important at all levels of schooling. Educators contacting parents early for positive interactions can help to change parents' perception of contact with schools as negative (Moles, 1999). At the preschool or kindergarten levels, the teacher may make an introductory phone call to build rapport and welcome their child to school before or during the first three weeks of the new academic year. To prepare for these important initial telephone calls, teachers should prepare notes regarding items to be discussed. During the conversation, McEwan (1998) recommends that the teacher sound enthusiastic, actively listen to the parent or family member, take notes during the conversation, and perform any needed requests by the parent. An essential requirement is that administrators support this activity and provide teachers with time and a private place to conduct the phone calls. At the secondary level, teachers might send a voice mail, e-mail, or newsletter with a welcome note, overview of the course, and course expectations.

Reaching-out methods throughout the school year include sending positive stickers or messages to the home. One school prints Happy-Grams so that teachers will send home notes to parents complimenting students for achievement or positive behavior (Redding, 1995). Parent/school journals connect families to their child's classroom teacher on a regular and intimate basis (Finnegan, 1997). To begin the process of using parent journals, classroom teachers encourage parents to write their ideas in a notebook or e-mail and send them to the teacher. The teacher responds to the comments and sends the journal or e-mail back to the family. This two-way dialogue continues throughout the school year.

At Hueco Elementary in El Paso, Texas, the principal developed a monthly Parent Communication Council so that families had a regular open forum (Funkhouser & Gonzales, 1998). The focus of this council is to listen and share concerns from the parents. In Lennox, California, the assistant superintendent asked family and community members to share perceived problems with the school at an Open Community Forum. During this open meeting, the parents, their children, and community expressed concern regarding gang harassment to and from school. Out of that meeting, the parents developed a neighborhood watch so children could safely walk to and from school without fear.

The personal approach to reaching out to parents is essential at those sites in which the cultures of the school staff and home differ or there is diversity among the school families. Diversity of cultures within a locality may generate mistrust and distance among the different culture groups. In Southern California, many localities report two to four cultures within the town. Espinosa (1995) noted that Hispanic parents do not seem to respond to written material, such as flyers or newsletters, even if these are published in the parents' native language, until direct personal contact has been created. Nicolau and Ramos (1993) remarked that in Hispanic culture the family is responsible for providing basic needs and discipline and the school's role is to instill knowledge. They noted a successful way to increase parent attendance at school events was parent to parent. The principal at one site encouraged parents familiar with the school to bring three other parents to a school meeting, preferably hosted at a community center outside the school. They report that these informal meetings, based on interests of parents, establish open connections between home and school. In the Mexican-American community the more personal the approach, the more the family will feel comfortable at the school (Kelty, 1997). Kelty (1997) found that Hispanic parents indicated personal contact by the school prior to an event was the reason they attended the event.

At Hillside Elementary School in Los Angeles, the Chinese principal acts within the cultural norm of these Asian groups—Chinese, Taiwanese, and Vietnamese. She extends a formal welcome to parents in Chinese as well as English, preparing newsletters in both languages. She remarked that Asian parents expect their children to attend school and the school to assume responsibility for the educational process. The work ethic of the Asian culture demands that parents spend many hours away from home. They respect schools that understand their cultural values and schedule school activities with deference to these values. These parents regularly attended school meetings out of respect for this principal, who spoke two Chinese dialects as well as English and wrote in fluent English and Chinese. Gate Elementary School in Los Angeles reaches out to the parents and offers the site for a Chinese School on Saturday so students may continue their study of Chinese.

Across cultures, ethnic groups, and gender, Moles (1999) reports higher parent involvement at schools if teachers' or parent liaisons make home visits to enlist family involvement. It appears that many parents feel more at ease and comfortable speaking within the intimacy of the home environment and with someone from the same culture.

REPORTING STUDENT ACADEMIC PROGRESS

A review of school practices indicates that parent-teacher conferences and school newsletters are the most pervasive methods for home-school communication (Hiatt-Michael, 2000). These findings also revealed that teachers and administrators consider these to be communication from the school to the home. The PTA (Stein & Thorkildsen, 1999) reported that a large survey completed by teachers indicated that the most important way in which parents can help their child is to attend a conference with the teacher. This section will deal with report cards and home-school conferences. A later section will discuss newsletters.

Report cards became a school practice at the same time that graded schools mushroomed across the country in the mid-1800s. Report cards emerged during modernization of the industrial society and provided standards and grades to rate each student's educational progress in school.

Report cards, currently considered the traditional form of school to parent communication, often are viewed as a punitive form of communication (Moles, 1999). However, report cards can be two-way communication if the district provides ways for parents to respond. Funkhouser and Gonzales (1998) propose that report cards include sections to request the parents' perceptions of children's homework activity, use of TV/e-mail time, pleasure reading, academic progress, or work on self-initiated projects.

Regularly scheduled parent conferences began to augment the ubiquitous school report card during the second half of the 20th century. Parent conferences grew out of the mental hygiene and teaching the "whole child" reforms during 1930s. During that period, teachers were hired to serve as school counselors in some schools, connecting the school and home. Progressive schools implemented the concept of the parent-teacher conference as a means to translate the new curriculum to parents. During the years following WWII, parent-teacher conferences rapidly expanded to other schools despite a burgeoning student school population and teacher shortages. These parent-teachers conferences connected the increasing numbers of urban and suburban parents to the modern school. These conferences provided an equal opportunity for every parent to participate and understand the academic curriculum and new instructional techniques. During this period, many school districts across the country prepared elaborate handbooks for teachers on parent conferencing.

Formally scheduled parent conferencing has become an accepted norm within all schools, private and public, across America (Hiatt-Michael, 2000b, 2001). Conferences tend to be held in fall at the same time the first student progress report or report card is due and then again in spring following testing and in preparation for next year's placement. These conferences seem to be a source of concern to new teachers. This is the one aspect of parent involvement that appears to receive attention in preservice training (Hiatt-Michael, 2000a).

Schools often regard parent conferences simply as a one-way personalization of the report card, but parent conferences offer opportunities for dialogue. During this dialogue, the teacher perceives the parent perspective. This perspective provides a basis for the teacher's knowledge of the family and the student. Redding (1995) reports that setting an agenda for a formal parent-teacher conference is considered desirable according to surveys of school district brochures on the topic. An agenda provides a structure and direction to the dialogue. Counselors indicate that setting the tone of the formal conference is essential for open dialogue in any culture. One approach is to have the teacher share one positive thing about the child, then the parent shares one positive thing about the child's work. Next round, the teacher raises one concern about the child's academic or social behavior; in turn, the parents share a concern in the same vein. This opens dialogue and provides a shared basis for communication and student-based decision making between teacher and parents.

Parent-teacher conferences can be a vital source of information for both parents and teachers. However, most teachers report receiving little or no training in conducting effective parent teacher conferences (Jonson, 1999). Moles (1999) and Foster (1994) recommend several strategies to prepare for conferences. Principals can provide information about conferencing during a professional development session, provide time and funding, use a variety of sources to publish upcoming conference dates, and survey parents. Teachers can plan the conference agenda with elicited parents' feedback, contact parents to schedule a convenient conference time and have samples of student work available for parents to view. During the conference, the teacher should focus on developing rapport and trust with the parent, emphasize the partnership between the teacher and the parent, exchange information with the parent, and discuss ideas to follow up at the completion of the conference.

Parent participation in family-school conferences is often high for students in the early grades but dramatically decreases for students in middle and high school grades. After the conference, there is often little communication between parents and teacher, home and school. That may be because the conference is one-way, school to home. In this one-way conference, the teacher tells the parents what kind of grades the student has, what his/her behavior is in the classroom, and whether or not homework is being completed satisfactorily. Collaborating with parents to assess their needs, using the parent-teacher conference as a means to connect and learn from parents, and maintaining a solution-based focus while working with parents can go a long way in establishing open, friendly and effective home-school communication (Rosenthal & Sawyers, 1996).

Involving the students seems to increase attendance at home-school conferences. One new approach is the student-led conference (Tuinstra, 2001). At the student-led parent conference, the student discusses his/her work and learning with his/her parents. As the student reflects on his/her work, several positive outcomes occur. First, the student learns to critically evaluate the work, noting areas for improvement and areas of mastery. Second, the student assumes the responsibility for, and pride in, the quality of academic performance and products. That responsibility extends to demonstrating to and discussing the work with one's parents. The student explains the goals and objectives of the work, which work was done to meet those goals and objectives, and the quality of the work in meeting those goals and objectives. The social dimension, namely, the student and parents discussing the student's work, solidifies the learning to the student and clarifies the quality of academic achievement to the parents. During these conferences, parents and students refine the student learning through continuing discussions.

The many benefits of student-led parent conferences make the practice worth pursuing at any K-12 school. Guskey and Marzano (2001) guided 13 teachers from different grade levels in northern Michigan to implement student-led conferences. They reported that parent participation rate was 95% and extended teacher participation to 11 schools within their service area. Comments from parents were very positive. The teachers indicated that class time was required to prepare the students to lead the conferences but that outside class time to prepare conferences was reduced. Parents felt that they learned more about their children's work at school. Students reported pride and personal satisfaction. Student-led conferences in other ethnic settings create similar findings.

HOME-VISITS

Home-visits by teachers or parent liaisons are perceived as one of the most beneficial parent communication activities (Winter, 1995). Home-visits are a contemporary method, with roots in the Social Reform era 1870–1920 (Bhavnagri & Krolikowski, 2000). Though the early attempts at home visits were to ameliorate home conditions that led to academic problems, home visits have shifted to an empowerment model. Through home visits, a strong personal connection is made between the school personnel and family members.

Children who view their parents and teachers working together develop a more positive attitude toward school (Bell, 1996). Home visits serve to provide teachers insights into their students' behavior and life outside of the school setting. During the visits, teachers establish a sense of community with the parent and child. Moles (1999) recommends that flexible scheduling, advance notification via phone or mail, detailed descriptions of the visit agenda and inclusion of the student in a fun activity are important items to consider in structuring home visits. Dodd and Lilly (1997) suggest that the teacher with the family develop a family portfolio during a home visit. This family portfolio provides insights to the teacher and helps the teacher understand the whole child.

Houston Independent School District (1997) report home-visits seem to increase school attendance, reduce number of reports for disruptive student behavior, increase completion of homework, assist to appropriately place students, and improve academic achievement. Home visits afford unique opportunities for the teacher to observe so many things about the child and his family. The teacher will note the organization within the home, parenting practices, and family interests. In addition, the parent is within his own domain and should feel more comfortable asking questions about the school, academic expectations, and other concerns. Jones (1997) described the benefits of a bilingual Navajo staff member who makes home visits to obtain parental viewpoints and to secure parental understanding. These visits have increased student attendance at the school.

At Patrick O'Hearn Elementary School in Boston, a core group of parent volunteers were recruited to visit parents whose child was new to the school (Mapp, 1997). This group of parents contacted each new parent and made arrangements for a personal visit at their home. This informal face-to-face connection made new parents feel welcome and comfortable to come to the school. Quickly, they reported that they knew people, felt at ease in the school culture, and were encouraged to become involved within the school.

In the traditional Asian culture, parents value privacy and perceive home visits as an invasion to that privacy (Rumjahn, personal communication, 2001). These parents positively respond to formal requests from designated authority figures such as the school principal.

The State of Maine mandates that teachers visit the homes of all prospective kindergarten students prior to the children attending school and supports that program with state funds. In most other states home-visit programs are financed by Title I or Head Start funds (Moles, 1999). In California, funds have been provided so teachers in some school districts are paid for extra time outside of class in order to visit parent homes. Though all research reports that home visits have positive outcomes for students, families, and teachers, Taveras (1998) findings from the teachers' perspective of home visits revealed that few teachers ever conducted a home visit. The primary barrier to home visits was lack of training in handling a home visit.

PARENT AND COMMUNITY LIAISONS

The parent or community liaison is a critical individual in promoting parent involvement. Since the school is the reaching out agent, it is helpful to have someone within the community do the reaching. The parent or community liaison knows both the accepted practices of the culture as well as the differences within certain families. Also, reaching out takes significant time. It is far easier for the teachers and administrators to work with one community liaison than to devote the required time to connect with all the parents within the class.

Using Title I funds, a principal at an urban Kansas City Magnet school hired a full-time parent liaison, who represents the African American community, the majority ethnic group at the school. She keeps the teachers informed about students and their families. In addition, she supports the school in numerous ways—organizing parent events such as school orientations, arranging home visits (averaging 10 per week), and assisting parents with referrals to agencies. At Alamo Navajo Community School in New Mexico, the community liaison is bilingual and makes regular home visits, interfacing between the language and culture of the teachers and that of the Navajo family. The Rodney P. Cox School in Dade City, Florida, utilizes a parent involvement teacher, two migrant home-school coordinators and one minority recruiter to conduct home visits. These community liaisons market the school's open door policy that ensures teachers will be available to parents whenever the need arises. The principal indicated that school attendance improved as a direct result of these home visits and that student test scores in reading and math increased, in part to this increased communication between home and school.

For school systems without such funds, Moles (1999) recommends that community liaisons be filled by members of an organized volunteer or PTA program. In small systems, he suggests that the position could be system wide rather than school-based. And, in large schools, parental liaisons might be assigned to grades, clusters, or departments.

NEWSLETTERS

Newsletters provide an informative and inexpensive means to communicate with parents. School districts, schools, and individual classrooms publish parent newsletters. Possible topics for inclusion encompass general items of information, school events, holidays and conferences, discipline policies, home activities parents can do with their children, and highlights of student or staff accomplishments. Moles (1999) recommends that the PTA, parent liaisons, teachers, and students be involved in the production of parent newsletters. Parents, teachers, administrators, and students may assist by providing articles or work. Newsletters should be available in the parents' language for limited or non-English speaking parents who are literate in their native language.

In El Paso, Texas, Hueco Elementary School publishes a monthly newsletter for parents, and many teachers create a weekly or monthly newsletter (Funkhauser & Gonzales, 1998). The director of parent literacy programs in California shared with colleagues that, at her child's school in San Jose, the teacher sends home a Monday night newsletter. The director and other parents at the school expect that newsletter and plan the week according to the school activities. In Irvine, California, student teachers work with their supervising teachers to prepare weekly parent newsletters. In my teacher education classes, I promote student editors of classroom and school newsletters to incorporate student thinking and writing into this form of home-school communication. Student participation promotes parental reading and a positive connection between classroom life and parenting.

Many schools utilize newsletters as a forum for parent surveys so two-way communication occurs between parents and the school. Schools use newsletters as the medium to solicit family volunteers for the library or lunchroom, ensure sign-up for the teacher/father breakfast or grandparent's day, and request parent opinion regarding a proposed new school policy.

A principal of a Chicago primary school, asserted that newsletters grant equal access to all parents concerning school information (Allen-Jones, 2001). Newsletters, printed in representative languages of the school, secure that all families have the opportunity to receive school news. She stated that "newsletters provide information about the school and are essential to the home-school communication process."

TECHNOLOGICAL CONNECTIONS

The installation and usage of telephones within classrooms can improve communication between parents and teachers. Phone calls allow immediate feedback, two-way communication, and high comfort level using this form of communication tool (Cottle, 1991; Henniger, 1981). Lucas (1994) indicated most respondents to a post survey on an educational list serve and internet conference groups agreed on the need to equip kindergarten through 12th grade classrooms with modern communications tools including telephone lines to be used predominately for voice and computer communications.

Moles (1999) suggested a strategy for teachers on how to use the telephone to connect with the home. In the beginning of the school year, teachers make introductory phone calls to each student. In addition, the teachers contact parents and briefly share with them the focus for the coming year. It was recommended that the phone calls be kept short and focused.

A parent-school telephone tree was recommended by parents as a way to overcome barriers to home-school partnerships (Davies, Bauch, & Johnson, 1992). Atenville Elementary School in Harts, West Virginia, regularly utilizes the telephone tree as well as personal home visits to encourage rural parents and their children to attend school. Each telephone tree parent calls 20–25 families. The phone tree provided a close link for the school family to inform others about events, silence rumors, share frustrations, and listen to the emotional and physical needs of the family.

Bittle (1975) conducted a research study to determine if communication could be improved between parents and teachers using recorded phone messages. The results showed that the system was used extensively. The inclusion of academic information in the daily message resulted in improved academic performance by every student, and families complied with recorded teacher instruction of a non-academic nature at a much higher rate than they did when these instructions were only sent home with the child in memo form.

Beginning in the late 1980s, homework hotlines were implemented by an ever-growing number of schools to improve student academic achievement (Bauch, 1998a). Each teacher at the school records a voice message describing homework or other class activities. Parents call the hotline number and listen to his child's teacher's message. The best practice for homework hotlines requires all teachers to place a daily message on the hotline. The schools that mandate regular daily messages by all teachers receive between 80–100% of the parents calling the hotline on a regular basis. This translates to improved student completion and submission of homework on a regular basis. In this voice-mail dialogue, the parents were encouraged to raise questions, express concerns, and leave messages for the teacher.

Follow-up studies revealed that parents report voice-mail systems let absent children know what homework needs to be completed (Bauch, 1998b). Two other findings are important from these studies. First, the more the parent used the homework hotline, the higher the parent expressed a positive attitude toward the school. Second, in schools using homework hotlines, school-wide student achievement scores in math and reading were higher the following year.

Using a voice-mail system, Nielsen and Finkelstein (1993) suggest setting up initial conferences between teacher, parents and students to collaborate and plan for the upcoming year. Cameron and Kang (1997) conducted a research study focusing on teachers and parents perceptions of their interactions using a voice mail system. Twenty-four families from kindergarten and a fifth grade class volunteered for the study. The parents were randomly assigned to the voice mail intervention group or the non-intervention group. Prior to the study, parents reported contacting their child's teacher approximately once every other week. During the trial study, parents reported contacting the teacher at least once a week. This resulted in a doubling of the number of parent contacts with teachers. The comparison group reported less than one contact every two weeks. The voice-mail group reported at least three contacts from the teacher per week. The comparison group reported less than weekly contact. This group indicated that written messages were their primary means of communication whereas 100% of the voice mail group noted voice mail messages as the primary means of communication.

Using e-mail, list serves, and World Wide Web is commonplace among business and professional establishments. However, schools have been less enthusiastic to adopt these forms of interactive communication. World Wide Web has a host of promising capabilities. The establishment of web pages could create an enticing interactive audio-visual forum for information between families, the community, and the home. In Beverly Hills, some classrooms create a web site showcasing their classroom and individual activities. Compton School District in Los Angeles area had a professional firm create Web sites for each school. Thus far, this form of audio/visual communication has been one-way from school to home. Besides being one-way, the negative aspect to promoting the Web and Internet use is that not all homes have the capability to access information via the Internet. Access appears to be related to socioeconomic status. Thus, the newsletter is presently the equitable way to share school information in most schools.

A research study by Weiss and Nieto (1999) focused on the use of electronic communication tools to connect families living in remote areas in Alaska with educators. Due to the remoteness of many Alaskan families, teachers and special education professionals serve students over a wide distance. Inclement weather often interferes with the teachers' ability to travel and work with the student in person. Most rural schools double as community centers in Alaska. This facilitates many families being able to use a computer because computers have been placed in these centers. Weiss and Nieto also reported several promising strategies that are being studied—the use of interactive web libraries, web bulletin boards and e-mail discussion lists.

Connor (2000) suggested that another way to enhance Internet access to parents is to equip the parent resource room at the school with a computer and an Internet connection. Maine School Administration District #3 provides computers to parents in schools as well as town sites. At Cane Run Elementary School in Louisville, Kentucky, five family technology nights each year increase parents' awareness and provide hands-on computer training for parents. Most public libraries have made free Internet access to anyone who holds a library card, though many families may be unaware that this service is available. Disney (2000), director of the Parents Information Network in Great Britain, reported that not all parents are computer literate. As information technology continues to progress, parents may require information technology education in order to possess skill level to work with the new technology.

EMPOWERMENT ISSUES

Power dynamics may be observed in all relationships within schools (Sarason, 1995) and these dynamics may assist or hinder the child in the school setting. Exchanging ideas and skills—communication—is the foundation of human relationships. However, social class and lack of cultural capital pose barriers to parents' ability to participate within the school setting (Finders & Lewis, 1994; Lareau, 1987; Pena, 2000). Parents from higher social economic levels tend to have more formal and informal social networks than parents from lower social economic levels. This lack of access inhibits their ability to get information and ultimately gain power within organized parental organizations and within schools (Pena, 2000). Most parents care and want to help their children learn and lead successful lives (Chavkin, 1993). However, the parents' and teachers' lack of understanding of how to help each other is a major barrier to creating proactive home-school collaborations.

In *How to Deal with Parents Who Are Angry, Troubled, Afraid, or Just Plain Crazy,* McEwan (1998) builds upon the importance of strong home-school communication and collaboration as the web for strong relationships between these two groups. She draws upon her experience as a school principal and shares a vast array of counseling techniques and ideas that are required by teachers and site administrators in order to deal with parent concerns. Such ideas include listening to and understanding the parents' viewpoint, working to develop a collaborative plan, providing emotional and information support to parents, and following up on action plans. Her ideas empower teachers and principals so that they can effectively work with families.

Finders and Lewis (1994) noted that educational institutions must change their perceptions of why parents may not participate in their child's education. They expressed the following reasons: personal failure in schools, time constraints, and language barriers. These echoed a survey by Davies, Burch, and Johnson (1992) on 42 schools that were part of the Family, School, Community network. The following strategies were reported by parents as a means for teachers and administrators to assist them: explain to parents how to help in their child's education, provide encouragement for parents to become advocates for their children, and establish rapport and trust while honoring the home experiences of the family (Finders & Lewis, 1994; Kirschenbaum, 1999). Schools can involve the limited English-speaking parents by translating materials into their native language, providing a bilingual parent coordinator, and/or having bilingual and multicultural materials within the school and on display (Bermudez & Padron, 1998; Moles, 1999).

Dunlap and Alva (1999) have noted several barriers that must be overcome in establishing successful school partnerships. One common barrier is that some families may feel alienated from the school due to a lack of knowledge about school operations. These parents may feel inadequate or unwelcome due to a difference of income, education, or ethnicity as compared to school personnel. This difference may result in the parent's perception that the school is indifferent to these feelings. When parents have these feelings, they tend to withdraw from the school environment. As a result, school personnel may assume that the parents are uninterested in school involvement. Another factor noted by Dunlap and Alva (1999) that widens the gap between school personnel and the families, is that many teachers and administrators come from another culture or another part of the town. They may not see themselves or the school as a part of the surrounding community.

These barriers can be addressed by reaching out to families and providing them the individualized attention, education programs, and services they need to become active participants and stakeholders in the school (Stein & Thorkildsen, 1999). When school personnel listen to parents, this provides insights to fruitful approaches that assure the school and families are working together as equal partners to make the school a central, learning institution for the entire community (Brandt, 1998). Family, school, and community partnerships flourish when they are based on mutual trust and respect for each other's values, perspectives and experiences. Schools need to demonstrate to families that diversity of culture and values is respected. Sielo, Sileo, and Prater (1996) have stated that home-school communication should focus on parents' influence on their children's education. These authors stated that school programs are effective if teachers and administrators perform the following:

1. involve parents as equal partners in problem-solving dialogues;
2. observe and participate in community activities;
3. develop mutual understandings and shared personal needs, hopes, and concerns by listening to parents and talking with them; and
4. inform parents of their rights and responsibilities with regard to improving the educational environment.

McCoy Elementary School in Kansas City, Missouri, demonstrates these practices in action. Billions of dollars have been spent in Kansas City Schools to improve test scores, but only McCoy Elementary School showed increased student achievement. This school consists of predominantly African-American families. George Cooper, the Caring Communities Site Coordinator at the school, described the reaching out efforts by everyone at that school to families in the community and how these outreach efforts resulted in higher student performance. Cooper informed me that "building and increasing support and participation in neighborhood governance is a major theme of the Caring Communities Initiative in Missouri." McCoy Elementary employs multiple approaches to connect with families. Cooper shared that focus groups are held in order to identify what parents perceive as needed services and programs. He remarked that the school utilizes newsletters, flyers and neighborhood publications to communicate with families. On Thursday evenings the school hosts family support groups "to increase communication between family members in the home and also between families and the schools." These meetings especially focus on children who have been truant and the family. In addition, teachers make individual home-visits to meet families and develop home-school expectations. All staff and parents diligently work toward building a caring community within the school.

CONCLUSION

Family and schools working together in the best interest of the student is the overarching goal of home-school communication practices. Many avenues and approaches lead to that goal—reaching out by the school, home visits, use of parents and community members as liaisons, newsletters, formal and informal conferences, and telecommunications. In return for the school reaching out, parents contribute knowledge and information to compliment the skills of teachers so that their children can achieve academically and socially. Families, schools and children benefit from positive and regular two-way home-school communication.

REFERENCES

Allen-Jones, G.L. (2001). *Home-school communications and the use of newsletters*. University Park, IL: Governors State University.

Bauch, J.P. (1998a, Oct. 30–Nov. 1)). Applications of technology to linking schools, families and students. *Proceedings of the Families, Technology, and Education Conference*, Chicago, IL. 1. ED425017.

Bauch, J.P. (1998b). *Parent involvement partnerships with technology.* Nashville, TN: Peabody College of Vanderbilt University.

Bell, S.S. (1996). Kindergartners respond to teacher visits. *Teaching and Change, 4*(1), 50–61.

Bermudez, A.B., & Padron, Y.N. (1998). University-school collaboration that increases minority parents involvement. *Educational Horizons, 66,* 83–86.

Bhavagri, N., & Krolikowski, S. (2000, Spring). Home-school community visits during an era of reform. *Early Childhood Research and Practice, 1.* (ERIC Document Retrieval Service n. ED 439 851).

Bittle, R.G. (1975). Improving parent-teacher communication through recorded telephone messages. *The Journal of Educational Research, 69*(3), 87–95.

Brandt, R. (1998). Listen first. *Educational Leadership, 55*(8), 25–30.

Cameron, C.A., & Kang, L. (1997). Bridging the gap between home and school with voice-mail technology. *Journal of Educational Research, 90*(3), 182–191.

Chavkin, N.F. (1993). *Families and schools in a pluralistic society.* Albany: State University of New York Press.

Conner, C. (2000). Rebuilding a parent program with technology. *Principal, 80,*(1), 61–2.

Cottle, W.E. (1991). *Improving communications between parents and teachers of middle school age students by the use of the telephone and other techniques.* Nova University.

Cushman, K. (1998). The family and essential schools: Mobilizing democracy toward equity. *Horace, 15*(1). [Coalition of Essential Schools: Providence, RI]

Davies, D., Burch, P., & Johnson, V. (1992, February). *A portrait of schools reaching out.* Center on Families, Communities, Schools and Children's Learning. Report no. 1.

Decker, J., & Majerczyk, D. (2000). *Increasing parent involvement through effective home/school communication.* Unpublished manuscript, Saint Xavier University, Chicago.

Disney, J. (2000, March 10). PINpoints: Parent Information Network. *The Times Educational Supplement no 4637 online,* p. 36.

Dodd, E.L., & Lilly, D.H. (1997). Family portfolios: Portraits of children and families. *Preventing School Failure, 4*(2), 57–63.

Dunlap, C.Z., & Alva, S.A. (1999). Redefining school and community relations: Teacher's perceptions of parents as participants and stakeholders. *Teacher Education Quarterly, 26*(4), 123–33.

Espinosa, L. (1995). *Hispanic parent involvement in early childhood programs.* ERIC Digest, University of Illinois, Urbana.

Finders, M., & Lewis, C. (1994). Why some parents don't come to school. *Educational Leadership 51*(8), 50–54.

Finnegan, E.M. (1997). Even though we have never met, I feel I know you: Using a parent journal to enhance home-school communication. *Reading Teacher, 51*(3), 268–270.

Foster, S.M. (1994). Successful parent meetings. *Young Children, 60*(1), 78–80.

Funkhouser, J.E., & Gonzales, M.R. (1998). *Family involvement in children's education:Successful local approaches.* Office of Educational Research and Improvement: Washington, DC.

Guskey, T.R., & Marzano, R.J. (2001). *Implementing student-led conferences.* Thousand Oaks, CA: Corwin, Press, Inc.

Henniger, M.L. (1981). *The telephone and parent/teacher communication.* Central Washington University.

Hiatt-Michael, D. (2000a). *Parent involvement as a component of teacher education programs in California.* Paper presented at American Educational Research Association Annual Meeting, New Orleans, LA. (ERIC Document Retrieval Service No. ED 441 771)

Hiatt-Michael, D. (2000b, November). *Working with parents and loving it.* Paper presented at the Association of Christian Schools International Teachers Convention, Anaheim, CA.

Hiatt-Michael, D. (2001, April). *Preparing preservice teachers for homes-school partnerships across the United States.* Paper presented at American Educational Research Association Annual Meeting, Seattle, WA.

Hoover-Dempsey, K.V., & Sandler, H.M. (Winter, 1995). Parent involvement in children's education: Why does it make a difference. *Teachers College Record, 2,* 310–331.

Houston Independent School District. (1997). *Absent student assistance program, precinct 7, 1996–97.* Houston, TX: Department of Research and Accountability.

Johnstone, T. (1997). *Case study of a school-based parent center in a low-income immigrant community.* Unpublished doctoral dissertation, Pepperdine University, Malibu, CA.

Jones, D. (1997). *Working with Navajo parents of exceptional children.* (ERIC Document Reproduction Service, No. ED 406 119).

Jonson, K.F. (1999). Parents as partners: Building positive home-school relationships. *The Educational Forum, 63*(2), 121–126.

Kelty, J. (1997). *An examination of Hispanic parent involvement in early childhood programs.* Master's Thesis, Grand Valley State University, Michigan. (ERIC Document Reproduction Service No. ED 420 406)

Kirschenbaum, H. (1999). Night and day: Succeeding with parents at School 43. *Principal, 78*(3), 20–23.

Lareau, A. (1987). Social class differences in family-school relationships: The importance of cultural capital. *Sociology of Education, 60,* 73–85.

Lucas, L.W. (1994). Say "YES" to telephone lines in the classroom. *ERIC Digest.*

Mapp, K. (1997, September/October). *Harvard Educational Letter.*

McEwan, E.K. (1998). *How to deal with parents who are angry, troubled, afraid or just plain crazy.* Thousand Oaks, CA: Corwin Press, Inc.

Moles, O. (Ed.). (1999). *Reaching all families: Creating family-friendly schools* [brochure]. Washington, DC: U.S. Department of Education, Office of Education.

Moles, O. (Ed.). (2000). *Reaching all families: Beginning of the school year activities* [brochure]. Washington, DC: U.S. Department of Education, Office of Education.

Nicolau, S., & Ramos, C.L. (1993) *Together is better: Building strong relationships between schools and Hispanic parents.* New York: Hispanic Policy Development Project, Inc. (ERIC Document Reproduction Serivce, No. ED 325 543)

Nielsen, L.E., & Finkelstein, J.M. (1993, August/September). A new approach to parent conferences. *Teaching K-8,* pp. 90–92.

Pena, D. (1998). *Mexican American parental involvement in site-based management.* Paper presented at the Annual Meeting of the Americna Educaitonal Research Association. San Diego, CA, April 13–17. (ERIC Document Retrieval Service no. ED 423 086)

Pena, D.C. (2000, April). *The social dynamics of parental involvement: Social capital, power, and control.* Paper presented at the American Educational Research Association Annual Meeting, New Orleans, LA.

Redding, S. (1995). *Parents and learning.* [on-line document]. Retrieved on 5/10/01 from the World Wide Web http://www.ibe.unesco.org.

Rosenthal, D.M., & Sawyers, J.Y. (1996). Building successful home/school partnerships. *Childhood Education, 72*(4), 194–197.

Sarasan, S.B. (1995). *Parental involvement and the political principle.* Jossey-Bass Publishers: San Francisco, CA.

Sileo, T.S., Sileo, A.P., & Prater, M.A. (1996). Parent and professional partnerships in special education: Multicultural considerations. *Intervention in School and Clinic, 31*, 145–53.

Simon, B. (2001, April). *High school-family partnerships: Effects of schools' outreach on family involvement practices.* Paper presented at the American Educational Research Association Annual Meeting, Seattle, WA.

Stein, M.R., & Thorkildsen, R.J. (1999). *Parent involvement in education: Insights and applications from research.* Bloomington, IN: Phi Delta Kappa International.

Taveras, G. (1998). *Home visits from the teachers' perspective.* (ERIC Document Reporduction Service No. ED 426 775)

Tuinstra, C. (2001). *Student-led parent conferences.* Doctoral dissertation in progress, Pepperdine University, Malibu, CA.

Weiss, T., & Nieto, F. (1999). *Using the Internet to connect parents and professionals: The challenges.* Albuquerque, NM: Rural Special Education for the New Millennium, 7.

Whalley, M. (2001). *Involving parents in their children's learning.* London: Paul Chapman Publishing Company Ltd.

Winter, M. (1995). *Home visiting: Forging the home-school connection.* Portsmouth, NH: RMC Research Corp. (ERIC Document Retrieval Service No. ED 405 075)

CHAPTER 4

PARENT-CHILD LITERACY PROJECTS

Francesca K. Pomerantz

"We now read 30–40 minutes each night."

"My son reads the stories to me from his new take home books every day."

"I read more often with my daughter and I sit down with her as directed by the teacher to do her homework."

"I gave my daughter a journal so when she reads a book she can write about what happens and also she can write down words that she learned from the book."

These quotes from parents illustrate what can happen at home when parents and teachers communicate and collaborate around students' literacy development. The students involved attended urban schools participating in the ReadBoston Family Literacy Project described later in this chapter. This chapter reviews model K-12 parent-child literacy programs and projects that can be implemented and sustained by teachers, administrators, and school districts without long-term support from external agencies or organizations. The projects are located in various geographic areas of the country and serve a diversity of students and parents. The intent of this chapter is not to provide a comprehensive review of parent-child literacy projects, but rather to present the broad range of actions teachers and administrators can take to involve families in their children's literacy development.

The important influence of parent-child literacy interactions on language and literacy development is widely acknowledged. Decades of research clearly support this idea. Parent involvement in children's literacy learning through storybook reading, listening to children read, and talking about books has been shown to affect a child's readiness for school literacy learning, ability to attend to print and school tasks, motivation to read, and reading achievement. (Anderson, Hiebert, Scott, & Wilkinson, 1985; Robinson, Larsen, & Haupt, 1996; Rowe, 1991).

For this reason, effective schools and teachers take an active role in encouraging parents to become and stay involved with their children's literacy learning. Taylor, Pearson, Clark, and Walpole (1999) investigated the school-wide and instructional practices that characterized elementary schools in which at-risk students were "beating the odds" in regard to reading achievement in grades K-3. The most effective schools and teachers had strong links to parents, including frequent parent-teacher communication and at-home reading programs. Kletzien (1996) described the practices of nationally recognized "Blue Ribbon" elementary schools, most of which had adopted school-wide reading programs that encouraged students to read at home, and parent involvement in out-of-school reading time.

Most of the projects included in this chapter focus on reading and writing. However, a few seek to involve parents in science and math, and demonstrate that parents and students can also benefit from parent involvement in these other "literacies." Projects included in the chapter have demonstrated their success in terms of high participant satisfaction, increases in quantity of literacy interactions between parents and children, increases in the quality of literacy interactions, and/or improvements in children's academic performance.

There are two kinds of "family literacy" or parent-child literacy projects: those that help parents support their children's school learning, and those that address both parent and child literacy learning (Handel, 1999, p. 7). This chapter includes descriptions of both types of projects. All effective family literacy projects, regardless of which category they fall into, share certain assumptions and characteristics. These basic themes are that:

1. Parents' level of education, English proficiency, income, ethnic background, or race do not play an important role in their ability to support their children's education;
2. Schools and teachers can influence the frequency and quality of parent–child interactions dealing with literacy;
3. Successful projects are attuned to the families, cultures, and communities they serve and take this knowledge into account when planning activities and curriculum and developing materials.

HISTORY: PARENT/CHILD LITERACY PROJECTS

Family literacy or parent-child literacy programs and projects developed as a response to "growing evidence that cycles of low literacy tend to repeat themselves across generations" (Handel, 1999, p. 15). Several studies and reports, including the 1985 National Assessment of Educational Progress, highlighted the connections between a mother's level of education and the reading achievement of her children. Lower maternal educational levels tend to correspond with lower paying jobs, poverty, and lower reading achievement on the part of children in the family. However, many children from poor family backgrounds whose parents did not finish high school or attend college, achieve high levels of literacy themselves. Consequently, parental education and income levels do not fully explain why some children succeed in school and others do not. As Handel (1999) noted: "Expectations and attitudes toward literacy, family routines, and resources of information and experience—the social capital that the family can provide—affect the growing child's literacy development, as does the interpersonal environment within the family" (p. 16). Parents who provide opportunities for learning by sharing books, interacting with children in literacy tasks (e.g., taking a phone message, writing a card), and modeling literacy through reading and writing themselves can positively influence their children's literacy development (p. 16). Consequently, the aim of most parent-child literacy projects is to foster book sharing and other literacy related activities within families. Many programs provide early childhood education, adult basic education, and joint parent-child literacy activities. Such programs grew in the 1980's as a result of federal legislation, the aim of which was to break the cycle of low literacy achievement within families (Handel, 1999, pp. 20–21).

In addition, evidence has highlighted the role of schools in promoting parental involvement in children's literacy learning and the significance of the interaction between the school and home. For example, in their investigation of home and school influences on literacy development, Snow, Barnes, Chandler, Goodman, and Hemphill (1991) found a strong relationship between teacher-initiated parent contacts and student gains in reading comprehension. In recognition of the influence of home and school interaction, "Title I regulations now make outreach to families a school responsibility in accordance with the National Education Goal of family-school partnerships" (Handel, 1999, p. 23). The rest of this chapter describes projects and programs that have successfully forged literacy connections between home and school.

The projects and programs included in the chapter are divided into three categories: (a) Those that are classroom-based and occur in the context of the school day; (b) those that are school-based but outside of the typical classroom routine, and (c) those that are district sponsored. The descriptions and references are intended to provide K-12 teachers and school administrators with a variety of strategies to establish family-school partnerships that support literacy development.

EFFECTIVE CLASSROOM-BASED PARENT-CHILD LITERACY PROJECTS

Home Response Journals

Morningstar (1999) and Shockley, Michalove, and Allen (1995) described how home response journals helped parents and teachers share information about children's literacy learning and development. Morningstar, a kindergarten teacher in Iowa, first shared Cochrane and Cochrane's reading development continuum with parents at a September parent information meeting (1992, cited in Morningstar, 1999). The continuum provided Morningstar and parents with a common vocabulary to describe a child's literacy behaviors, understand a child's stage of literacy development, and develop appropriate teaching strategies. She then invited parents to share their observations of their child's home language and literacy activities in a weekly journal. Some parents shared observations and others asked questions that gave Morningstar the opportunity to share strategies. For example, one parent wrote: "Sean is starting to sound out words. I think he is going to have a big interest in reading like his sister did. Do you sound out words a lot in class?" In response, Morningstar wrote,

> At school Sean enjoys a variety of language opportunities. He has made original puppets for a show, worked at reading beginning readers, and "played school" by reading big books with a partner. I continue to encourage him to use a variety of strategies to figure out an unknown word as he reads. Some examples (you can also offer him while he's reading at home) include:
>
> Saying blank for an unknown word or skipping it,
>
> Deciding what word would make sense,
>
> Using a picture clue,
>
> Deciding if he knows a word that rhymes with the unknown word, or
>
> Sounding it out.
>
> The more strategies he is comfortable with using, the better reader he will be. I am really proud of how dedicated he is to learning! (p. 695)

Morningstar's strategy to encourage and develop a partnership with parents carried over to her parent-teacher conferences. At the conferences, Morningstar first asked parents to tell her about their child's literacy at home. As parents shared their observations about their child at home, Morningstar contributed her observations of the child in the classroom. Together, the parent and Morningstar decided which stage the child was at on the reading development continuum and shared ideas about specific strategies to encourage each child's development.

Thirteen out of 19 parents participated in the conferences and home response journal effort. Morningstar realized that some parents might find journal writing difficult because of busy schedules or because they were not proficient readers or writers themselves. She also noted that the responsibility of replying to thirteen parents in the journals each week was overwhelming. Consequently, she decided to "condense the paperwork by having one fourth of the class return their journals each week. Providing parents a month to respond may encourage those with busy schedules by giving more time to make observations", while allowing the teacher to reply to a more realistic number of journals" (p. 696). Morningstar and the parents who participated felt that the journals and conferences helped the teacher and the parents understand each child's literacy development and how to nurture it.

In their book *Engaging Families,* Shockley, Michalove, and Allen (1995) described a similar effort to develop a partnership between parents and teachers around children's literacy learning. Shockley and Michalove were first and second grade teachers respectively at an elementary school in Athens, Georgia, and Allen a professor in language education at the University of Georgia. They created a series of practices designed to connect parents and teachers in Shockley's first grade class which then carried over to Michalove's second grade class with the same group of children and parents. The practices included: (a) Asking parents to tell the teachers about their child in a letter, (b) keeping home reading journals, (c) telling family stories, (d) promoting family reflections on their child's reading and writing progress, and (e) fostering group discussions with parents.

Each child had a home reading journal that she took back and forth from the classroom to home along with a book from the classroom library. Children chose books every night and "reading together and talking about books was the heart of the homework" (p. 20). Three school nights in first grade and two nights in second grade, families were to talk about the book with their child and record the child's responses to the book in the journal. The teachers responded to each journal entry. Shockley, Michalove, and Allen explained that, "each family developed its own uses for the journal, including talking about books, illustrating, sharing information about the child's literacy development, occasionally conducting business, and sharing concerns" (p. 20). Furthermore, "the reading, talking, and journal writing process gave every family a dependable time to spend together around books. Several parents commented that the structure helped them do something they wanted to do, read with their children, at times when the routines of everyday life might otherwise have intruded" (p. 70). All of the parents and children in first and second grade participated in the journal writing.

The teachers also invited the parents to write and share a family story with the class and created a class book of the stories. Through this effort, parents and family members modeled writing and storytelling for their children. In addition, the teachers created "learning albums" for each child that included reflections on the child's learning by the child, the parent, and the teacher, as well as other forms of literacy assessment. These learning albums were shared at parent-teacher conferences. The teachers also invited the parents and other caretakers to seven after-school meetings that focused on topics such as how the parents wanted to structure homework.

At the end of the second year of the project, the teachers asked parents what difference, if any, the home-school practices had made. Shockley, Michalove, and Allen reported that "much of the conversation concerned the journals" (p. 26). They wrote, "to a person, these family members said that the opportunities to be actively involved with their children's reading and writing, and with their children's teachers were very important to them" (p. 26). One parent wrote to the teachers:

> I was so glad for the "homework." It gave me the opportunity to be in the "scholastic" part of his learning. I can appreciate it and I feel that it has helped Brandon's learning. I remember when the journals first started I would read to Brandon. Towards the end Brandon read to me. He was eager to learn more words so that he could read more, so he learned!"(p. 27)

Respect for the families permeated the teachers' behaviors regarding the journals and may help explain the positive response and the 100% participation. Sometimes parents directed their children to do literacy related tasks that the teachers did not perceive to be developmentally appropriate. For example, a parent might use the journal to have a child spell words from the book. The teachers might share other ways of using the journal, but they never expressed disagreement with the parent. Another family member read Bible stories with a child instead of the book the child brought home from the classroom library. This decision was also respected. When the student or parent did not write in the journal, the teachers simply wrote "no response." No child or parent was scolded for not writing in the journal. The teachers understood that sometimes circumstances made it difficult or impossible to write. However, when a pattern of not writing persisted, the teacher asked the child to tell her about the book and then to write it down in the journal. Parents who did not speak English or had low levels of literacy found a way to participate in the journals that was welcomed and respected. They copied parts of the text into the journal and/or drew pictures. They were encouraged to listen to their child read and to tell the story from the illustrations.

Take-home Books

Many projects focus on students taking books home from the classroom to read with family members. Such projects often involve establishing classroom libraries of quality children's books, incorporating routines for book selection, tracking the numbers of books read, and sending home letters and information for parents. The following section describes four such projects which provide compelling evidence that when teachers and schools incorporate sending books home from classroom libraries and provide outreach to families around literacy, students read more at home and are more motivated to read in general.

The Running Start Program was developed by Reading Is Fundamental (RIF) to increase first-grade children and families' access to quality children's literature, to involve families in children's literacy development, and to increase children's motivation to read (Gambrell, Almasi, Xie, & Heland, 1995). The program was implemented at many urban and suburban schools throughout the United States. Teachers involved in the program chose and bought children's books for their classrooms. The children were asked to read, or have someone read to them, 21 books during the 10-week program. After children had read 21 books, they were able to choose a book to keep and receive a certificate. Teachers received a handbook of ideas and activities to involve the children in reading and were provided with materials such as a poster, stickers, bookmarks, and certificates. Each child kept track of his/her progress toward the 21 books by putting stickers for each book read on a "personal challenge" chart (Gambrell et al., 1995, p. 146). Family members received suggestions for reading activities to do with children. In addition, teachers created more opportunities for children to read or be read to during the school day. Books read at home and at school counted toward the 21-book goal. Finally, families were invited to a "Reading Rally" where reading was celebrated with skits, readings, and music. Additionally, families were provided with information about how to support their children's reading. At the rally all family members received a book.

Gambrell (1993, cited in Gambrell et al., 1995) conducted two studies to evaluate the program's influence on children, parents, and teachers, particularly in regard to the effects of the program on reading motivation and family literacy practices. The first study, conducted in 49 schools in nine states, involved 7000 first-grade students, 4000 parents, and 320 teachers. Before the program started, the researchers surveyed children and families to assess the children's motivation to read and family involvement in reading. Teachers were also surveyed to assess their classroom literacy practices and instruction. The same surveys were again administered after the end of the 10-week program. The pre- and post-test analysis "revealed statistically significant increases in children's reading motivation and involvement in literacy activities" (p. 149). Children spent more time reading independently and with family members, and these children were more motivated to read as a result of the Running Start program. Furthermore, "there were statistically significant increases in the amount of time parents and family members reported spending with their children reading books and discussing books and stories. In addition, parents reported that the program increased their child's motivation to read and reading proficiency level" (p. 149). The teacher surveys revealed that teachers sent more books home and learned more about children's literature as a result of the program.

The second study examined the effect of Running Start on first-grade students who were members of ethnic and racial minority groups in four urban schools. Four schools that did not participate in the program served as a control group. The experimental and control group schools were matched in terms of number of students enrolled in the reduced cost lunch program, number of students eligible for compensatory reading programs, and ethnicity. This study involved 500 children, 350 parents, and 23 teachers. At the conclusion of the 10-week Running Start program in the experimental schools, all of the children, parents, and teachers from the eight schools completed the surveys. In addition, 109 children from both the control and experimental schools were interviewed about their motivation to read and reading activities.

Again, the results revealed that Running Start had positive effects on reading motivation and family literacy practices. Gambrell et al. (1995) stated that "when compared to the children in the control schools, the children in the Running Start program were more motivated to read, spent more time reading independently and with family members, engaged more frequently in discussions of books with others, and took more books home to read" (p. 150). The parent and teacher surveys also confirmed the findings from the first study.

Robinson, Larsen, and Haupt (1996) investigated the effects of a similar take-home book program for kindergarten students. Their study examined whether taking home picture books would increase the amount of books read and the amount of time spent reading at home, and if books would be lost or the procedures cumbersome for the teacher. Seventy-five children from two different schools at unspecified locations participated in the study. Each school had two kindergarten classrooms taught by the same teacher (one in the morning and one in the afternoon). At each school one of the classrooms participated in the take-home book program (the treatment group) and one did not (the non-treatment group). One school served a low-income neighborhood and the other served a middle-class neighborhood. Therefore, there were students from both low socioeconomic homes and middle-class homes in the group that received the program. Each of the four classrooms received a set of 40 quality picture books. However, students in the two classrooms participating in the take-home book program were given 10–15 minutes every day to select a book to take home. Parents were surveyed by telephone every week for 12 weeks and asked to report family literacy activities, including instances when their child looked at or read a picture book and who read with the child.

The researchers analyzed their data with statistical procedures and found that "for all children, treatment subjects read significantly more books at home than did subjects in the no-treatment comparison group" (p. 254). In addition, children in the treatment group read significantly more minutes on the sample days than children in the non-treatment group. Importantly, there were no differences between the children from low socioeconomic backgrounds and middle-class backgrounds in terms of amount of reading or who read with the child. Over the 12-week period, children in the treatment group took home books 73% of the time. Only one book was not returned. In addition, teachers reported that managing the take-home book program and checking the books in and out was not disruptive to their curriculum or too time consuming.

The ReadBoston Family Literacy Project, a part of the city's literacy campaign, was designed to (a) establish K-5 classroom-based lending libraries and accompanying reading response activities that encourage families to read at home with children for 20 minutes a day, at least four times per week, and (b) establish twice yearly, individual 20–30-minute parent-teacher conferences that focus on literacy. In order for a school to receive project assistance, 95% of the teachers had to agree to implement the lending libraries and conduct individual parent-teacher conferences. With technical and financial assistance from ReadBoston, the teachers establish classroom lending libraries, send home books (and audiotapes in some cases) at least once per week, send letters to parents explaining the purpose of the books, chart the number of books read by each child, and incorporate reading contracts and/or parent/child response activities into homework routines. The reading response activities vary among teachers and schools and may include writing a summary of or drawing a picture based on the book, writing in a reading journal, creating a book cover or an advertisement, or simply recording the book title and minutes read on a reading contract.

Teachers at participating schools conduct twice yearly, individual parent-teacher conferences that provide parents with suggestions about helping their children with reading at home. ReadBoston also helps the schools hire and train "Parent Liaisons" (usually parents, community members, or school staff) to track participation in lending libraries and conferences and to reach out to nonparticipating families and students. The project started in 1998 in two schools and has expanded every year to now include a total of 15 schools, 245 classrooms, and approximately 4,600 students. Schools are provided with funding for books for three years, after which time the cost of maintaining the classroom libraries must be incorporated into each school's budget. All of the elementary schools involved are part of the Boston Public School system (Pomerantz & Sampson, 2001).

An evaluation consisting of interview, observation, and survey data was undertaken to assess the project's effectiveness in meeting its goals and to discover the ways in which the lending libraries and parent/teacher conferences influenced parents, teachers, and students. The evaluation focused on the following key questions: (a) What are the outcomes of the parent-teacher conferences for teachers, parents, and students? (b) What do teachers, parents, and students do with the classroom lending library books? (c) Can a classroom-based lending library, reading response activities, and/or parent-teacher conferences increase the quantity and quality of parent-child literacy interactions?

Parents and teachers volunteered to be interviewed for the evaluation and received a set of books in appreciation of their participation. Twenty teachers and 21 parents participated in structured interviews, which were audiotaped and transcribed. Six hundred and eighty-one parents out of 2,135 (32%) at nine schools returned written surveys evaluating the project. Forty-two teachers responded to surveys at six schools. Evaluators observed 12 parent-teacher conferences and conducted three "case studies" in which parent-child pairs were observed reading a book from the classroom lending libraries, the parent was interviewed, and the parent-teacher conference observed. The Adult/Child Interactive Reading Inventory (ACIRI) was used to help focus the parent/child reading observations (DeBruin-Parecki, 1999). Site visits were conducted at all 15 schools to observe how the teachers used the lending libraries, and to collect information regarding notable practices, participation rates in the home reading programs, and attendance rates at parent-teacher conferences.

The site visits and conference observations confirmed that the majority of teachers implemented the project as intended. Attendance at parent-teacher conferences ranged from 68%-99% per school in the 1999–2000 school year, with most schools achieving more than 75% attendance. Participation in home reading (as documented by sign-in/out forms, reading contracts, etc.) ranged between 75%-96% depending upon the school, with most classrooms achieving more than 80% participation.

In surveys and interviews, parents and teachers overwhelmingly affirmed the value of the individual conferences and the home reading programs. Teachers cited improvements in attendance, homework completion, home reading participation, behavior, and academic progress as outcomes of the conferences. Teachers also cited increases in the frequency of parent contact after the first conference, suggesting that the conferences may increase parents' confidence regarding interacting with teachers and the school. In addition, several teachers mentioned that the conferences increased their empathy for parents and students and that they increased support at school when they realized home support was limited. Parents reported that they learned about their child's progress, and how it is assessed, how reading is taught, and how to foster reading at home.

As many as 78% (529) of the parents returning surveys reported that the home reading program (books and reading response activities or reading contracts) increased the number of times per week they read to their children or their children read independently. For many families, reading at home increased an average of two times per week as a result of the home reading programs. The surveys did not address whether the books, the response activities, or the reading contracts were the primary factor involved in increasing the amount of reading at home. For some families, the increase may have been due to greater book access, for others the response requirements may have structured home reading, and for others both may have been equally important. However, many parents indicated that they would like their children to take home more books, suggesting that increased access to books is a greatly appreciated and critical component of the program.

The three case studies revealed more in-depth information about the various ways the books and conference information were used by parents and children, and illustrated the need for more specific teacher/parent communication. The case studies suggested that parents and students benefit from demonstration and modeling of specific reading strategies. In one observed parent-teacher conference, the teacher modeled, with the child, the kinds of strategies the mother could use at home. The parent/child reading observation occurred three weeks later and the mother had adopted the strategies modeled by the teacher. In another parent/child reading observation, however, the mother required that the kindergarten child read a book to her that was far too challenging for his reading level. The teacher had not made it clear enough to the parent that the books should be read to the child and had never explained how to tell if a book was too difficult. In the third case study, the teacher told the mother that the child must read at home and the parent tried to comply. However, the child's reading skills were well below his second-grade level and he did not like to read. This mother needed clearer instructions on how to involve her child in reading. Additionally, she needed advice on how to encourage her son to read instead of pressuring him to read.

The ReadBoston Family Literacy Project, Kindergarten Take-Home Book Project, and Running Start evaluations make it clear that classroom lending libraries have the potential to increase the amount of reading parents and children do at home. However, the ReadBoston Family Literacy Project evaluation also suggests that parents may need more information from teachers about how to use the books. The parent-teacher conference is an excellent opportunity to offer such information, and the more specific and individualized that information is the greater its usefulness to the parent and child.

The benefits of sending home books with audiotapes have also been demonstrated (Blum Koskinen, Tennant, Parker, Straub, & Curry, 1995; Koskinen et al., 1999). Researchers conducted two studies in which a total of 171 first-grade students had increased access to books both at school and at home. The students were both English speaking and non-English speaking. The teachers and students were divided into one of four groups as follows: Those that had (a) group shared reading, (b) group shared reading and daily rereading of books at home, (c) group shared reading and daily rereading of books with audiotapes at home, or (d) unchanged reading instruction at school. Teachers in the first three categories created "book-rich" environments by adding books to their classroom libraries (Koskinen et al., 1999, p. 432). The results from "comprehension and fluency assessments as well as teacher, parent, and student questionnaires and interviews revealed enhanced comprehension and motivation for all the students" in classrooms in the first three groups (p. 432). Similar to the findings of the other studies cited above, "home-based reading with and without audio support increased many students' reading interest and promoted parental involvement in literacy activities" (p. 432). However, the audiotapes had special benefits for the English as Second Language students. Teachers and parents reported that the audiotapes were "especially motivating for some second-language learners" (p. 440). The audiotapes also created more opportunities for some children to interact with family members around reading because the entire family could listen to and improve their English from the tapes.

Home Literacy Portfolios

Paratore, Hindin, Krol-Sinclair, and Duran (1999) explored the uses of home literacy portfolios and how they could enhance parent-teacher conferences for both parents and teachers. Their study took place in a diverse urban community and involved four parent-teacher pairs. The mothers participating in the study were immigrants and native Spanish speakers from El Salvador, Guatemala, Peru, and Puerto Rico. Their children were in Spanish bilingual classrooms and were in kindergarten, first grade, and third grade. The mothers attended classes at a family literacy project sponsored by a local university and the school district (discussed later in this chapter). They were instructed to observe their children's literacy practices at home and to collect samples in a "family literacy portfolio." They were asked to include samples of their child's drawings, stories, and letters, as well as their own written observations. The mothers were also taught ways of sharing the portfolio samples with teachers during parent-teacher conferences. The four classroom teachers involved in the study attended three seminars led by the principal researcher in which they discussed articles about home-school partnerships and family literacy, as well as the family literacy portfolios.

The teachers tape-recorded their parent-teacher conferences. A total of eight conferences were analyzed. Parents and teachers also participated in three to four interviews each at the beginning of the study, immediately after the conferences, and at the end of the study. Among the findings was the fact that when literacy was discussed, parents and teachers shared the conversation and were equal participants. Interestingly, when any other topic was discussed teachers dominated the conversation. Thus, the portfolio seemed to give parents the confidence and opportunity to share how they supported their children's learning. It provided teachers with the chance to affirm and encourage what the parents were doing, to connect school literacy activities to what parents and children were doing at home, and to give suggestions about ways parents could build upon the home literacy activities. Teachers, as well as parents, learned from the conferences. In one case, the teacher learned more about the child's abilities, in another the teacher learned that the child was more advanced than she previously believed, and a third case led the teacher to pay greater attention to a child's writing. Thus, the portfolios "led parents and teachers to new insights and understandings about children's uses of literacy at home and at school" (p. 74).

Parents in the Classroom

Nistler and Maiers (2000) implemented a project that brought parents into the classroom to engage in literacy activities with their children in order to "enhance their understanding of literacy development and provide the confidence and support necessary to contribute to their children's literacy development" (p. 670). Maiers, a first-grade teacher in the inner city of Des Moines, Iowa, invited parents or other family representatives to attend her class with their children on selected Fridays from 8:45 until 11:30 a.m. Thirteen sessions were held the first year she implemented the program and 15 sessions were held the second year. Participation increased slowly over several months, but attendance grew to more than 90% in years one and two. Maiers recruited parents by making a visit to their home, by sending written fliers at the beginning of each week a session was to be held, and by making reminder phone calls a day or so beforehand. Babysitting and transportation were provided if necessary, but younger siblings and infants were also welcome to attend the sessions.

Each session consisted of the parents, children, and teacher sharing a poem, and then breaking into four parent/child groups in which parents guided children to reconstruct the poem lines written on sentence strips. Children cut the sentence strips up into words and put the poem together again. They glued and illustrated a copy of the poem into a personal "Poem Book." The whole group read and sang a song. They cooked a simple food with attention paid to basic math concepts (measurement, counting, etc.), vocabulary related to cooking, and reading a recipe. Additionally, parents and children participated in the literacy and math stations in the classroom, including dramatic play, math manipulatives, magnets, music, reading corner, and the art center.

The teacher kept a journal throughout the program and interviewed a family representative for each child at the beginning, middle, and end of the year. Interviews were audiotaped and transcribed. Nistler, a university professor, attended the sessions and noted his observations. Nistler and Maiers found that the program encouraged parents to do similar literacy activities with their children at home, including reconstructing texts with cut up sentences and words, cooking and reading recipes together, reading stories, and providing a space at home for school work, materials, and books. Parents' confidence in their abilities to help their children increased, as did their understanding of what was expected at school.

In addition, it was very clear that the personality and persistence of the particular teacher involved was critical to the program's success. When she left for an eight-week maternity leave, participation in the sessions dropped down to three family members. Nistler and Maiers identified several crucial aspects of the teacher's role. First, she made "simple gestures," such as welcoming and saying goodbye to everybody who entered or left the room, taking and sharing photos of the families who came to the sessions, and asking parents for advice about child-rearing, in addition to the intensive recruitment measures already mentioned (p. 677). The project is particularly notable for its uses of both traditional school literacy activities (the centers, the poem activities) and more typical "home" literacy experiences,

such as cooking and singing. In this way, parents wer\
uses of literacy, " as well as affirming the value and pc\
learning potential of "everyday home activities" (p. 678

Teachers Involve Parents in Schoolwork (TIPS)

Researchers at Johns Hopkins University, working toge\ ... with teachers in Maryland, Virginia, and the District of Columbia created the Teachers Involve Parents in Schoolwork (TIPS) project to help parents support their middle school children's homework assignments (Epstein, Simon, & Salinas, 1997). The TIPS homework assignments are interactive and require that students complete or discuss their work with a family member. Assignments might include interviewing a family member, discussing a topic, or reporting a parent's experiences. All of the assignments include "a section for home-to-school communication in which parents indicate whether the student was able to discuss the homework, whether they enjoyed working on the activity together, and whether they learned something about what the student is learning in class" (p. 1).

Two studies have been conducted regarding the effects of TIPS language arts and science assignments (Epstein et al., 1997; Van Voorhis, 2000). The first examined whether TIPS language arts homework activities "contributed to students' writing scores and report card grades over one school year, beyond what would be predicted by the students' initial skills, and how students and families reacted to the TIPS process" (Epstein et al., 1997, p. 1). The study involved 683 sixth and eighth grade students attending two different schools in Baltimore, Maryland. The students were mostly African-American. The schools served poor families and had low achievement rates in comparison to other city middle schools. Three writing samples were collected in the fall, winter, and spring, as well as attendance records and report card grades. Additionally, students and parents completed surveys evaluating TIPS. The researchers found that the TIPS activities positively influenced students' scores on the writing samples. In addition, those students who completed more TIPS homework activities received higher language arts report card grades. Interestingly, "students with lower report card grades were more positive about TIPS than were more successful students, indicating that TIPS may help keep some of these students engaged in homework even if they do not like school very much" (p. 2). Parents liked the TIPS assignments and felt TIPS provided them with information about what their children were learning in school. Importantly, their participation was not correlated with their socioeconomic status. Also notable was the fact that the teacher's attitude toward TIPS (as measured by the survey) was associated with the students' attitudes toward it. Thus, "if teachers conveyed belief that TIPS is important, students had more positive attitudes about interactive homework" (p. 2).

The second study (Van Voorhis, 2000) examined the effects of Science TIPS on sixth and eighth grade student's science achievement, homework completion, family involvement and attitudes toward science. Two hundred and fifty-three students participated in the study from ten classes taught by four teachers at a diverse Maryland middle school. The teachers and researcher created 18 TIPS science homework activities that were connected to the school curriculum. Each assignment included a letter to the parent that described the activity and its due date, the purpose of the activity, the materials, the steps to complete, the report or chart to display results, conclusions/discussion, a home-to-school communication section and a parent signature. Six of the classes received these interactive assignments and four of the classes received the same assignments without the interactive components (e.g., the letter to the parent, the home-to-school communication section, questions for students to ask parents). The teachers developed test questions to test the students' knowledge from the assignments. Students and parents completed surveys evaluating the assignments. The researcher found that the TIPS interactive assignments promoted more family involvement than the non-TIPS assignments and that students who completed more homework (TIPS or non-TIPS) and involved parents (whether or not the assignment asked them to) had higher science achievement and more positive attitudes toward science. Thus, the study demonstrated the importance of family involvement in science homework and a strategy to promote it.

Teen Parents and Family Literacy

Parent/student literacy projects at the high school level are scarce, probably because students are expected to be increasingly independent and responsible for themselves as they get older. However, one teacher in a high school with a number of teen-age parents saw the opportunity to prepare high school students to read to their own children (Enz & Searfoss, 1995). The teacher designed a children's literature unit to teach students about selecting books that appeal to and encourage young children to read, and expressive reading strategies. The class was designed to help the teens make the connection between early family reading and success in school. Each student was paired with a first grader from a nearby elementary school for nine weeks. During the hour-long, weekly sessions, each high school student read with and coached a beginning reader. The success of the program was made evident by the almost perfect attendance of the high school and elementary students at the weekly sessions, a high rate of homework completion, and an enthusiasm for reading the children's books even when the high school students' were poor readers or did not like reading. In addition, several of the high school students reported that they read to their siblings or children more often as a result of taking the class.

Several important points emerge from the studies in this section. First, teachers can play a very important role in encouraging and influencing parent/child literacy interactions. The teacher's attitude, enthusiasm, organization, and persistence often make the difference between a family's participation or non-participation. Second, increased access to books is often an influential and vital aspect of parent-child literacy projects. Third, high participation in parent-child literacy projects grows over time and sometimes requires intensive recruitment and outreach on the part of the teacher or school coordinator. However, the studies in this section, as well as the following sections, illustrate that most families, regardless of socio-economic status or education level, are willing and able to help their children succeed in school.

EFFECTIVE SCHOOL-BASED PARENT-CHILD LITERACY PROJECTS

The following section addresses parent-child literacy projects that provide instructional services to adults and/or children outside the typical class-room context. These parent-child literacy projects are usually taught by classroom teachers, often initially trained by university staff or staff developers from outside organizations. The following section provides several examples of these types of projects, including those aimed at increasing family involvement in reading and math.

Public Television and Family Literacy

The Family Literacy Alliance demonstrated how a public television series based on books, such as Reading Rainbow, could promote family literacy in a variety of settings, including schools (Liggett, 1995). Coordinators at participating public television stations trained teachers and staff to implement the FLA model at their respective sites. In the Family Literacy Alliance model, teachers lead sessions for parents and children that include watching Reading Rainbow together, reading and discussing the book, and completing a related arts and crafts project. For example, after watching a Reading Rainbow episode that presented a book about families and adoption, parents and children discussed their own families. Materials to make collages were supplied so that parents and children could discuss

ily portrait. At one school, K-2 teachers invited parents and
end sessions every two weeks in the evening. Parents and
enthusiastic and "the teachers shared the creative results of
activities on bulletin boards throughout the school. Soon
the school were asking, 'Can me and my Mom [and/or Dad]
come too. (p. 212). An evaluation of the program at several sites found
that the FLA program increased parents' and children's interest in books
and reading. The evaluators concluded that the FLA approach and use of
public television programs "can create interest in reading" among "people
who have been intimidated by books and libraries" (p. 208). The FLA
model is particularly practical because it makes use of public television: a
resource available to most teachers, children, and parents.

Family Math

Family Math, for grades K-8, was designed by Virginia Thompson at the
University of California, Berkeley in the early 1980s. The purposes of the
program's parent/child sessions are to promote conceptual development
and math strategies and to help parents support their children's math skill
development. During the sessions, parents and children work together to
solve math problems involving manipulative materials. Problems might
include geometric concepts, spatial relationships, interpreting data, esti-
mating, communicating results, and the importance of math to careers
(Bobango & Milgram, 1993). The activities are designed to be consistent
with the standards set forth by the National Council of Teachers of Mathematics. The instructors are often classroom teachers who work on a voluntary basis. Brodsky, Fish, Gross, and Urso (1994) undertook an evaluation
of Family Math implemented at a K-8 school in Brooklyn, New York. The
teachers implementing the program received 12 hours of training by Virginia Thompson and implemented three two-hour sessions for parents and
students after school or on weekends. The evaluation focused on students
in grades four through six and addressed several research questions: (a)
Did participating students show higher gains on math assessment measures
than comparable students? (b) Did parents and students develop more
favorable attitudes toward math? (c) Did Family Math impact on family
involvement with the school? (d) Did teaching Family Math affect classroom teaching?

The evaluation included student attitude questionnaires, parent questionnaires, evaluation forms, teacher and parent interviews, tests of students' conceptual math abilities, and standardized math achievement tests.
The evaluators compared the assessment data for the students participating in Family Math with a matched control group of students who did not

participate over a two-year period. Most students and parents did not attend all three Family Math sessions. In the 1993 group, 61% of the students and families attended two or more sessions and in the 1994 group, 64% of the students and families attended two or more sessions. Results indicated that participation in Family Math had a statistically significant positive effect on students' scores on the assessment measures for those students who attended Family Math two years in a row. This suggests that more Family Math may lead to improved performance because of the additional math experience or increased parental participation. However, it is also possible that students attending Family Math for two years have highly motivated parents to begin with, which positively affected their performance. Other findings from the evaluation suggested that parents liked the program, learned how to help their child with math, and learned how math was taught at school. Parents reported that it was more enjoyable to do math with the child after the sessions and that they were more likely to incorporate math into daily activities. They also reported greater confidence in approaching teachers and the school. Additionally, teachers observed increased confidence on the part of students and parents. Some of the Family Math teachers also reported changing their classroom practices to include more hands-on activities and greater emphasis on problem-solving skills.

Effective Partners in Secondary Literacy Learning

As noted previously, there are not many parent-child literacy projects at the high school level. This may be due to the perception that it is difficult to involve parents of older students or because it is assumed that teenagers do not want their parents to be closely involved with their education. However, Cairney (1995), a university professor, found that his own project and research with parents of secondary school students in Australia "provided little reason to support these assumptions" (p. 522). Six parents requested his help establishing a parent education program to "support and raise parent participation in children's literacy learning and study skills in grades 7–10" (p. 522). The parents had participated in a parent-child literacy project at the elementary school level and wanted a similar program at the secondary level. The parents, teachers, and researchers developed a proposal for the "Effective Partners in Secondary Literacy Learning" project and secured funding. Initially, 17 adults and 57 children (aged 12–17) participated. The school was located in a predominantly low-income suburb of Sydney, Australia, and had a low level of academic achievement in comparison with other secondary schools. Parents attended 11 two-hour sessions taught by a project coordinator or guest speakers (including classroom six-week period. The content of the sessions included the …g and writing processes, learning strategies (e.g., summariz-…es, research techniques), and the use of computers for word …Home tasks" were assigned to parents that involved trying one …ing strategies with their child and/or talking with their child ab… …choolwork. Each session included the presentation of a strategy, practice with the strategy, and discussions of the new information and parents' experiences with the "home tasks."

The project was evaluated through parent surveys and interviews with parents, teachers, and students. Parents reported a high degree of satisfaction with the project. They acquired new strategies and information about literacy and learned how to help their children, improve communication with their children, and gain confidence. Teachers changed their attitudes and expectations about parents' roles in their children's education and perceived an increase in parental involvement in school activities. Both teachers and parents reported positive influences of the project on students. They indicated that as a result of parental participation in the project and the "home tasks," students developed new skills, had higher personal expectations, increased their self-confidence, and improved their relationships with their parent(s).

The Partnership for Family Reading

The Partnership for Family Reading (Handel, 1999) was designed to facilitate adult and child literacy development and to help elementary school teachers be family literacy educators. The program began as a partnership between Montclair State University and the Newark, New Jersey school system. It started in one school in 1987 and, over eight-years, grew to include 34 schools. It is now institutionalized in 10 schools and continues there without university involvement. Teachers and other school staff volunteered for the training, involving two days in the fall and one day in the spring. They then implemented five to six Family Reading sessions for parents at their schools throughout the school year. Each session (designed for parents of children in grades K-3) included introducing a children's book, modeling a reading strategy using the book (such as making predictions, creating questions, connecting personal experience to the book, etc.), practicing reading the book in pairs, and discussing the book and the issues it raised. Parents then borrowed copies of the book to read at home or in the classroom with their child. The atmosphere of the sessions was informal, social, and participatory. Childcare was provided or younger children were invited. Sessions were conducted in Spanish and English and translators were provided for other languages. Participants were mostly mothers.

The effects of the program were evaluated through pai
and interviews. Parents reported that they improved thei
skills through the program and increased their interest in
brought more books into their homes (through visits to the p
as a result of attending the sessions and read more interactive
children. They enjoyed the social relationships fostered by the s   ...s and
gained new insights about their role in their children's education. Teachers reported that children whose parents attended the sessions grew more
interested in classroom reading. Importantly, the teachers who taught the
Family Reading sessions changed their classroom teaching to include more
focus on reading strategies and read more stories to their students.

One of the reasons that the Partnership for Family Reading grew from
one to 34 schools was because of "district endorsement" (Handel, 1999, p.
52). The projects discussed previously were initially implemented by individual teachers or schools, but the school district, often in partnership with
a university or external organization, can be a powerful catalyst for the
implementation and establishment of parent-child literacy projects. The
next section describes two projects with significant district involvement and
support.

PARENT-CHILD LITERACY PROJECTS IMPLEMENTED BY SCHOOL DISTRICTS

Megaskills

Chavkin, Gonzalez, and Rader (2000) explored the reasons behind ris-
ing test scores and parent and student enthusiasm in a previously low per-
forming school district on the Texas-Mexico border. Each school in the
district (K-12) had implemented a home-school program called Megaskills.
Teachers, parents, and students chose the model. The district provided the
funding for the training and the space, equipment, food, and materials
necessary for parent workshops. The workshops were designed to give parents strategies and activities to build students' "megaskills": Confidence,
motivation, effort, responsibility, perseverance, caring, initiative, teamwork, problem solving, common sense and focus. Dorothy Rich is the
author of *Megaskills: How Families Can Help Children Succeed in School and
Beyond* (1988) and the founder of the Home and School Institute, a nonprofit organization, that provides training to school and community members interested in implementing Megaskills activities in the classroom and
in parent workshops. A description of Megaskills and suggested activities
can be found in Dorothy Rich's book. Examples include encouraging the
development of effort in children by talking about one's work in daily con-

versation, creating study spaces for children and home-school boxes for school belongings, and teaching responsibility by having each child in the house take turns waking everyone up for school and work.

In the district studied by Chavkin, et al. (2000), 95% of the students are Hispanic and are mostly from low-income families. Prior to the implementation of Megaskills, the district performed very poorly on the state assessment test compared to others in the state. Principals, parents, and teachers believe Megaskills made a difference and helped the district improve. The researchers collected surveys from five schools (including elementary, middle, and high schools) and more than 1,600 students and families. School staff, parents and students were randomly selected for mid-year and end of year interviews. The researchers also collected achievement, behavior, and attendance information. They found improvement trends in the students' performance on state tests, including reading and math, as well as improvements in behavior (in terms of the number of students referred for disciplinary actions). In addition, parent attendance increased at school activities. Parents and teachers indicated that the program improved the school climate and provided parents, teachers, and students with a common vocabulary that encouraged learning skills and success at school and at home.

The Intergenerational Literacy Project

The Intergenerational Literacy Project (ILP) started in 1989 as a partnership between a university and a local school system. The school system is located in a diverse, urban community in which 66% of students speak English as a second language and 85% are from low-income families (Paratore, Hindin, Krol-Sinclair, & Duran, 1999). The purposes of the project are to support adult literacy development, help parents support their children's literacy development, and educate parents about schools and how to help their children succeed. The project is situated in an early learning center (pre-kindergarten through grade 1) where parents attend classes four days or three evenings per week for two hours per class. Each class is taught by two teachers (graduate students at the university or public school teachers from the district) and three tutors (college work-study students or former program participants). There are many instances of partnership between the district and the project in support of home-school connections. The school district funds the salaries of the director and one teacher, provides the space, and pays teachers to attend workshops about home-school partnerships led by the project director. Additionally, project staff contribute to family literacy events at the district schools and participate in school system committees that help set policies. Classroom teachers in the district refer parents to the project (Krol-Sinclair & Paratore, personal communication, March 12, 2001).

The classes give adults opportunities to read and respond to stories, poems, and articles of interest, provide books and literacy strategies to share with children (the project has a library of multilingual and multicultural books that parents can take home), and offer a context in which to share experiences related to parenting and family literacy. The classes are conducted in English but the parents' first languages are often used in small group and individual discussions with the teachers. On-site childcare is provided. In the morning program, children aged three and four attend an on-site preschool designed to facilitate language and literacy development, and infants and toddlers are cared for by qualified teachers and tutors. In the evening, childcare is provided for children of all ages.

Several studies have evaluated the effects and influence of the ILP (Paratore, 1993, 1994, cited in Paratore, Melzi, & Krol-Sinclair, 1999). Attendance at classes is higher than most adult literacy programs and parents involved make "more rapid gains in literacy achievement" (p. 11). In addition, participating parents increase their literacy interactions with their preschool and school-age children. Paratore et al. (1999) examined the school experiences of 12 children whose parents participated in the ILP classes for five to nine months. Data sources included report card grades, school attendance records, referrals for special services, parent/child/teacher interviews, and parents' reported family literacy practices. The researchers "came to understand that, for these children, success in school was a complex process, dependent on both the actions of parents and teachers separately, and perhaps most importantly, on their interactions" (p. 107). In the eight cases where the children experienced a moderate to high degree of success in school, parents and teachers established "linkages" (p. 109). For example, teachers and parents shared information, ideas, and concerns when children were dropped off or picked up from school, and/or teachers asked parents for specific help on homework assignments. Students who were successful in school also had effective classroom instruction and had frequent literacy interactions at home with their parents.

Four of the students had difficulty in school. There was no single reason these children were failing. Some of the children were affected by their families moving a great deal, divorce, low motivation, a possible learning disability, poor school instruction, and inconsistent support at home. Three of the four children "lacked consistent, daily routines for the practice of family literacy" as well as "collaboration between parents and teachers ... high quality school instruction ... and a consistently high level of motivation to learn" (p. 111).

Importantly, this study demonstrated how family literacy practices and programs can help parents and children succeed but also illustrated the limitations of such programs. The authors wrote, "although family literacy programs are important and may make important contributions to children's ultimate school success, they cannot and will not, by themselves 'correct' the problem of underachievement..." (p. 114).

CONCLUSION

Clearly, the evidence indicates that parent-child literacy projects are worthwhile. When projects are respectful of parents, sensitive to cultural differences, and include parents in planning and development, they can be very helpful in meeting parents and students' needs for greater information, strategies, books, and skills. As the evidence in this chapter demonstrates, home response journals, parent-teacher conferences, parent workshops and classes, take-home books and tapes, parent participation in classroom literacy activities, and interactive homework have the potential to involve families in children's literacy development. But parent-child literacy projects should not be considered the panacea for school failure. Instead, parent-child literacy interactions and the projects that nurture them are one important factor among many influencing success in school, and, as such, should be part of any classroom, school, or district plan.

REFERENCES

Anderson, R.C., Hiebert, E.H., Scott, J.A., & Wilkinson, I.A.G. (1985). *Becoming a nation of readers: The report of the Commission on Reading.* Washington, DC: National Institute of Education.

Blum, I., Koskinen, P., Tennant, N., Parker, E., Straub, M., & Curry, C. (1995). Using audiotaped books to extend classroom literacy instruction into the homes of second-language learners. *Journal of Reading Behavior, 27* (4), 535–561.

Bobango, J., & Milgram, J. (1993). Establishing Family Math. *Middle School Journal, 24*(5), 44–47.

Brodsky, S., Fish, M., Gross, A., & Urso, J. (1994). *An urban family math collaborative.* New York: The Graduate School and University Center of CUNY, Center for Advanced Study in Education. (ERIC Document Reproduction Service No. ED 379 154)

Cairney, T. (1995). Developing parent partnerships in secondary literacy learning. *Journal of Reading, 38*(7), 520–526.

Chavkin, N. F., Gonzalez, J., & Rader, R. (2000). A home-school program in a Texas-Mexico border school: Voices from parents, students, and school staff. *The School Community Journal, 10*(2), 127–137.

DeBruin-Parecki, A. (1999). *Assessing adult/child storybook reading practices* (Report #2-004). Ann Arbor, MI: Center for the Improvement of Early Reading Achievement, University of Michigan.

Enz, B., & Searfoss, L. (1995). Let the circle be unbroken: Teens as literacy learners and teachers. In L. Morrow (Ed.), *Family literacy: Connections in schools and communities* (pp. 115–128). Newark, DE: International Reading Association.

Epstein, J. L., Simon, B. S., & Salinas, K. C. (1997, September). Involving parents in homework in the middle grades. *Phi Delta Kappa, Research Bulletin #18.*

Gambrell, L., Almasi, J., Xie, Q., & Heland, V. (1995). Helping first graders get a running start in reading. In L. Morrow (Ed.), *Family literacy: Connections in schools and communities* (pp. 143–154). Newark, DE: International Reading Association.

Handel, R. (1999). *Building family literacy in an urban community.* New York: Teachers College Press.

Kletzien, S.B. (1996). Reading programs in nationally recognized elementary schools, *Reading Research and Instruction, 35*(3), 260–274.

Koskinen, P., Blum, I., Bisson, S., Phillips, S., Creamer, T., Baker, T. (1999). Sharing reading, books, and audiotapes: Supporting diverse students in school and at home. *The Reading Teacher, 52*(5), 430–444.

Liggett, T. (1995). The Family Literacy Alliance: Using public television, book-based series to motivate at-risk populations. In L. Morrow (Ed.), *Family literacy: Connections in schools and communities* (pp. 206–217). Newark, DE: International Reading Association.

Morningstar, J. W. (1999). Home response journals: Parents as informed contributors in the understanding of their child's literacy development. *The Reading Teacher, 52*(7), 690–697.

Nistler, R., & Maiers, A. (2000). Stopping the silence: Hearing parents' voices in an urban first-grade family literacy program. *The Reading Teacher, 53*(8), 670–680.

Paratore, J.R., Hindin, A., Krol-Sinclair, B., & Duran, P. (1999). Discourse between teachers and Latino parents during conferences based on home literacy portfolios. *Education and Urban Society, 32*(1), 58–82.

Paratore, J.R., Melzi, G., & Krol-Sinclair, B. (1999). *What should we expect of family literacy?* Newark, DE: International Reading Association.

Pomerantz, F., & Sampson, H. (2001). *An evaluation of the Read Boston Family Literacy Project.* Unpublished manuscript.

Rich, D. (1988). *Megaskills ®: How families can help children succeed in school and beyond.* Boston: Houghton Mifflin.

Robinson, C., Larsen, J., & Haupt, J. (1996). The influence of selecting and taking picture books home on the at-home reading behaviors of kindergarten children. *Reading Research and Instruction, 35*(3), 249–259.

Rowe, K.J. (1991). The influence of reading activity at home on students' attitudes towards reading classroom attentiveness and reading achievement: An application of structural equation modelling. *British Journal of Educational Psychology, 61,* 19–35.

Shockley, B., Michalove, B., & Allen, J. (1995). *Engaging families: Connecting home and school literacy communities.* Portsmouth, NH: Heinemann.

Snow, C., Barnes, W., Chandler, J., Goodman, I., & Hemphill, L. (1991). *Unfulfilled expectations: Home and school influences on literacy.* Cambridge, MA: Harvard University Press.

Taylor, B., Pearson, P.D., Clark, K., & Walpole, S. (1999). *Beating the odds in teaching all children to read* (Report #2-006). Ann Arbor: Center for the Improvement of Early Reading Achievement, University of Michigan.

Van Voorhis, F. (2000). *Tales of TIPS: A quasi-experimental investigation of science interactive homework in the middle grades.* Paper presented at the 10th International Roundtable on School, Family, and Community Partnerships, New Orleans, LA.

CHAPTER 5

FAMILY CENTERS IN SCHOOLS

Expanding Possibilities for Partnership

Vivian R. Johnson

"Parents trust the district and they ask principals for information about sending their children to college," said a bright young teacher. He knows this happens because he and his sister grew up in the community in which they teach. Their mother requested information in family centers in local elementary and middle schools that helped her children get college education, Master's degrees and teaching credentials. Always an active parent in the schools, the mother continues to assist in the family centers in the schools where her son and daughter teach.
—R. & B. Estrada (personal communication, 2000).

THE DEVELOPMENT OF FAMILY CENTERS IN SCHOOLS

This powerful example of family-school-community connections illustrates the definition of family centers. They are places where parents and other family members connect with school staff and community participants to gain information, and implement programs in support of children, families, educators and communities. The development of family centers is a promising practice because these special places in schools promote families' involvement in children's learning (Johnson, 1993, 1994b; Johnstone, 1997). In the illustration above, a parent in the predominately Latino Lennox School District in Los Angeles County gained information from a family center that assisted her son and daughter in preparing for college. After

85

receiving their college education, Master's degrees and teaching credentials, these young people returned to the Lennox community to teach. In the family centers in each of the schools in which they teach, their mother continues working to assist other parents in gaining information about college opportunities for their children. Despite the fact that Lennox is a low-income community, expectations are high (Johnson, 2000). The cycle of information sharing and mutual assistance is widened and deepened in the connections made in the family centers in these schools. Ever expanding opportunities for family-school-community partnership results from these connections. Family centers are a specific school practice that supports the expansion of these connections because they encourage broader participation by families that may be hesitant to become involved in schools (Johnson, 1994a). In their study of school programs and parents' attitudes, Dauber and Epstein (1993) note the importance of school activities that encourage participation:

> The strongest and most consistent predictors of parent involvement at school and at home are the specific school programs and teacher practices that encourage and guide parent involvement. Regardless of parent education, family size, student ability, or school level ... parents are more likely to become partners in their children's education if they perceive that the schools have strong practices to involve parents at school. (p. 61)

CHANGING ATTITUDES REGARDING PARENTS' ROLES IN EDUCATION

Educators' traditional attitudes toward parents was that they should come to school only on invitation. Children's performances and open house were special times when parents were expected to be at school. In addition, they were expected to participate in the bake sale, and other fundraising events. If children misbehaved, parents were often asked to come to school to discuss their youngsters' problems. The idea of parents coming in and out of the school at any time was seen as intrusive and a challenge to teachers' professionalism. Tradition held that parents should support schools from home by making certain that homework was done and children were at school on time. Parents and teachers provided "separate spheres of influence" based on their separate contributions to children's growth and development. Urie Bronfenbrenner challenged tradition in his 1979 classic book *The Ecology of Human Development: Experiments by Nature and Design*, by promoting the study of human development in context.

Emphasizing the importance of relationships, Bronfenbrenner noted that, "In ecological research, the principal main effects are likely to be interactions" (p. 38). In an extension of Bronfenbrenner's theoretical orientation, Epstein in Chapter 1 provides a graphic representation of the ecology of children's development by representing family, school and community as "overlapping spheres of influence" in children's lives. In her conceptual model, the overlapping spheres may be pushed together or pulled apart by forces within a child's ecological environment. My research on family centers is conducted within this framework (Johnson, 1993, 1994b).

An earlier challenge to traditional roles of parents and teachers came from the passage of the Elementary and Secondary Education Act in 1965. Parental oversight and sign off were required for school programs designed for children from low-income families. Desegregation plans, mandating inclusion of parents on school councils provided a third challenge—this time to traditional school governance. A fourth challenge came from the national call to action following the 1983 publication of *A Nation at Risk*. Since that alarm was sounded, educators have regularly requested parental assistance in school reform efforts. A decade later a poll of 1,000 public school teachers by *Education Week* (May 19, 1993) showed that increasing parental involvement in schools was one of two top priorities on their national educational agenda.

BRIEF HISTORY OF FAMILY CENTERS

A relatively new example of family-school community partnership, family centers are an example of a strong practice that has been expanding during the past 15 years. I conducted the first study of the centers in 1991 through the network of the League of Schools Reaching Out sponsored by the Institute For Responsive Education in Boston. The League included more than 70 schools from Puerto Rico to Hawaii engaged in a variety of activities to improve children's learning through enhanced partnerships with families and communities (Davies, Birch, & Johnson, 1992). Thirty-one of the League schools had family centers and 28 of the 31 returned a survey requesting information about the centers. Twenty-three were elementary schools, three were middle schools and two were junior high schools. The following discussion of family centers will therefore focus on schools at those levels. Eight features of family centers were identified by the survey respondents: *definitions, initiation, names, space, staff, funds, hours of operation, and activities.*

Definition of a Family Center

Defined as special places in schools where family members can meet, plan, and implement programs, family centers are also places where school staff and community volunteers are invited to collaborate in support of children's academic and social development. A particular emphasis in the definitions provided by family center participants was the importance of the *designation* of a special place in schools for families. The provision of "a place of their own" for parents in schools signals a change in attitudes regarding parents' role in education.

I (Johnson, 1993) argue that the idea of a special place for parents in schools represents a significant symbolic and structural change in schools' relationship with families. Parent rooms or family centers, as these special places are usually called, are a feature of school restructuring that has received less attention than school-based management, for example, but are a development that require close examination because they represent a profound change in the way educators view the role of parents in schools and the way parents view their role in their children's formal education.

Initiation of Family Centers in Schools

Changing definitions of parents' roles in their children's formal education prompted the establishment of special places for families to gather in schools. From the 1991, study of family centers, following is the information received regarding the age of the 28 centers surveyed in 14 states.

In a 1993 article, I noted that the development of parent/family centers is a recent process in most schools. With the exception of one center that evolved from a PTA effort that began in 1924, and another center that began in 1979, all the centers began within the last five years. Most were started as a result of (1) parents' request for a place of their own, (2) teachers' and parents' request for space to work together more closely, (3) implementation of a district policy of parental involvement, or (4) principals' leadership.

Names of Family Centers

Family center names vary. However, most were called "parent centers" or "parent rooms" during the first study. During visits to centers in the 1990s, I found more named "Family Center." Other names indicate ideas about use by a range of participants. Examples include Learning Lab for Students and Parents, Parent-Community Networking Center and Community

Room. Interviews with center participants indicate a uniform concern about promoting family-school-community cooperation, collaboration and partnership within these special places in schools.

Space: The Importance of "Structure"

Family centers are a structure that takes family-school-community partnership off the margins of school life and brings it into the daily life of schools. Families are structured into the school space. There is a place for them in the school, so they are clearly expected at any time. Parents and other family members have to sign in and observe other school rules regarding visitors, but they are visitors with a room of their own. In their special space, family members make decisions about furnishings, activities, hours and procedures. The initiation of a family center changes the structure of relationships between the adults (parents and teachers) in the overlapping spheres influencing children's lives. The traditional structure is one in which family and community members visit schools only on the invitation of teachers and other school staff. When a space is designated, families are no longer simply invited guests in schools. They are sometimes hosts, who reach out to other families and "reach in" to invite teachers, other school staff and community participants to join them in a wide range of programs in support of children's development. By structuring families into schools, educators symbolically change their status from outsiders to insiders (Johnson, 1993). The change is important because research studies indicate the existence of poor communication between families and schools, and parents report they are uncertain what to do to help their children with school work (Dauber & Epstein 1993; Johnson, 1991b). In the family center, parents have a place designed to make them comfortable about asking questions and opportunity to share experiences with other parents. Explaining her participation in a family center, one parent said: "The main reason is that I enjoy the children so much. I always feel welcome anytime I come into the Family Center. Everyone is so nice and makes you feel at home" (Johnson, 1996, pp. 3–5). Greetings increase parents' feeling of comfort and a space increases their feelings of belonging. Feelings of comfort and belonging in school increase the possibility that parents and other care givers will become partners with schools in promoting children's academic performance. Involvement not only benefits children, but also parents, as noted by a grandfather's statement at a family center in Boston. "Now, my granddaughter ... is really giving me an education. I'm helping her, and she's helping me. I'm trying to bring my education up to date and get my GED. And she helps me at night" (Johnson, 1990, p. 21). Winters (1993) examined the effects of school participation on African American mothers in urban schools in low income communities.

> African-American mothers have benefited by discovering and rediscovering skills and abilities. A number have emerged with a keener sense of responsibility, commitment, and a fierce determination to improve their lot in life. They elect to further their education or seek employment training. Their newly found strength is reinforced as they extend themselves in helping others. (p. 111)

Family centers provide space where parents can gain information, explore issues, develop skills and help others.

Parent Information Centers and Parent Resource Centers

Differences in initiation and space distinguish family centers from Parent Information Centers and Family Resource Centers at the community or state level. Family centers located inside schools, and those initiated by school staff, but located offsite, are distinguished from information or resource centers by structural and symbolic differences. Because family centers are initiated locally, they modify the local school organization pattern by structuring families into school life. Because space for family centers is allocated by local school staff, their local action signals the symbolic change for families from outsiders to insiders. The contrast is between local action that can be closely observed and distant action that is usually unobserved. In contrast to locally initiated family centers, parent information centers and family resource centers are usually initiated by staff within city or state governments or agencies. These centers may be located in a particular school, but local staff, parents and the community have not initiated the action. The distinction was described in Johnson (1993) based on a study by Glenn, McLaughlin, and Salganik (1993).

> Parent or family centers in schools are different from parent information centers (PIC), another innovation becoming more common across the country. The two differ in origin and function. Parent centers are usually initiated by parents in consultation with principals and teachers or they are sometimes initiated by teachers or principals. They are located in or near, and usually serve, a particular school. Parent information centers, on the other hand, are offices that are centrally located in a community and set up by school departments to provide a range of information to parents about school assignments and district services. The difference is significant—parent centers often represent a parent initiative and are usually operated by parents. PICs represent a school initiative and may or may not be operated by parents. Some PICs offer various types of parent training programs requested by parents, how-

ever, most PICs are primarily information centers and referral offices related to children's school assignments, especially in school desegregation plans. (pp. 2–3)

In addition to information, some district-wide family centers offer a wide range of family support programs. In Buffalo, for example, parents from all schools in the district participate in programs at a center that include activities for parents with their teenagers. Federal funding also supports statewide Parent Information Resource Centers (PIRCs) that are often information clearinghouses (Leontovich,1999).

Space: Size and Location of Family Centers

Varying in size from a few feet at the edge of a library to complete classrooms, school-based family centers usually serve a particular school and they are located in or near that school. When space is limited, parents and teachers find that an unused area in the basement, or a space in a stairwell might serve as a place for parents to meet, plan, and implement programs. The space may be insufficient for meetings as parents discovered at the Tomasita School in Albuquerque. Their solution was to store materials and supplies in a space shared with the custodian and the school's physical education equipment. The space was named "Parent Room" rather than "Center" and meetings were held elsewhere.

My research (Johnson, 1993) revealed that lack of a "Center" has not deterred parents in the school from active participation. They find other meeting space within the school and use the Parent Room for storage, including storage of children's clothes in a clothing bank, and storage of a popcorn popper used in fund-raising. Once a month, parents make four hundred bags of popcorn which are sold to children as an after-school snack for twenty-five cents. Funds collected from the popcorn sale are distributed to each class in the school on a rotating basis and teachers, parents and children in the class decide how to spend the money. Funds have been used for field trips, classroom equipment and mateials for special projects such as science or art projects.

In San Diego, California, expanding enrollments reduced the space available for family centers in most schools. A very creative solution has been used to address this challenge—a mobile Parent Center. A school bus has been outfitted with tables, chairs, and other equipment bolted to the floor. Materials in a variety of languages are stored on the bus and it travels throughout the city for a scheduled program at school parking areas. Parents come aboard and gather for a wide range of parent education classes.

Instructors share information, show books for home reading and assist parents in making materials for home use in reinforcing school skills.

A Family Center Apartment

Similar activities occur in a very different setting in Fairfax County, Virginia. When Susan Ackroyd, principal of Parklawn Elementary School, realized that over half of her students lived in the same housing complex, she decided to get an apartment in the complex for a family center. Activities include parent curriculum workshops, family literacy, after school tutoring and connections to community agencies. The nearly 800 students attending the school come from more than 37 countries and speak 34 languages. Staffed by a full-time teacher and a full-time hourly instructor, the family center brings this diverse cultural community together in a wide range of programs of family school-community collaboration (Johnson, 2000).

Staffing Family Centers

Family center staff may be paid or voluntary. However, if staff were voluntary, survey respondents in the 1991 study indicated fundraising efforts to fund a paid position. Interviews with principals and center participants reveal general agreement that staff should be paid because the job is demanding and payment promotes stability and status in the position. Center coordinators are often parents of current or former students at the school. Teachers, or former teachers sometimes staff centers as well. In some schools, Title One funds are used to fund the center including the coordinator's position (Johnson, 1993).

Funding Family Centers

Funding for family centers is rarely stable. Most center staff seek funding sources constantly and many coordinators mention funding as their major problem. Funding support includes some combination of donations, often from business partners; school funds; Title I funds; and fundraising activities in the center.

Equipment in centers is often donated and sometimes books and other materials are donated as well. Staffing is the primary expenditure, followed by materials for participants. Telephones, television and VCRs were in half of the 28 centers surveyed (Johnson 1993, 1994b).

Hours of Operation in Family Centers

Center hours are flexible in response to participants' schedules and hours vary considerably. Some centers are open several hours a day, weekends and for special school events like Open House, Family Math Night, or performances. Others are open during the regular school day and reopen for special events. After school tutoring sessions or parent meetings may be the only time some centers open if there is no regular staff person. School events during December holidays and May or June graduation often increase activities in family centers. They are often the places where family members, teachers, students, and community participants meet to plan, and sometimes store equipment, for these events. The three variables that most likely influence family center hours are funding, parents' work schedules, and school activities (Johnson, 1993, 1994b).

Activities in Family Centers

Family Center activities link schools to families and communities. When these activities are examined within Epstein's (1987) Overlapping Spheres of Influence, the centers may be viewed as connectors within this conceptual framework because their activities bring families, schools and communities together. Increased interaction among the three spheres, occurring in or promoted by family centers, can create a dynamic connecting force to develop greater overlap among the spheres. Family centers are a promising school practice because greater overlap increases opportunities for collaboration among families, schools and communities. Within the model of Overlapping Spheres of Influence, Epstein has created a framework for studying school, family, community interaction. Activities occurring within family centers can be categorized within Epstein's (1995) six types of involvement: Parenting, Communicating, Volunteering, Learning at Home, Decision Making and Collaborating with the Community. Examples within each category follow.

Epstein's Type 1: Parenting
Analysis of data collected from the 28 schools in the first study published in 1993 revealed that family centers are used for meetings, workrooms, tutoring spaces, and gathering places before and/or after school events. Following is a brief description of prevalent activities.

All (28) schools reported that their parent/family centers are used to provide parent information and nearly all centers conduct parent workshops or classes on a variety of topics in response to parental needs. The next two areas in which most assistance is provided to families are social service referrals and child care. More than half of the schools noted those types of assistance. About one third of the schools' centers have lending libraries offering books, audiotapes, videotapes and toys, in that order. One school also loans globes. About a third of the schools also coordinate home visits, translate materials from English to the language spoken at home and also translate for parents attending meetings at schools. In addition, seven reported computer classes for parents, six reported health and nutrition classes and five reported adult education and English as a Second Language classes. (Johnson, 1993 p. 8)

In Family centers, Type I activities often involve a combination of parent education and response to basic needs. For example, some family centers have food banks where families can purchase food at low costs. Parents may form a cooperative in which they take turns purchasing or bagging groceries, worth $50, available to families for $1 per bag. In many centers, these food banks continue until the activity can be turned over to another agency in the community. In addition to food banks, some family centers also sponsor needed health services for families. In the Benson Elementary School in the Lennox section of Los Angeles County, health screening services were provided by the UCLA Medical Center. Therefore, Type I (Parenting) and Type VI (Collaborating with the Community) activities were combined at the school. The principal, Dr. Thomas Johnstone (1997) described an important health service event illustrating this combination.

> The Buford Elementary School parent center Grand Opening/Health Fair was a crucial and pivotal event in exposing and addressing the needs of the Benson community and determining future directions for parent involvement. The health fair provided the spark to bring the community together and the opportunity for the school to address a number of the community needs identified in an April 1993 Parent Survey…, including clothing distribution, food distribution, substance abuse education, police assistance, counseling and various forms of medical services. (p. 58)

Health screening at the Fair revealed a large number of medical and dental problems that could not be addressed locally because of a lack of health services in the area. Two hundred eighty-seven people were screened and the vast majority with medical conditions received no follow-up because they lacked health insurance. One hundred two children screened were found to have dental cavities; none sought treatment.

Concerned about the health of the community, the parent involvement team from the Buford School wrote a proposal to bring health services to the community. The team, including parents from the school, two doctors from UCLA, the principal and a social worker, was unsuccessful in the first attempt to receive funding, but later received a Healthy Start implementation grant of $300,000 for direct health services in the community. Health Fairs, similar to the screenings at Buford Elementary School, were extended to six other schools in the area (Johnstone, 1997, pp. 60–63). Concern about the health needs of the community focused the efforts of the parent involvement team at the school and expanded collaboration with community resources.

In under served low-income communities, Type I activities in Epstein's framework represent a very important response to families' basic needs related to food, clothing and health. Family centers provide a special place in schools where basic needs of families can be acknowledged and plans developed to address them. Johnstone (1997) notes that community outreach was strengthened as parent involvement grew in the early years of the center. Clothing and food distributions were expanded along with classroom and parent field trips. Schools are not health or social welfare agencies. However, by finding ways to assist families in addressing their basic needs through collaborative activities, schools increase communication (Type II) and expand the opportunity for activities in Type III (Volunteering) and Type IV (Learning at Home). This progressive development in the Types of parent involvement activity is seen in the movement from Type I to Type IV at the Benson Elementary School. Parents involved in Type I family development were encouraged to remain at school to volunteer (Type III) after their morning English as a Second Language classes. During a 90–minute orientation replacing Back to School Night, parents were given information regarding ways to get involved in their children's education. (Types II and IV. Family school-community partnership in Types III and IV at the Buford Elementary School was expanded through a range of activities that increased Communication which is Epstein's Type II involvement.

Epstein's Type II: Communications

In their study of minority parents and their youth, Ritter, Mont-Reynaud, and Dombusch (1993) report

> There is a consistent pattern: Parents who are deferential to and less comfortable with teachers and schools are less likely to attend school programs and discuss problems with the schools. Lower parent involvement by some ethnic groups is associated with trusting schools or a lack of ease in dealing with schools. (p. 118)

Family centers are a school practice designed to address problems of ease and comfort and improve home-school communication because expanded communication is a primary focus of these special places in schools. Describing the importance of positive home-school-community communication, Family Center Coordinator Mercedes Pacheco notes that she felt uncomfortable when she first started volunteering at Memorial Academy Middle School in San Diego. However, she "started talking to people, because things that go on in the school are our responsibility" (Leontovich, 1999, p. 5). She began volunteering 14 years ago and combined her efforts with those of other parents, teachers, and administrators. Memorial Academy is a welcoming school for parents and the community and Ms. Pacheco continues to "smile at them, walk with them, talk with them, and ask questions" (Leontovich, p. 5). The family center also has an activity in which communication is expanded by powerful silence rather than speaking. When students misbehave in a classroom, teachers may request "Parent Presence." With the knowledge of the principal, several parents from the family center go to the class the next time it meets. They simply sit in the back of the room and observe the class. Their silent presence communicates a powerful message to students and the misbehavior almost always stops (Johnson, 1994b).

Epstein's Type III: Volunteering

Family centers are often the places in schools where volunteering is coordinated. Family members' skills, talents, and interests are matched with students' needs for tutoring and teachers' needs for assistance in classrooms or on field trips. In their analysis of National Education Longitudinal Study of 1988 (NELS:88) data, Catsambis and Garland (2000) report that changes in types of involvement, including volunteering, may occur, between grades 8 and 12.

> Parent-initiated contacts about academic programs and volunteering are also higher in high school than in the middle grades. Overall, the big change in parent/school communication between the two school grades, namely 8th and 12th, occurs in communications about parents' involvement in academic choices and school activities. Levels of communication about students' individual progress do not change much between the two grades. By the 12th grade, 41% report contacting the school about volunteering and 46% report contacting the school about the school's academic program. (pp. 9–10)

The finding in the NELS: 88 Study that 41% of 13,500 twelfth-grade parents surveyed noted that they contact the school about volunteering is an indication of how common this activity is in family involvement in schools. My interviews at the elementary and middle school levels with parents, teachers and administrators (Johnson, 1993, 1994b) revealed the importance of family centers in coordinating well planned and continuous outreach orientation and training for volunteers. Outreach to parents through personal contact was noted as especially important through phone calls, and speaking with parents whenever they are in school. Community outreach includes announcements at religious institutions, colleges, agencies, and businesses. Volunteering is defined and explained in terms of flexible opportunities in classrooms, offices, and field trips. In their invitations, schools provide examples of activities in addition to tutoring and office work. Examples include: demonstrating a skill or hobby to a class, inviting students to visit businesses, showing slides and artifacts from trips to student interest groups and corresponding with a student with similar interests about a project or research topic. School administrators also note the importance of having a plan for screening volunteers to ensure school safety. Orientation for volunteers provides an opportunity to explain the school mission and particular goals and objectives of curriculum for each grade. It is also crucial for their functioning within school schedules and following school procedures. At orientation sessions, volunteers share information about their skills, talents and interests to determine matches with students' needs. Following orientation, volunteers can be given specific training to prepare them for classroom assistance, tutoring, office work, or field activities. Frequently, the family center is the place where the training occurs and family center coordinators arrange the logistics of volunteer assignments within a school. Some volunteers move into paid positions as aides in schools. At Myles Park Elementary School in Cleveland, a school-wide Title I school, there were six educational aides.

> The Educational Aides are an integral part of the school staff and join teachers and principal in finding ways to enhance education for children. One example is a summer enrichment program initiated by Mathews and Rogers and implemented with the principal's and teachers' assistance in curriculum development. The summer program grew out of concern about poor reading scores two years ago (1989). Enlisting assistance of teenagers to help with younger children, the parents developed a school and community program for sixty-two children, K-6 for six weeks during the summer. Reading skills building, field trips to the zoo and other enrichment activities combined to bring about improved behavior along with higher reading scores. (Johnson, 1991a, pp. 36–37)

Epstein's Type IV: Learning at Home

Some parents develop homework-focused activities in their daily family lives as they organize activities to assist their children in reinforcing school skills. In his study of parents' homework-focused parenting practices, Clark (1993), describes parents' specific homework-related behaviors

> ...as parenting practices (e.g., providing a setting conducive for homework completion, equipping the child with skills for resolving homework problems, making resources available to the child, providing positive parental homework guidance, exposing the child to role models of active learning,

and monitoring during homework). The data showed that most parents of both high and low-achieving students were enacting some of the positive behaviors that contribute to student achievement. Most parents were providing a quiet place to study, sending the children to school regularly, providing a regular time for home-study activities, and expecting children to complete homework assignments. To be academically successful, students apparently needed their parents (or other adults) to expose them to an array of additional support behaviors. Uneven levels of parenting skills were especially apparent between parents of high and low achievers with regard to parent-child learning patterns (e.g., monitoring of children's home-study behavior and parents' expectation for their children's education) and parent-personality patterns (e.g., feelings about children's learning and perceptions about their ability to support their children's homework). (pp.103–104)

Support for children's homework was provided to parents through the family center at the Ellis Elementary School in Boston (Johnson, 1991b). During home visits, special school aides, called Parent Support Workers, assisted parents in reinforcing school skills through modeling rather than tutoring. The program began when a random sampling of parents was asked how the school could be most helpful. When 80% of the responding parents said they wanted to learn how to help their children with schoolwork, the Parent Support Workers Project was launched through the school's family center. Two Latina and two African American women were selected as home visitors for the project. All four women were long time community residents with college training and extensive experience in supportive activities with families. Their training for the Parent Support Workers project included techniques for building on family strengths, modeling versus tutoring skills, explanations of homework expectations by teachers, and activities to link home and school. Each support worker visited ten families weekly and documented progress in weekly reports. As Swap (1990) noted, these aides

> ...offered parents friendship; support for parenting concerns; information, modeling and feedback about how parents can support their children's learning at school; referral information about (e.g., finding improved housing, medical care, or summer program information; and greater connection to the school through information about school activities, hints about communicating with teachers, and support for getting more involved at the school. (p. 51)

Recent evidence that school support for home learning can improve children's academic performance is indicated by Henderson's (2000) report of a ten-year effort at the O'Hearn Elementary school in Boston. In 1990, the school was near the bottom of the cities' 78 elementary schools on students' reading performance. A home reading program was launched with a contest to encourage students to read more books. A family center was opened in the school in the same year. The following year, the school increased the number of books available for students to read at home and developed a reading contract. The contract required that all students read or be read to at home 15–20 minutes four days a week. Fifty percent of the students participated in this effort. In order to improve participation, the following year, parents from the school visited every incoming family and took a book for each child in the family. After a few years, participation rose to 84%. In order to gain further improvement, parents, teachers and administrators increased their contact with families who were not participating in the home reading activities. Henderson reports the results of this continuous effort over a 10-year period:

> As of the middle of the 1999–2000 school year, 95 percent of O'Hearn students now participate regularly in the home reading program. Over the years that we have promoted home reading, our students' performance on standardized tests has also shown steady and dramatic improvement. O'Hearn's recent scores on the Stanford 9 reading test put the school above the national average and near the top of Boston's elementary schools. (p. 48)

This school's home reading program is not solely a function of its family center. It is an activity of the entire school. However, during the ten-year period in which the home reading program has been developed and expanded, the family center has been a hub of activity—welcoming families into the school with breakfasts, family math nights and school information sessions. Having a strong family center in the school reinforces the outreach needed to improve participation in home reading.

Epstein's Type V: Decision Making

In my 1991 survey of 28 schools in 14 states, respondents reported that governance was the area of greatest parental involvement. Seventy-five percent of the responding schools indicated that their family centers sponsor school-decision making meetings. District requirements for parental and community involvement in school restructuring efforts and school-based management also increase participation in this area. In addition to providing space for meetings, family centers provide a place to discuss, explore and examine important decisions affecting the school. One parent noted during an interview: "I have used the Parent Room to do planning for School Based Management with the Principal"(Johnson, 1996, p. 115). Other parents noted that their participation in the family center gave them a greater sense of safety and belonging.

> **Parents' Comments**
>
> "It makes you feel like you belong here" (Johnson, 1994b, p. 37).
>
> "This school makes me feel like I'm included and my thoughts matter" (p.38).
>
> "Great opportunity to meet with other parents and discuss a variety of topics--as adults—while children are able to play with others in a safe and fun environment" (Johnson, 1996, p. 57).

At the Buford Elementary School in Los Angeles County, Johnstone (1997) reported that following the implementation of Epstein Type I activities responding to families' basic needs, the parent center shifted priorities during the next two years to develop parents' leadership capacity. The development of leadership capacity in parents, was itself, an evolutionary process. Parents with a willingness to lead emerged early in the parent center program, but with no existing tradition of parent leadership initiative, the nurturing of this parent leadership took time and patience to develop. For the first two years, parent leaders gained confidence. By year three, they were actively fund-raising $12,000 and demonstrating a willingness to initiate involvement at the PTA district and state levels (p. 92).

Epstein's Type VI: Collaborating with the Community

Family centers serve as linkage agents connecting schools to families, social service agencies, churches, organizations, colleges and universities, as well as businesses. Therefore, collaboration between schools and communities is often coordinated in family centers. Following are examples from my 1993 report of survey responses from 28 schools in 14 states. Most schools report some type of business church or other type of community partnership. Universities are mentioned less often than businesses. Lions Clubs, Rotary Clubs, police departments, or divisions, military units, law firms, health centers, block associations, a musician's association, and a local Red Cross were also mentioned as examples of school partners (Johnson, 1993, p. 11).

School-family-community collaboration has expanded during the past two decades as educators reached out to families and communities to request assistance in supporting children in school. Partners and other volunteers provide a wide range of aid including tutoring, equipment, funding, and special programs, such as career days. Many family centers develop listings of community resources available to assist families with social services. Information about community activities for children during the summer and other school vacations is especially valuable for families. Announcements of food distribution, clothing exchanges, employment opportunities and job training are often found on family center bulletin boards (Johnson, 1994b, 1996). By providing information about community resources, family center staff combine Type I (Parenting) and Type VI (Collaborating With The Community) activities.

School, family community collaboration opportunities were expanded nationally in December 1995 with the launching of the Family Involvement Partnership for Learning. The national effort is a joint project between the U.S. Department of Education and more than 170 organizations. By signing an "Employer's Promise for Learning," organizations commit themselves to support family involvement in education through family-friendly work policies. Released time for participation in their children's schools, as well as opportunities for flex time in employment are examples of suggested policies. Included among current participants in the collaboration are Hewlett Packard, Wells Fargo & Co., GTE (now Verizon), United Airlines and the U.S. Army (U.S. Department of Education, 1996). In addition to giving employees an opportunity to become more involved with their children's schools, this corporate commitment increases organizational and company options in providing human and other resources to schools (Johnson, 1998). For example, donations of equipment, such as computers, may expand opportunity for both students and their families to learn technology. At the Holland Elementary School in Boston, computers donated by the business partner are used by students during the school day and for a computer course (in English and Spanish) offered evenings for parents. At Memorial Academy middle school in San Diego, a local business gave $12,000 worth of $50 gift certificates to be used in their store by parents volunteering at the school. The activity was coordinated through the family center. Community groups may provide parent workshops as well as other types of resources. At the Horton Elementary School, also in San Diego, workshops in cultural context were provided in the family center by a Latino organization called The Parent Institute, and an African American organization called the Center for Parent Involvement in Education. Both groups provided parent education and support to assist parents in learning about ways to assist their children by reinforcing school skills at home. Workshop sessions also focused on community activism to involve other parents and gain community support for schools as well as training in assisting other parents when their children experienced difficulty in school. School administrators note their desire to expand school-community collaboration as a means of addressing complex family needs. Many indicated the need for better connections to social services to assist families with adult education, job training, and support services for children and adolescents (Johnson, 1993).

CONCLUSIONS

Family centers provide a place in school that brings adults together from families, schools and communities who share in the care of children. Centers represent a promising practice because evidence shows that programs in these special places in schools, can address barriers to family-school-community partnership related to norms, knowledge and comfort.

Norms

Tradition dictates that, parents and teachers meet in formal ways dictated by the norms of Open House and Parent-Teacher Conferences. These formal meetings are not the natural ways that adults come together to discuss children's growth and development. Moreover, differences in roles may strain teacher-parent relationships despite their desire to form partnerships. Lightfoot (1978) argues that home-school relationships are embedded in a pattern of role-related conflict.

> Families and schools are engaged in a complimentary sociocultural task and yet they find themselves in great conflict with one another. One would expect that parents and teachers would be natural allies, but social scientists and our own experience recognize their adversarial relationship—one that emerges out of their roles as they are defined by the social structure of society, not necessarily or primarily the dynamics of interpersonal behaviors. (p. 20)

A century ago, parent-teacher interpersonal relationships were likely to be informal as well as formal, because teachers were more likely to live in the communities in which they taught. They saw their students and students' parents in a variety of community places including the grocery store, sports events and religious activities. Adults encountered each other within a wide range of interpersonal activities in which they developed a sense of mutual accountability in raising children. In contrast, changing demographics have created educational institutions in which few, if any of the teachers live in the neighborhoods in which they teach. Schools are therefore challenged to find programs and practices to develop partnerships with parents and community partners that will enhance adults' mutual accountability for children's academic and social success. Noting that partners recognize their shared interest and responsibility, in the following quote Epstein (1995) stresses the importance of creating partnerships to care for the children we share:

> If educators view children simply as *students*, they are likely to see the family as separate from the school. That is, the family is expected to do its job and

leave the education of children to the schools. If educators view students as *children*, they are likely to see both the family and the community partner with the school in children's education and development. (p. 701)

Winters (1993) also examined accountability in parent-teacher relationships. As an aspect of participation, shared accountability shifts the power and improves the basis for negotiation and understanding between those functioning within the social system of the school. This is particularly pertinent where there are differences of educational achievement between school personnel and residents in disadvantaged urban communities. Accountability serves a leveling function. Expectations on both sides are altered, changing the school's expectations and appreciation, as well as that of parents. In the context of shared tasks and shared accountability, blame is reduced. As a valued stance, accountability is transferable to other experiences and interactions (pp. 106–107).

Family centers are a promising practice in the development of mutual accountability for children because they signal welcome and a school's expectation that parents and other community residents will come because there is a place for them in the school.

Knowledge

In attempting to develop partnerships to promote mutual accountability for children, parents and teachers often have a mutual problem. They lack knowledge about each other. Not only do formal meetings and lack of frequent social contact decrease their opportunities to interact as adults caring for children they share, parents and teachers are uncertain about outreach to each other. Teachers report lack of training in ways to develop partnerships (Becker & Epstein, 1982; Epstein, 1985). Parents report lack of knowledge about how schools work or what is expected of them in assisting their children (Chavkin & Williams, 1993; Dauber & Epstein, 1993; Ritter, Mont-Reynaud, & Dornbusch, 1993).

Comfort

In addition to lack of knowledge, parents and teachers are often uncomfortable with each other. The discomfort may be a function of the nature of schools as powerful institutions of assessment. Schools have the power to greatly influence children's futures both by what they do and what they fail to do. School performance is very consequential for children; yet, teachers are often uncertain about how to explain curriculum and testing to parents.

For some parents, school procedures, curriculum, testing, and expectations remain a mystery despite the fact that they attended schools. Other parents report feelings of intimidation because they were not good students.

> People who performed well in school as children and understand school structure as adults are likely to come to school. All others are less likely to come unless special outreach programs are developed to contact them. It is not surprising that people for whom school was a painful experience in childhood, or whose children are having academic or social problems in school are not anxious to go into schools. Parents who do not speak English well or those who do not understand school curriculum or organization are also unlikely to come to school. The people least likely to come are those under the constant stress of poverty or personal problems, including concern about meeting basic needs for food, shelter, health, safety, and clothing. (Johnson 1994b, p. 33)

Having a place of their own in schools is helpful, parents report because it gives them an opportunity to gain information about how schools operate, explore curriculum with teachers, share experiences with other parents and learn skills to assist their children in schools. Family centers are a promising practice because they provide a wide range of classes and workshops in response to needs parents express. These activities include: computer classes, GED, ESL and literacy classes, and workshops on school curriculum and children's development. Parents report that participation in family centers increases their comfort levels in relationships with schools and improves their knowledge about how schools work.

Parents Comments

"Some parents stood outside and invited me in for a cup of coffee. They were very welcoming and I felt that this place is OK."

"I feel safer being in the school and knowing he's getting the treatment he needs."

"This school is a friendly place to want to be"!

"By being here, I learn what's expected in the next grade my child will attend and I can get him ready."

"My perception of people and how children should be educated has changed. The scope is not so narrow now. I know the possibilities now" (Johnson, 1994b).

Expanding possibilities is the purpose of education. Family centers are a promising practice because they assist in bringing families, schools and communities closer together in that endeavor.

REFERENCES

Becker, H.J., & Epstein, J.L. (1982). Parent involvement: A study of teacher practices. *Elementary School Journal, 83,* 85–102.

Bronfenbrenner, U. (1979). *The ecology of human development: Experiments by nature an design.* Cambridge, MA: Harvard University Press.

Catsambis, S., & Garland, J.E. (2000). *Parental Involvement in students' education during middle school and high school* (Report No. 18). Baltimore, MD: CRESPAR.

Chavkin, N.F., & Williams, D.L., Jr. (1993). Minority parents and the elementary school: Attitudes and practices. In N.F. Chavkin (Ed.), *Families and schools in a pluralistic society* (pp. 73–83). Albany, NY: State University of New York Press.

Clark, R.M. (1993). Homework-focused parenting practices that positively affect student achievement. In N.F. Chavkin (Ed.), *Families and schools in a pluralistic society* (pp. 85–105). Albany: State University of New York Press.

Dauber, S.L., & Epstein, J.L. (1993). Parents attitudes and practices of involvement in inner-city elementary and middle schools. In N.F. Chavkin (Ed.), *Families and schools in a pluralistic society* (pp. 53–71). Albany: State University of New York Press.

Davies, D., Burch, P., & Johnson, V.R. (1992). *A portrait of schools reaching* (Report No. 1). Baltimore, MD: Center on Families, Communities, Schools, and Children's Learning.

Epstein, J.L. (1992). School and family partnerships. In M. Alkin (Ed.), *Encyclopedia of educational research* (6th ed.). New York: Macmillan.

Epstein, J.L. (1994). Theory to practice: School and family partnerships lead to school improvement and student success. In C.L. Fagnano & B.Z Weber (Eds.), *School, family, and community interaction: A view from the firing lines* (pp. 39–52). Boulder, CO: Westview Press.

Epstein, J.L. (1995). School-family-community partnerships: Caring for the children we share. *Phi Delta Kappan, 76*(9), 701–712.

Epstein, J.L. (2001). *School, family, and community partnerships: Preparing educators and improving schools.* Boulder, CO: Westview Press.

Fantuzzo, J., Davis, G., & Ginsburg, M. (1995). Effects of parent involvement in isolation or in combination with peer tutoring on student self-concept and mathematics achievement. *Journal of Educational Psychology, 87,* 272–281.

Glenn, C.G., McLaughlin, K., & Salganik, L. (1993). *Parent information for school choice: The case of Massachusetts* (Report No. 19). Baltimore. MD:Center on Families, Communities, Schools and Children's Learning.

Henderson, W. (2000). Home reading: The key to proficiency. *Principal, 80*(1), 46–48.

Johnson, V.R. (1990). Schools reaching out: Changing the message to "good news". *Equity and Choice, 6*(3), 20–24.

Johnson, V.R. (1991a). The many partners of miles park elementary school. *Equity and Choice, 7*(2), 35–39.

Johnson, V.R. (1991b). *Home visitors link school to multicultural communities. Community Education Journal, 18*(4), 15–16.

Johnson, V.R. (1993). *Parent family centers: Dimensions of functioning in 28 schools in 14 states* (Report No. 20). Baltimore, MD: Center on Families, Communities, Schools and Children's Learning.

Johnson, V.R. (1994a). Connecting families and schools through mediating structures. *The School Community Journal, 4*(1), 451–455.

Johnson, V.R. (1994b). *Parent centers in urban schools: Four case studies* (Report No. 23). Baltimore, MD: Center on Families, Communities, Schools and Children's Learning.

Johnson, V.R. (1996). *Family center guidebook.* Baltimore, MD: Center on Families, Communities, Schools, and Children's Learning.

Johnson, V.R. (1998). Family centers: The new human resources paradigm at work and school. In M.G. Mackavey & R.J. Levin (Eds.), *Shared purpose: Working together to build strong families and high performance companies.* New York: AMO-COM.

Johnson, V.R. (2000). The family center: Making room for parents. *Principal, 80*(1), 26–31.

Johnstone, T.R. (1997). *Case study of a school based parent center in a low-income immigrant community.* Unpublished doctoral dissertation, Pepperdine University.

Leontovich, M. (1999). Experts say parent centers are helpful. *Title I Report: Compensatory Education's Comprehensive News Source, 1*(10), 4–8.

Lightfoot, S.L. (1978). *Worlds apart: Relations between families and schools.* New York: Basic Books.

Ritter, P.L., Mont-Reynaud, R., & Dornbusch, S.M. (1993). Minority parents and their youth: Concern, encouragement, and support for school achievement. In N.F. Chavkin (Ed.), *Families and schools in a pluralistic society.* Albany: State University of New York Press.

Swapp, S. (1990). *Schools reaching out and success for all children: Two case studies.* Boston: Institute for Responsive Education.

Winters, W.G. (1993). *African American mothers and urban schools: The power of participation.* New York: Lexington Books.

U.S. Department of Education. (1996, January/February). *Community Update, 32,* 1.

CHAPTER 6

FAMILY PARTICIPATION IN DECISION MAKING AND ADVOCACY

Don Davies

Participation in decision making and advocacy in school affairs provides parents and other community members a forum to acquire and practice democratic principles. These opportunities can contribute to the development of a more civil and democratic society and to more effective schools for all children.

BASES FOR FAMILY INVOLVEMENT IN DECISION MAKING AND ADVOCACY

Introduction

Decision making and advocacy have always been the most controversial forms of parent participation in schools, and the most stoutly resisted by many teachers, administrators, and school boards. Decision making and advocacy are inherently political and deal directly with issues of power and control. A survey by the National Center for Educational Statistics in the mid-1990s revealed that "in general, public elementary schools do not include parents in decision making to a great extent..." (National Center for Educational Statistics, 1998, p. iii).

I write as an advocate of increased participation by families and communities in educational decision making, using the first person on occasion. I draw heavily on my own experience and studies over the past 30 years with the Institute for Responsive Education. My own studies over the years suggest that many teachers and administrators appear to doubt that parents have anything of great value to offer on educational matters. This doubt is especially strong when the families are poor, are recent immigrants, are from minority groups, or have cultural backgrounds different from the community's dominant ones (Davies, 1988).

As an advocate of school-family-community partnership I have been encouraged about the recent surge of interest in the topic by policymakers, educators, and researchers. Along with increased acceptance of the partnership idea, there has been some positive increase in practices in local school districts and schools. The widespread adoption of Joyce Epstein's National Network of Partnership Schools is evidence of this, as are reports from many states and cities about extensive efforts to involve families and the community in school reform initiatives.

I propose two primary purposes for increasing parent participation in school decision making and advocacy that are especially important in the early years of the 21st century.

> **Purposes for Family Involvement in School Decision Making**
>
> Parent participation in decision-making and advocacy will contribute strongly to school reform so that all students can achieve academic success with high standards.
> Parent decision making in school governance will provide community members a forum to acquire and practice democratic practices. These opportunities will contribute to the development of a more civil and democratic society.

Many states have sought to support partnerships through legislation and by offering training and information services in the state education agencies. Dozens of federal programs require or encourage one or more forms of parent or citizen participation. Under Richard Riley's leadership as Secretary of Education, the U.S. Department of Education stepped up its efforts to promote the partnership idea. Oliver C. Moles (this volume, Ch. 2) provides a good overview of federal programs.

This chapter will first describe the bases for family involvement in decision making, identify varieties of activities and reasons for family participation, and offer some historical background. The remainder of the chapter will focus on five types of family involvement in school governance activities that can provide an enhanced role for families and the community in decision making and advocacy. The five types of activities are:

1. School governance councils to give a stronger, mandated role to parents and the community;
2. Organized grassroots activism to push for changes in school practices and policies;
3. School-sponsored collective participation in planning and action;
4. Independent organizations serving as "critical friends" to both support and criticize the schools; and
5. Principals leading their schools to make democratic decision making a part of the school culture.

Varieties of Decision Making and Advocacy Activities

The traditional practices of parent involvement, participation, or partnership have been significantly broadened to encompass a wider range of activities and functions. Within Epstein's six types of family partnership activities, the fifth type is identified as parent decision making and advocacy (Epstein, this volume, Ch. 1, 1995). The National Center for Educational Statistics (1998) reports that parent involvement within schools is occurring but at varying levels. Approximately, one-third of the schools report a high degree of parent involvement in decision making another third report a moderate extent; and a third a limited extent. A substantial majority of public elementary schools reported having an advisory group or policy council that includes parents. This was the case more often in larger schools and schools with minority enrollments of more than 20%. Schools with advisory groups that include parents report giving more consideration to parent input into school decisions than schools without such groups.

The terms "decision making" and "advocacy" in the title of this chapter are interpreted in dramatically different ways in practice. These terms can be applied to either individual or collective efforts to affect education. Individual family members can participate in the planning and approval of educational programs and services for their own children, as in the Individual Education Plans required in special education programs. As individuals, they can seek to influence decisions about their own children made by school staff. They can vote for candidates, bond issues, and ballot referenda. They can write letters to the editor or officials, appear at school board or city council meetings, or lobby the school board, the city council, the legislature, or Congress.

Collectively, family members may join with others in community-based organizations working on school issues—to lobby, protest, do research, join with school staff to seek improvements in school practice or results, or pursue other forms of advocacy. These collective efforts can be supportive of and collaborative with educators or confrontational and adversarial. The efforts may be in one neighborhood or citywide, independent, or linked to national organizations, universities, or corporate interests.

Families may elect to work through school-based organizations, including PTA's and other parent associations, booster clubs, school site councils, or action teams seeking to influence school decision making and policies. In these activities, families choose to participate in planning and problem solving within the school culture.

Families face other decisions about participation. They may be loyal and support their children's school, backing existing policies and practices. Or, if they are dissatisfied, they can raise their voices, individually or collectively, to try to change the school. Opting out of the school for another school in the same district, for another school district, a private school, a charter school, or home schooling represents parent choice, which is another common and legitimate form of participation and influence. While I recognize the importance of all of this variety, I will consider only collective, organized approaches for this chapter.

Why Family Participation in Decision Making?

The *argument* that appeals most to policymakers and business and foundation officials is that various forms of parent/family partnership are linked to student academic achievement. This argument has come to the fore as policymakers and educators have moved toward substantial school reform, including a new curriculum based on higher academic standards and accountability, including high-stakes standardized tests. Many of the proponents of school reform have recognized that the changes they seek are not likely to work or be sustained without the support and assistance of families and the community. Hence, many state, federal, and private educational reform initiatives include encouragement or requirements for school, family, community partnership, sometimes including participation in decision making and collaborative planning.

However, the evidence to establish a direct link between participation in decision making or forms of school governance is limited. The sections below on the school councils in Chicago and Kentucky include some encouraging evidence. Along with many proponents, I argue that, if partnership contributes to the conditions that promote student academic achievement, the linking argument is plausible. For example, establishing a school site council may help to increase test scores in reading *if* the actions of that council lead to more parents supervising homework at home, the establishment of good classroom libraries, or policies that lower class size.

A strong pragmatic argument for giving parents a real voice in school affairs is that such participation can help to increase the support of parents and other community participants for the schools. Such interest and support could be reflected in willingness to increase taxes for the schools. The school councils in Kentucky and the work of the Southwest Industrial Areas Foundation offer some confirmation of this point. The work of these groups will be discussed in later sections of this chapter.

A third argument, often skipped over by educators, is the contribution that organized participation of parents and other citizens can make to revitalizing democracy and building civic leadership. A basic democratic principle is that people should have opportunities to influence decisions that affect them. I am among those activists and social commentators who argue that parent participation in school decision making and advocacy is one important way to realize this principle and to contribute to building a civil society. I maintain, often without much support from other educators, that participation is not just a means but also a worthwhile end itself if it contributes to strengthening our democratic society. Both Robert Putnam (2000) and Ernesto Cortes (1993) support this view, using social capital theory to explain the power of voluntary associations in an effective democratic society.

Being consistent about the values of democracy requires recognizing the right of parents to organize and advocate for their own interests and preferred policies. This right prevails even when their views are unpopular and/or the predominant voices in a school or community consider them "extreme" or "unwise." Examples include opposition to teaching evolution, support for Afro-Centric curriculum, support for or against Gay and Lesbian student organizations, or opposition to distribution of condoms.

There are also many arguments offered against increased partnership or power sharing. Chief among these is the protection of the prerogatives, status, and expertise of the education profession. Some educators argue that enhanced professional status for teachers will lead to greater public recognition of their work and higher salaries, making possible recruiting and keeping more high quality teachers. Decreased efficiency is another caution raised against participation. Some argue that efficient planning and management require schools to limit and control interventions by outsiders, including parents and community residents. Many also contend that firm professional control is needed to protect the schools and the community from narrow or special interests and community conflict, arguing that elected or appointed school boards can best represent diverse community interests.

Historical Perspective

Since the end of Word War II, the question of what role parents should have in decisions about the schooling for their children has been a matter of considerable national interest. During the late 1940s and 1950s, the period of the baby boom—mushrooming population, escalating costs, and the huge population shift to the suburbs—the question was considered largely non-controversial. The primary mode of parent involvement was supporting the schools and advocating increased funding. According to the historical review by Fruchter and his colleagues (1992), the typical activities were parent conferences, PTA fundraising events, and classroom and school support activities, buttressed by homework monitoring, report card review, and supervision of field trips. During this period, participation was clearly class structured and tended to bypass economically disadvantaged parents (McLaughlin & Shields, 1987).

The extensive participation of low-income and minority parents in schooling issues emerged for the first time in the mid-1960s, fueled by the Civil Rights Movement and other grassroots stirrings. New people from formerly excluded groups participated in new ways, producing a crisis of participation (Davies, 1979b; McLaughlin & Shields 1987). This crisis included the community control struggle in New York City and in other minority communities around the country, the emergence of Indian-controlled schools, voucher proposals coming then largely from the left, and the rise of scores of grassroots organizations in the cities, often racially or ethnically based. The methods of Saul Alinski, Paulo Freire, and Ralph Nader were studied and emulated. Many new organizations arose to promote opportunities for expanded citizen participation.

Governments at all levels responded to the crisis of new participants demanding a stronger voice by initiating requirements for "maximum feasible participation" and mandated participatory councils of many different kinds. Much grassroots activism was channeled into government-subsidized service activities and advisory mechanisms. Many of these mechanisms were implemented at the level of tokenism or information sharing (Arnstein, 1971; Davies, 1979a; Gittell, 1979). Local districts and state governments responded to the threats of community control by decentralization measures.

The Nixon and Reagan eras were much quieter on the citizen participation front. During this period, several states became concerned about the inadequate quality of their public schools and embraced the idea of decentralization. This decentralization process would provide some authority to individual schools and grant some authority to school councils, which included parents and teachers. The hope of some policymakers was to stem the tide of citizens who were disenfranchising themselves from civic activity. Civic activity of all kinds —including voting, volunteering, membership in civic organizations —was declining, as extensively documented by Robert Putnam (2000). For example, the membership of the national PTA declined by at least half from its peak of about 15,000 members.

In the 1980s through the 1990s, the policy of decentralization spread to many school districts. These districts adopted various forms of school-based management approach to reform. These adoptions were partially in response to the growing national concern about school quality. This concern was fueled by the Department of Education's report *A Nation at Risk* and international studies which showed American students faring badly in math and science compared to those in other developed countries. School-based management plans often included some kind of school council. In the 1990s, school reform became a major political issue in many states and an important priority for the Clinton administration. Partnership ideas were important in some but by no means all of these developments.

FIVE TYPES OF ACTIVITIES

I have categorized five types of family involvement in school governance activities that will provide an enhanced role for families and the community in decision making and advocacy. To reiterate, the five types of activities are:

1. School governance councils to give a stronger, mandated role to parents and the community;
2. Organized grassroots activism to push for changes in school practices and policies;
3. School-sponsored collective participation in planning and action;
4. Independent organizations serving as "critical friends" to both support and criticize the schools; and
5. Site principals leading their schools to make democratic decision making a part of the school culture.

In selecting a few examples in the above five types of activities, I know I have missed many potentially promising examples and have excluded many other possibilities because of space limits. The five categories encompass many but not all of many forms of collective participation. My personal biases will be apparent. Some of the material is based on documents, the Internet, and e-mail communication provided by the organizations themselves, some on the work of outside observers, or commentators.

What was the most important criterion I used to call a practice *promising*? I looked for schools, programs, projects, or organizations that plausibly will contribute to making public schools better for all students, including especially those students now being left behind, and at the same time exhibit democratic procedures and contribute to the strengthening of democratic communities. Most of the practices for local school councils described below were developed during the 1980s and 1990s and reflect the national and local concern about school reform as we enter the 21st Century.

Local School Councils: New Approaches to School Governance

Starting in the 1970s there was a significant trend toward decentralized school decision making or site-based management. Educational reform was the main purpose of the legislation in many states. California, South Carolina, and Florida were among the first states to promote site-based management and school councils. The point of many plans was to devolve some authority for some decisions from the superintendent and central office to the building principal and to establish a council of parents, and teachers. Other community representatives and older students were also sometimes included. The language creating the councils in most states and cities that have incorporated this plan typically suggests, "shared decision making," but typically the councils played a largely advisory role and had only nominal authority in matters of personnel, budget, and school program (Davies, 1979a; Malen & Ogawa 1988; Smylie et al., 1992). Two major exceptions to this situation are Chicago and Kentucky, where school councils were mandated and given substantial authority.

Chicago's Local School Councils

One of the boldest and most controversial changes in urban school district governance was the Chicago School Reform Act of 1988, in which the Illinois Legislature decentralized administrative power and gave parents primary decision making authority in the Chicago Public Schools. The major force behind the legislation was the push for school reform in the city, which had been called by President Reagan's Secretary of Education William Bennett, "the worst school system in the United States." The reform effort began with the election of Chicago's first black mayor, Harold Washington, in 1988 and was backed strongly by business groups, educational reform advocates, and many community organizations representing grassroots constituencies. The new law was opposed by the Chicago Principal's Association and given lukewarm endorsement by the Chicago Teachers Union (Fruchter et al., 1982).

The law required each school to elect a Local School Council with a majority of parent and community representatives and a parent chairman. Unlike legislation in other states (except Kentucky) that sought to mandate parent participation in decision making, the Illinois act gave the Local School Council power to hire and fire the principal, approve the school budget, and review and approve a required school improvement plan. A council consists of six parent representatives and two community representatives, elected by parents and community representatives; two teachers, elected by the school staff; the school principal; and in high schools, an elected student. The chair must be one of the six parent representatives. In 1997, in Chicago's 540 public schools, there were approximately 3,200 parents, 1,080 community representatives, and 1,080 teachers, and 540 principals. The members are by far the largest number of elected public officials in the state (Consortium on Chicago School Research, 1997).

The school principal was given wide authority to hire all of the rest of the school staff, including teachers. Councils hire the principals for a four-year, performance-based contract. The curriculum is largely the responsibility of a professional committee composed primarily of teachers. The council's budgetary authority includes local funds which not nonnegotiable, such as the 80% locked-in centrally to salaries, and state discretionary funds for educating low-income students.

From the beginning the new structure has been controversial (Consortium, 1997). The proponents saw the reform as producing stronger and more accountable school leadership, greater attention to teaching and learning and student achievement, and improved facilities and safety. Opponents questioned whether parents and community representatives, particularly in the poorest neighborhoods, would have the capacity and interest to govern their schools.

In 1995 the Legislature made several changes in the reform act, but, after a prolonged fight, kept the basic structure of school-based decision making intact (Designs for Change, 1998, p. 3). The revised law gave the Mayor broad new system wide power, replacing the school board with a five-person Board of Trustees and a chief executive officer [CEO], limiting the scope of bargaining to wages and benefits, excluding working conditions, and weakening the power of the teachers' union. The new CEO and the Trustees have sweeping power to reconstitute low-performing schools and dismiss (rather than transfer) school staff. According to Donald Moore, this has created "ongoing conflict between the Local School Councils and advocates for local school initiative, on the one hand, and an aggressive central administration, on the other" (Designs for Change, 1988, p. 4).

There have been many studies and much journalistic reporting regarding this Chicago Public School reform. It seems clear that the Local School

Councils have been successfully institutionalized in many schools, but not in others. A 1995 study by the Consortium on Chicago School Research (1997) surveyed parents, teachers, and principals. Some of the most important results are summarized below.

There are three distinct levels of council functioning. Fifty to 60 per cent appear to be relatively high functioning. These follow good procedures, work well with their constituencies, have considerable internal capacity, and are a proactive force for school improvement. Another quarter to a third of the groups share some of these characteristics, but are more likely to follow the initiatives of the school staff and be less proactive. The remaining 10 to 15% report more serious problems and appear to lack the capacity to govern.

On the question of a council's ability to govern, 23% of the members gave *very* positive response and another 38% gave a positive response. Thirty percent had a mixed response, and only 9% were negative about the Councils' capacity.

The council membership overall resembles the racial and ethnic composition of the city. This means that 1,800 African American parents and 700 Latino parents are now serving as elected public officials and hence gaining the skills associated with this experience.

From 60 to 80% report training of council members on issues including their roles and responsibilities, understanding the school improvement plan, understanding the budget, how to select and evaluate the principal, and encouraging parent involvement. The amount of training on substantive issue would seem to far exceed that typically offered to school board members and school site councils across the country.

Most councils take their responsibilities of selecting and evaluating the principal seriously. Fifty-six percent report very comprehensive or comprehensive evaluation procedures; 22% report minimal evaluation, and 12%, none at all. About 80% of all respondents reported that their council interviewed several candidates for the principal's job, checked references, and sought input from non-council parents, teachers, and community residents. The principal respondents were, not unexpectedly, more modest in their appraisal of the principal selection process than were teacher and parent members.

Similar positive results were found on the council's involvement in the school improvement process. More than half of the councils report active or very active involvement, including helping to develop and review the plan, sponsoring community forums, and regular monitoring. About a third of the councils reported only moderate involvement, and 19% indicated that their council was inactive.

Less involvement is reported in the budget process. This limited involvement may be explained because a significant portion of the budget is nonnegotiable, about 80% allocated to fixed salaries. Less than a quarter of the councils appear to be highly involved in the budget process; 60% moderately involved. The rest report only minimal involvement, deferring to the principal in budget matters.

An overwhelming majority of respondents report that their council was not involved in such problematic behaviors as pressuring the principal to spend money inappropriately, using influence to get jobs for friends or relatives, overstepping their authority, or being dominated by conflict. Only about 8% indicated that some unethical conduct had occurred. In the context of urban school politics nationally, these results are encouraging.

Some of the differences between the most effective and least effective councils are important to note. There were no major differences reported in terms of member educational levels or occupational status. The least productive councils received less training or no training at all, had less knowledge and skill in meeting behavior. Members of least productive councils were more likely to report in-fighting, lack of trust, lack of agreement on priorities, and sustained conflict. Members of the most productive councils almost unanimously (96%) rated their principals positively or very positively. Only 57% of the members of the least productive councils had the same positive views.

Julie Woestehoff of Parents United for Responsible Education concluded in 1998 that there was ample evidence that the accountability that came with the councils "has been a key factor in the improvements in our schools." (Woestehoff, 1998, p. 1). She applauds the hard work, dedication, and lack of corruption exhibited by the Councils. Historian Michael Katz goes farther and asserts that the Local School Councils' success "demonstrated the viability of democratic governance and the fallacy behind the assumption that highly centralized bureaucracies are inescapable in urban education" (Katz, 1995, p. 205).

A recent study focused on the 85% of elementary schools that had exhibited low test scores in 1989 and discovered that approximately 40% of these schools were carrying out a systemic approach to reform and many others were carrying out unfocused initiatives. Schools with councils, described as democratic and functioning effectively, were much more likely to be carrying out system restructuring of their educational program (Designs for Change, 1998, pp. 66–69).

The researchers concluded, "A political practice that engages a broad base of people who have a stake in the local school and who sustain discussion about educational issues can create valuable social resources to support systemic restructuring efforts" (Designs for Change, 1998, pp. 35–36) There is a downside to this optimistic finding. Consortium researchers found that the social organization and practices of almost all of Chicago's high schools had changed little as a result of the reform law and characterized the high schools as a case of institutional failure.

Another elementary school study shows a significant trend of improved scores in reading achievement, identifies several practices which differentiate the more successful schools from the less successful ones (Designs for Change, 1998, pp. 52–64). Two of these factors (with a statistically significant positive relationship) were "Local School Council Contribution" and "Teacher Outreach to Parents." This link between student academic achievement and a school governance variable is significant and is one of several factors that make the Chicago governance reform promising.

"Strong Democracy" was the pattern of school politics that reflected the theory of change underlying the 1988 law. The reformers hoped that the shift of authority and resources to the school site, that the new law made possible, would lead to increased involvement in important decisions by parents, the community, teachers, students, parents, and the school's principal. Such a shift would, in turn, stimulate fundamental school improvement. These hopes have not been fully realized, but the belief that a substantial number of schools have reached or are moving well toward a collaborative and democratic approach is good news (Bryk, 1993).

What Seems Especially Promising about the New Structure for Governance in Chicago?

1. The extensive research points to the success of many parent-led governance councils, including a link between successful councils and improved student achievement.
2. The Chicago reform was achieved through a collaborative effort of community based organizations and business leaders.
3. The success of many Chicago Local School Councils underlines the potential that grassroots parents have both the interest and ability to contribute positively to the governance of their own schools.
4. Democratic collaboration between and among council members (teachers, parents, and principals) is a characteristic of successful councils.
5. A reform such as this greatly broadens the participation of grassroots parents and citizens in civic life, offering valuable civic experience to thousands of people who were previously excluded from such opportunities.

School Councils in Kentucky's Reform Program

In 1990, the Kentucky Legislature enacted one of the most far-reaching and comprehensive educational reform acts of the last century. The action was triggered by a State Supreme Court decision, which described the state's school system as inadequate, inefficient, and, ineffective.

The most radical aspect of the Kentucky Education Reform Act was the shift of significant authority from the district to the school level with the required participation of parents and teachers in the school-based decision-making process. Each school is held accountable for results, through rewards and sanctions for improved student achievement (David, 2000). The legislation required every school to create no later than 1996 a school council composed of two parents, three teachers, and the building administrator (or multiples of these numbers, for larger councils). Their peers elect parents and teachers for one-year terms. The law requires the council to select the principal and then consult with him or her about other staffing decisions. Council authority extends to policies about curriculum and instruction, materials, assignment of staff and students, within-the-school-day scheduling, extracurricular programs, use of space, discipline, and classroom management. Principals cannot veto council decisions, except that the principal has the final word on hiring teachers and other staff. By 1994 about two-thirds of the schools had established councils; the others waited until the 1996 deadline.

The Kentucky councils have made school decision making much more democratic and have increased participation of both parents and teachers in school governance. More than 3,900 teachers and 2,800 parents are council members across the state, and thousands more serve on committees established by the councils, including an estimated 24,000 teachers (Office of Education Accountability 1999). In addition, minority representation has increased from 16 to over 700 (David 2000, p. 211). The presence of 700 or more minority (mostly African American) public officials in Kentucky has to be counted as an important step in the political development of the state.

David (2000), who has done the most extensive studies on the school councils in Kentucky for the Pritchard Committee for Academic Excellence, asserts: Structurally councils exist in every school in which they are required. The councils have hired more than 900 principals. Councils have created by-laws and policies as required by law. They have set up committees, hired staff, and developed improvement plans as required by the state. There are problems to be sure. Many councils are run totally by the principal; others have parents or teachers with personal agendas. Many superintendents would like more say in the selection of principals; parents would like a stronger voice. Yet, overall, a new structure in place that seems to be working as smoothly as, in some cases more democratically than, the structure it has replaced (p. 209).

David points out that the most striking thing about the results so far is what has not happened: There has been little conflict. The prediction that power struggles and resistance would eat up enormous amounts of time has not been realized. There have been fewer complaints than anticipated, and most districts made and continue to make good faith efforts to carry out the law. *Boone County v. Bushee*, which reached the Kentucky Supreme Court, reaffirmed the authority of school councils.

What Do Councils Do? David recounts how school councils have created bylaws and developed policies for discipline, curriculum, hiring, professional development, and other things. For many schools this is the first time written policies have existed—no small accomplishment for a group of people typically unfamiliar with setting policy. Councils are making many important decisions, including hiring principals. The hiring process now is generally viewed as more rigorous and sophisticated, as well as more open, than before councils were involved. Although this aspect of school-based decision making raises considerable debate among administrators, the fact is that councils have selected more than 900 principals, and there have been few serious problems. The percentage of minority principals selected is still small but has increased, suggesting that those councils are no worse and probably somewhat better than superintendents on minority hiring.

David reports that council discussion and decisions tend to focus on extracurricular activities, discipline, and facilities, and on making sure that they are doing things by the rules—such as rules on announcing meetings and appeals. A study by Aagaard, Coe, and Reeves (David, 2000, p. 313) reveals that approving school improvement plans and hearing reports about curriculum and instruction are afforded much council time but not much discussion. The issues that engender discussion are the hiring decisions that councils are obligated to make, sports, issues of teacher concern such as discipline code, and the everyday concerns of many parents such as student uniforms.

There appears to be little opposition to the new decision-making structure, and no major efforts to change or weaken it are reported by the Pritchard Committee (1999), which serves as an independent monitor of Kentucky Education Reform Act. This committee praises the commitment of school officials and advocates at the local, regional, and state levels. The committee claims, "there has been remarkable progress in decentralizing the governance structure of education in Kentucky." They note that the school councils have drawn thousands of parents more directly into the education decision-making process and given teachers more authority in their schools. The committee also concluded that too few families and parents are engaged as full partners in the education of their children and the idea of broad community responsibility for educating all children has not become part of most communities' behavior. This situation is a serious challenge for the next years of governance reform in Kentucky.

The Institute for Education Research reports that few councils seem to have taken a major role in changing the curriculum or instructional program, although that has begun to change as more councils take on responsibility for preparing or assisting with the school's improvement plan. A few schools have made significant policy changes that influence classroom practice, but these are the exception (David, 2000, p. 314; Kentucky Institute for Education Research, 1997).

The Pritchard Committee confirms this assessment (David, 2000). They report that "…Councils have been slow to change the academic practices of most schools, indicating a clear need for better training of councils members in interpreting test scores and developing strategies for improvement." The vision of the law's architects has not been fully achieved. The notion that the councils would be the main engine for changes in curriculum and instruction has not been realized on a major scale as yet, but, according to David (2000), parent and public opinion about the new structure tends to be quite positive.

A number of steps have been taken recognizing the uneven performance of councils across the state and the potential for being more effective. The councils have formed a statewide organization, the Kentucky Association of School Councils, a nonprofit group that works across the state to help school councils improve their performance. The law requires that new council members have 30 days to complete the required six hours of training. The Kentucky Department of Education has increased its standards for council trainers, issued a list of endorsed trainers, and required principals to submit names of all school council members and evidence that they have met the training requirements.

The most extensive effort to increase the efficacy of the mandated councils and of other parent leaders has been initiated by the Pritchard Committee for Academic Excellence and the Kentucky PTA. This training effort is described in the section Independent Organizations as Critical Friends.

One study by Wilkerson & Associates (1999) indicates that school council members are more positive than parents as a whole group or the general public regarding how well Kentucky Education Reform Act is functioning. For example, when asked how well Kentucky's content standards were working to improve teaching and learning, 77% of parents on the school councils answered "very well" or "moderately well," compared with 57% of parents as a whole group and 52% of the general public.

> **What Seems Especially Promising about the New Decision-Making Structure In Kentucky?**
>
> (1) The legislation makes the school councils' authority clear and comprehensive, touching all the important areas affecting the improvement of student academic performance.
> (2) The fact that the governance structure is embedded in state law insures that council authority will not be eroded every time there is a change in superintendent, principal, or school board. The need for training of council members was recognized, and substantial efforts are being made.
> (3) The spirit of the law and its implementation in Kentucky is collaborative not adversarial. Teachers (as well as parents) have substantially more say over the important matters affecting their work than was the case in the traditional decision-making structure.
> (4) Thousands of new people—teachers and parents, including minority parents—have a direct role now in running Kentucky's schools—a substantial step ahead for democratic governance.

Grassroots Activism

Grassroots civic action should be seen as at the heart of urban school reform and the revitalization of urban communities rather than as an exotic sideshow or a throwback to the 1960s. Civic action is an essential element in creating the social capital necessary for strong, democratic communities and strong, democratic schools (Putnam, 2000; Shirley, 1997). Organized community group action is also essential as political pressure on urban school officials to make needed improvements to enable all students, regardless of family background, to achieve academic success with high standards.

I give an important place on my list of promising practices in family decision making and advocacy to the revival of grassroots activism, and offer here brief discussion of just two examples, one new effort in Boston, and a well-established program in Texas, among many that could be included. In addition, I will discuss briefly two grassroots training programs that are directly relevant to supporting grassroots activism.

Boston Parent Organizing Network [BPON]

Boston Parent Organizing Network [BPON] is an ambitious effort begun in 1999 to connect more than twenty grassroots community organizations in Boston to help their efforts to be effective advocates for improvement in the Boston Public Schools. It represents an important effort to engage and empower parents and other community members for school reform. The Network has attracted the interest of civic leaders and of major area foundations, which have provided substantial startup funding. The organization has a full-time director, Michelle Brooks, and is housed at the Institute for Responsive Education, which serves as its fiscal agent. Ms. Brooks is a long time parent and community activist.

The purpose is to organize a diverse constituency of parents and other community members to support and advocate for the improvement of the Boston Public Schools. The long-term goals include building parent and community power and developing parent leaders who will effectively advocate for change. BPON (1999) seeks to achieve:

1. Collaborate on moving a parent-set agenda for improving schools;
2. Develop strategies to improve educational outcomes for children;
3. Exchange ideas and information;
4. Nurture parent leadership that focuses on accountability and equity in schools; and
5. Build partnerships that support educational excellence.

This initiative is based upon common beliefs around the engagement, empowerment, organization, and mobilization of diverse constituencies of parents, students, families and other community members. These beliefs are the foundation of their work and are the guiding principles for BPON and its member organizations. These guiding principles, include the following:

1. Parents and families are the most effective advocates for their children and must be continuously engaged to take the lead in organizing and advocating on behalf of their children;
2. Parents must be organized and empowered to affect change in the Boston Public Schools;
3. Parents, families and students are a key source for identifying educational issues for organizing and mobilization;
4. Organizing, which actively engages and supports low-income families and parents of color, is critical to improving Boston Public Schools and student achievement;
5. Educational organizing must actively solicit support from the broader community;

6. When existing community-based organizations form alliances and coalitions focus on building citywide strategies, they can have a major impact on education;

7. Collaboration among community-based organizations and parent organizing groups will provide linkages and create a power base for parents to become more effective agents for school improvement; and

8. Establishment of a network of community-based organizations, parent organizations, and advocacy groups can provide shared resources to develop leaders, exchange information and best practices, provide support, and build citywide capacity.

I have selected some activities from four Network members. ACORN published a study entitled *So That All Can Learn* with recommendations for school system-wide improvement. Parents organized and hosted a Boston City Council hearing on educational issues and a community forum on Boston Teacher's Union contract. ACORN is a local chapter of a national community ogranization with chapters in many places.

The Black Ministerial Alliance hosted twelve educational summits at member churches and established Educational Action Committees at ten churches The Alliance spearheaded "Voices for Children," a citywide coalition of parent and community-based groups advocating for change and increased accountability in the teachers union contract.

The Dudley Street Neighborhood Initiative established a community education committee to focus on developing a community vision for education and shaping the organizing efforts. Members formed working partnerships with two neighborhood schools. Utilizing a particularly impressive graphic approach, members hosted a community meeting at which parents and community residents posted more than 250 issues on the "Wall of Concern."

The Greater Boston Interfaith Organization conducted the "A Place to Live and a Place to Learn" campaign, which advocated for and was instrumental in legislative increases in education spending for public schools. The organization sponsored several meetings with parents to identify issues. A result was the initial steps to organize parents at one middle school.

An example of grassroots political activity for the network occurred in the fall of 2000 when BPON member organizations came together in a campaign to restore funding for a state program that provides funds to urban school districts to supplement the cost of desegregation. BPON members launched a petition drive and collected more than 1200 signatures demanding reinstatement of the funds. The governor and legislature reinstated the funds with such resounding local support for the program.

The BPON utilizes a variety of communication devices: a quarterly Newsletter; an on-line web site and list-serve; networking conferences; and the development of a resource library that includes research about community organizing for school reform, home/school/community partnerships, and family engagement.

> ## What Seems Especially Promising about BPON?
>
> 1. It brings together for united planning and action formerly separated and largely unconnected community organizations. They have demonstrated their capacity for political impact.
> 2. Its existence has increased the number and importance of school reform efforts by many of its member groups.
> 3. BPON sponsors hope that it will spur the development of similar efforts in other cities.
> 4. It has the potential to reach and give increased voice to several of the least well-connected and least powerful sectors of the community

The Southwest Industrial Areas Foundation [SIAF]

The Industrial Areas Foundation is the home base of a national network of broad-based, multiethnic, interfaith organizations in primarily poor and low-income communities. The noted, radical community organizer Saul Alinski in Chicago founded this organization in 1940. The network includes about 40 programs in 16 states.

Ernesto Cortes, Jr., who has developed a systematic approach to organizing parents to engage in improving the public schools, formed the Southwest Industrial Areas Foundation (SIAF) in 1974. The SIAF approach has attracted widespread journalistic and scholarly attention. Cortes has become internationally known as a writer, speaker, and advocate for school reform and public engagement. His vision stresses both school reform and the strengthening of democracy. In a recent Education Week Commentary, Cortes wrote:

> What educators are beginning to realize is that, without the support and engagement of the parents and community leaders at the grassroots level, any attempts at improving the public schools will be ineffective. Public engagement is not mobilization around fears and frustrations, nor is it another easily applied formula for education reform. Meaningful public engagement is a long-term process requiring a patient investment of sustained effort ... When parents and community members are truly engaged, they are organized to act on their own values and visions for their children's future. They do not just volunteer their time for school activities or drop their opinions in the suggestion box. They initiate action, collaborating with

educators to implement ideas for reform. This kind of engagement can only happen through community institutions—public schools, churches, and civic associations. These institutions provide the public space where people of different backgrounds connect with one another ... The Industrial Areas Foundation is a network of just such broad-based institutions. Our members teach families how to become engaged in the public life of their communities, including their public schools. (Cortes 1995, p. 34)

In 1992 the SIAF began the Alliance Schools in Texas, a school reform initiative that in 1999–2000 included 129 schools with almost 90,000 mostly low-income children in all parts of Texas. According to Dennis Shirley (1997), Cortes and his associates learned important lessons from the Industrial Areas Foundation's sometimes not-successful efforts at school reform in the 1960s. For example, the Chicago Public Schools closed down the Woodlawn Experiment within two years because the participants questioned and confronted existing authorities and policies. These participants experienced the damaging the opposition of entrenched school bureaucracies, such as those in Chicago. Cortes and the SIAF developed a collaborative style, working with power holders such as superintendents and school board leaders. Rather than confrontation, SIAF leaders emphasized the language of mutual accountability and gained the confidence of a broad spectrum of civic educators and parent and civic leaders.

Cortes enlisted the Texas Education Agency as a cosponsor and obtained some state funding for participating schools. The support of the state education agency began under Democratic Governor Ann Richards, but the support was maintained by newly elected Republican Governor George W. Bush and the appointment of a new Commissioner of Education. In addition, Cortes secured the involvement and support of many Texas business leaders and corporations as well as key members of the legislature in both parties. As a result, SIAF obtained substantial grants from several national foundations.

The Alliance Schools use a community-organizing model that emphasizes dialogue between parents, teachers, administrators, and community members about their hopes and goals for their children. The model emphasizes a variety of approaches to connect parents and the community, as described in a concept paper prepared by the Industrial Areas Foundation for the National Alliance for Restructuring Education (IAF, 1994). These different approaches result in information collection, information dissemination, collaborative decision making, and parent advocacy. These approaches include individual meetings, house meetings, strategic planning meetings, neighborhood meetings, and training sessions.

At individual meetings—one-on-one conversations (not surveys) between parents, teachers, administrators, community members initiated by a community organizer seek to identify the issues of concern in the community.

House meetings are small group meetings for neighbors or clusters of individuals who have expressed interest. These sessions seek to form networks of relationships.

Strategic planning meetings have as their purpose developing a plan of action. The plan usually begins with a "situational audit" conducted by teams of parents, teachers, administrators, and community people to identify opportunities and threats facing the school and its community. Another step is the development of a mission statement, which is usually presented to the larger community for their approval.

Once the plan is formulated, it is presented to the larger community including all groups of stakeholders such as community organizations, churches, businesses, elected officials, parents, and school personnel. This neighborhood meeting provides the forum for full community participation in the plan.

Training sessions include opportunities for parents and school staff to discuss their vision for the school, discuss new roles for parents at school, plan neighborhood meetings around the issues of importance, and organize what SIAF calls "Walks for Success." "Walks for Success" is a method of parent outreach to meet and talk with large numbers of parent on an individual basis about their concerns and acquire educational theory and practice that affect the children. In addition, the SIAF and the Alliance Schools sponsor regional and statewide conferences, bringing in outside speakers such as Howard Gardner, Ted Sizer, and Jim Comer to speak.

The Alliance Schools are located in many of the poorest districts and schools in the state. The SIAF's collaboration with the state education agency has given the effort greatly increased credibility within school districts and communities. However, this reform effort has run into most of the same barriers and resistance that other reform efforts face. The initiative also faces the complex and differing multiracial, multiethnic political realities of Texas's cities and economically strapped small towns and rural areas.

SIAF had to exercise great patience and diplomacy during their work with school principals. Some principals were eager to participate because of the lure of state money and waivers from state regulations. However, some of these principals either misunderstood the concept of parental engagement for school reform or never intended to cultivate it in the first place. This misunderstanding required either terminating the relationship with some of the initial schools or establishing clear frameworks of mutual accountability. Shirley offers examples of how important it is for Alliance Schools to have help from political allies and from the Texas Education Agency to help them cut through inevitable bureaucratic snags. The program also has links with several of the universities in the state, which offer technical assistance and training, and with interfaith organizations in several of the cities. Another major feature of the SIAF approach in schools is leadership training for parents and educators, including helping parents and educators develop their ability to collaborate with other parents.

The Alliance Schools initiative has achieved many successes along with some disappointments. There is encouraging news on the academic achievement front. The SIAF reports that in the 84 schools that were Alliance Schools in both 1999 and 2000 state test administrations the pass rates improved at more than double the pace of the state for math, reading, and writing. Pass rates for economically disadvantaged students in the Alliance Schools improved at a greater rate than for all students in these schools, indicating some closing of the economic gaps. The schools that were in the Alliance program for three years or more have even stronger pass rates (The Alliance Schools Initiative, 2001).

Shirley (1997) offers detailed achievement test scores from 1996, showing a very mixed picture. He asserts that all but two or three of the schools have emerged from "the rock-bottom achievement level." Middle school achievement gains have not been as good as the elementary schools, but two of the three participating high schools (Jefferson Davis in Houston and Roosevelt in Dallas) in 1995–96 had the largest achievement gains of any high school in their respective districts. Shirley concludes that overall the schools are moving in the right direction.

Standardized test scores are only a part of the picture in assessing the progress to date of the initiative. Hundreds of teachers, parents, and community leaders credit the program for having revitalized their schools and neighborhoods, pointing to a wide range of health, housing, safety, and employment issues that have been addressed.

What Seems Especially Promising about the Industrial Areas Foundation and Alliance Schools?

1. The program sees parents as citizens in the fullest sense—change agents who can transform the culture of inner city schools and neighborhoods.
2. The IAF community organizing approach has been tested and improved over many years.
3. It is well-suited to low-income communities and schools with the most serious problems.
4. As adapted in Texas the approach has achieved credibility in part by being collaborative in spirit and stressing links with local and state officials and agencies, business

leaders, foundations, interfaith organizations, and universities.

5. The SIAF/Alliance School philosophy and goals are clearly spelled out providing ideological cohesion and consistency.

6. The program has shown that it is possible to draw hundreds of organizations and agencies into the process of school reform—faith-based organizations; community action and neighborhood associations, business; universities; and social service, and health and cultural institutions government agencies.

Training for Grassroots Leadership

With the upsurge of partnership activity across the country have come hundreds of training programs and projects sponsored by school districts, community-based organizations, universities working in school projects, state and national organizations, and state departments of education. The programs vary from a few hours to a year or more. They are largely face-to-face events, but increasingly parent training offerings are available on-line through organizations such as the Family Education Network.

I have selected just two examples that seem especially interested and promising to me, from hundreds of possibilities. In addition, the Commonwealth Institute for Parent Involvement in Kentucky and the Learning Path program in Chicago are described in the section on Independent Organizations as Critical Friends.

The Right Question Project. Founded in 1991, The Right Question Project, is based in Somerville and Cambridge, Massachusetts, but operates nationwide. Headed by Dr. Dan Rothstein, Right Question Project's stated objectives include enabling parents to support, monitor, and advocate for their children's education. They also seek to help community organizations build stronger constituencies.

Their approach is based on the premise that low income parents care deeply about their children's education but do not know how to monitor quality or push for improvement. Many do not know how the system works. Unlike many other approaches to training, the Right Question Project does not stress providing information to parents but sponsor workshops that focus on helping parents ask and make use of the answers to questions, such as: What is my child learning? Is the teacher teaching what my child needs to know? If not, what do I do?

The Right Question Project approach to training emphasizes having the participants work together to name information that they want and need, formulate questions, reflect on the knowledge that they gain, and formulate plans for advocacy and accountability. The trainers use simulations, role-playing, and discussion. They emphasize three roles that parents can play: To support their children's education, to monitor their educational progress, and to advocate for meeting their needs when necessary.

Unlike many other training programs Right Question Project has a strong democratic ideological framework, summed up in this quote from an organizational profile from the Right Question Project Web site:

> We believe all people have a right to participate in decision-making processes that affect them. We also believe that to have a strong democracy, good public institutions and a healthy society, we need more people who have the skills to participate effectively. Since 1991 Right Question Project has been working throughout the nation to share skills for effective participation with people in traditionally low and moderate-income communities. (RQP Web Site, www.rightquestion.org).

The project staff outlines the main outcomes that they believe their program can accomplish. For parents these are critical thinking, confidence, ability to plan and act, and the ability to apply the skills used in other situations. For schools, the hoped-for outcomes include improved home-school communication, less confrontational attitudes, and more productive interactions between the school and parents. For communities, outcomes might be greater capacity for citizen participation and the development of leadership potential (Maurici et al., 2000).

Some of the recent projects of Right Question Project include the following:

1. In New Jersey: The Patterson Education Fund has offered Project workshops to parents as part of an effort to prepare a strong local constituency for public education once state-sponsored receivership of the school district ends. Participants in Project workshops have actively used their skills to advocate for their own children's education and to hold accountable school officials from the local to the state level.
2. In Washington, DC, the parent advocacy and reform project, Tellin' Stories, has incorporated the Project approach in their effort's to increase parent participation in school district decisions, build a diverse parent-based organization, and cultivate new parent leadership.
3. In Kentucky, the Pritchard Committee on Academic Excellence has incorporated Project curricula and techniques into their Commonwealth Institute for Parent Leadership.

**What Seems To Be Promising about the
Right Question Project?**

1. Democratic ideology is the guiding framework.
2. Teaching parents and other community members to ask
   good questions is a good start to helping people learn
   how to understand and change policies in schools. .
3. The methodology can be applied in many different settings.

Institute for Responsive Education's Parent Leadership Exchange. In late 2000 the Institute for Responsive Education initiated a New England regional training and network program, which aims to establish a continuing resource for increasing leadership skills for parent leaders; provide networking opportunities; share best practices; and provide technical assistance and training on issues most critical to parent leaders. Karen Mapp is President of the Institute.

The new program seeks to "prepare and assist parent leaders to help schools and communities develop effective school, family, and community partnership and will emphasize increasing capacity of both school and community-based organizations to support efforts to help all children achieve high academic standards" (Institute for Responsive Education, 2001). The participants include parent liaisons or parent coordinators working at school, community-based organizations, and parent leaders from school leadership teams and/or school site councils at both elementary and secondary levels.

The Exchange is emphasizing both educational and political/decision-making skills and educational skills, seeing no conflict between the two. An example is from one of their first training workshops. One session was on "Best Practices of Family Involvement," another on "How to Approach Politicians with Education Issues," offered by a state senator.

**What Seems Promising about the Institute For Responsive
Education [IRE] Program?**

1. The IRE Exchange offers continuous support and follow-
   up after training events.
2. The participants include both school and community
   leaders together, helping to bridge the usual gap
   between school and community-based action.
3. IRE draws on its well-tested model of partnership as the
   basis for the training.

School-Sponsored Collective Participation in Planning and Action

For many decades some schools and school districts seeking to make changes or address serious educational problems have employed a variety of ways of involving parents and other community residents in their planning efforts. Sometimes these efforts have been largely window dressing, but in many other cases they have been real and helpful.

In the 1990s this kind of participation has picked up steam as schools faced new, content-laden curriculum requirements, a major increase in standardized achievement testing, new forms of accountability to many dissatisfied constituents and policy makers, and myriad social problems facing children and their families. When school leaders take seriously the benefits of family and community participation in their efforts to respond to these challenges, I have seen a positive increase in the influence and decision-making opportunities of both family members and community representatives and substantial positive results.

Two quite different promising examples of this approach to planning exist. One is the National Network of Partnership Schools at the Center on School, Family, and Community Partnerships, developed by Joyce Epstein at John Hopkins University and described in the first chapter. The other is the Parent-Teacher Action Research Program developed at the Institute for Responsive Education.

Action Teams in the Partnership Network

This important new program is described in Chapter 1 of this volume. This chapter also offers good examples of the work of Action Teams. The growth of the network is evidence that many educators and their partners in the families and communities see it as a promising approach. The Action Team concept is especially promising because it functions within a clear theoretical framework and has a firm research base. The approach is consistent with the participatory style of planning and action recommended by organizational development specialists in business and education.

Institute for Responsive Education's Parent-Teacher Action Research

In the early years of its organizational life, the Institute for Responsive Education began to explore participatory action research as a concept and methodology to empower parents, teachers, and other community residents to become effective agents for educational decision making, advocacy, and school reform. They built on the work of Parker Palmer and Eldon Johnson, who defined action research as a tool for political empowerment and problem solving. Over the years they employed this methodology in several projects in schools and communities.

The Parent-Teacher Action Research Project, IRE's largest action project during the 1992–1995 period, was carried out under the auspices of the federally-funded Center on Families, Communities, Schools, and Children's Learning. This project involved about 150 people in eight schools in seven quite different urban and rural American neighborhoods from Boston to San Diego. The participants in each school represented parents, teachers, principals, school specialists, students, social service agencies, community organizations, and universities.

Their approach is based on the following three principles: collaboration; research for action—studies that have practical use for practitioners in schools; and the importance of policy as a barrier or facilitator for change in schools, with changes in policy as one potential result of the action research. The steps of the process include the following:

1. Forming a team and agreeing to collaborate. The teams consist of parents or other family members, teachers, the principal or assistant principal, an older student (in schools with higher grades) and sometimes one or more representatives of community organizations;

2. Choosing or approving an outside facilitator. Sometimes the facilitator is a faculty member or graduate student from a university or a person from an organization or center with experience in participatory research;

3. Agreeing on goals and more specific objectives;

4. Determining constituent interests, concerns, and priorities through surveys, interviews, home visits, focus groups, or other methods planned and carried out by team members;

5. Designing and implementing a plan for action or for further study; and

6. Compiling results, reflecting on what has been learned, designing a plan for action based in what has been learned.

In a relatively pure form of participatory action research, the team decides on the question or questions to be studied, gathers data, analyzes and reflects on the results, and plans and carries out an action. In modified versions, such as that followed in this project, the area of study was determined in advance, namely how to increase family involvement in our school. A plan was developed and implemented by the team, and the results studied. There is no single, agreed-on model of participatory research. Research takes many forms depending on the circumstances and the participants.

One example from the Project is the Atenville Elementary School, in West Virginia in an economically poor section of Appalachia. With the leadership of the principal, some teachers, and the PTA, the team set out to study and improve communication between families and the school. The school reached out to the least connected families through a variety of means: a church-based parent center, a parent-to-parent phone chain, and home visits. The action research team documented project results by compiling portfolios on children's progress and their family's involvement. Positive changes were noted in an increase in family and student expectations for student success and increased enrollments in summer support services.

Parents are reported to be more organized and vocal about decisions that affect their children. When the county school board adopted a plan to reconfigure the grade structure of the district, the Atenville Action Research team gathered extensive data from home visits and observation. They presented their data to the county board and asked that the k-6 structure be maintained. The board, impressed by the action research team's data, reversed its decisions. Both parent participation in all aspects of school and student achievements have increased substantially at least in part because of the action research team and the parent involvement and community outreach work that it helped to initiate (Office of Educational Research and Improvement, 1997 p. A-8).

Participatory action research has not been widely adopted in public schools, possibly because its implementation seems daunting to many teachers and administrators in schools accustomed to thinking of research as something that belongs to specialists in universities. But, I believe that the concept has considerable promise.

What Is Especially Promising about Parent-Teacher Action Research?

1. Participatory research including parents and teachers can be an empowering experience for parents and can provide a solid basis for proposed policy changes.
2. The process is well suited to small-scale studies in which the participants are interested in a moderate and collaborative approach to change.
3. The process, when done well, demonstrates the link between research, action, and structural and policy changes.

Independent Organizations as Critical Friends

My experience over the past 30 years has taught me that efforts to initiate and sustain substantial and authentic participation of parents and the
community in school decision making are much more likely to succeed if
there is support from independent community organizations. Organizations that are hostile to the public schools and seek their elimination are
much less likely to be useful in efforts to improve those schools. Organizations, if they are to be effective in bringing about school change, must be
free and capable to be critical of the schools when necessary and to use a
variety of strategies of advocacy and influence.

I use the term "critical friends" as an umbrella term to describe organizations that are both supportive of the public schools, seek to improve and
not destroy them, but at the same time can be critical and know how to
press for change. These organizations fit the model described as promising
by David Matthews, when he wrote:

> Those trying to reconnect the public schools and the public by bringing the
> community's agenda to the schools rather than the school's agenda to the
> community will be worth watching. They stand a better chance of returning
> ownership to the public and benefiting from that reclaimed responsibility in
> the community. (Pankratz & Petrosko, 2000, p. 244)

Such organizations can be very useful as vehicles to family and parent
participation in advocacy and in influencing school-decision making. Over
the years, the Institute for Responsive Education has reported on the work
of such groups and recorded their successes and problems (Davies, 1981).

Below are brief discussions of three currently active organizations that
seem to be promising examples of "critical friend" organizations.

Parents for Public Schools

Parents for Public Schools began in Jackson, Mississippi in 1991 as a
movement to stem the tide of white flight from the public schools after
desegregation. The organization is now a national in scope with an organizational presence of about 50 chapters in 16 states. The mission has moved
far beyond keeping middle-class parents in the public schools. Most of the
chapters are in districts which have a significant minority enrollment but
have retained a core of middle class enrollment and supporters. The Executive Director is Ms. Kelly Butler. The national organization encourages its
local chapters to fit the "critical friends" mode. This mode encourages
strong support for the local public schools. The approach is balanced with
vigorous political efforts to influence school practices and policies in the

direction of higher academic standards for all children and stronger links between the schools and parents and the community.

The founding chapter in Jackson continues to be active with biracial membership and leadership. This chapter is reported to have become an important force in the community for improved schools. Some examples of their recent advocacy work include:

1. Worked to support a rejuvenated PTA in the Casey Elementary School (in which the organization began its work), which was part of a successful school improvement effort. The effort made it possible for the school to progress from the district's endangered list to Blue Ribbon School category;
2. Provided political strong support for a successful $31 million bond issue, the first success in 25 years;
3. Persuaded the district to adopt a site-governance policy; and
4. Provided leadership for establishing a community task force to tackle some persistent problems that the school bureaucracy has been reluctant to confront (e.g., overcrowded classes, high dropout rate).

The national organization has vigorously encouraged local chapters to adopt a strong advocacy stance on the problems and issues important to them. In most cases the chapters are working in situations where there is no other active parent/community leadership working for school improvement in the "critical friend" mode. The chapters vary widely in level and quality of activity,

Some examples of work by Parents for Public Schools chapters that are functioning well include:

1. *Charleston, South Carolina:* The chapter filed lawsuit to resolve a stalemate and move school board ahead on teacher raises. The City of Charleston joined the suit. The State Supreme Court ruled in their favor. The chapter's mission includes "bringing the entire community into the effort of improving public schools for all children, not just our own."
2. *Little Rock, Arkansas:* The chapter kept alive a hard won strategic plan for school reform in spite of its vulnerability during a superintendent transition.
3. *Syracuse, New York:* The chapter provided the leadership for an equity project to engage the broader community and public school parents in tackling curricular, instructional and facility issues.
4. *Cincinnati, Ohio:* The chapter led conversations with a powerful teacher union during contract negotiations to keep management

and union leaders focused on student achievement, not just financial issues.

5. *Waco, Texas:* The chapter forced the hand of the local school board to hold its budget sessions in public by threatening intervention by the attorney general to enforce the open meetings law. Later, this chapter succeeded in having three of its leaders elected to the school board.

6. *Greenville, North Carolina:* In spite of intense opposition by the superintendent, the chapter developed and got funded a training program for parents from all parts of the city, including the housing projects. The multi-year initiative included training in policy issues and advocacy as well as how to support children's learning at home.

Many other local chapters are struggling to get started, to develop their niche in their own community, to gain a base of membership that cuts across social class, racial, and ethnic lines, and to get needed financial support. Only a few of the chapters have been able to achieve enough funding to afford staffing. The national group considers staffing as one important factor for chapter viability. In some cases school districts have been supportive and helpful to Parents for Public School chapter efforts. However, in a number of other cases they have had a neutral or even somewhat hostile reaction.

What Seems Especially Promising about Parents For Public Schools?

1. Parents for Public Schools is one of the few organizations, national or local, recruiting families to stay in or come back to public schools. They are distinct in their efforts to maintain diversity in public schools, to transform their involvement into advocates for all children, and engage them in advancing an equity agenda.
2. The local chapters focus on district policies and change, rather than on individual schools.
3. The chapters are community-based not school-based.
4. Parents for Public Schools is not reluctant to stress aggressive advocacy by parents along with strong support for public schools. Their strategy is to create a permanent, embedded role for parents in school systems and not simply focus on specific issues.
5. The credibility and resources of the national organization are assets to the local chapters.

Designs for Change

Designs for Change was formed in 1977 with the mission of being a catalyst for major improvements in the public schools of the 50 largest cities in the United States, with a particular emphasis on Chicago. A Year 2000 brochure describes the organization as unique in the nation in combining high quality applied research and direct involvement in aiding reform. The Executive Director is Dr. Donald Moore. The organization is one of several local groups that worked hard and effectively for the passage of the Chicago Reform Act. Since 1977, DFC has served as a monitor, critic, and supporter of the reform effort undertaking several important studies and offering training and support to Local School Councils.

Example organizations' current projects include the Network for Leadership Development which advises and assists Local School Councils, teachers, principals, and parents in planning and carrying out basic educational reform to improve student achievement, especially literacy. They are working directly with five low-income schools, providing leadership for a citywide project to encourage independent student reading, and producing resource guides and advising any school in the city.

A second project is the Chicago Policy Reform Program, which studies school system structure and policy and advocate changes. For example, they worked with other Chicago community organizations to resist changes proposed by school district officials in the Local School Council aspects of the law. After a difficult struggle, the legislature defeated attempts to weaken the Local School Council authority.

A third project is the Learning Path Institute, an independent, degree-granting program to prepare and assist active parent and community members to become skilled leaders for educational change in major cities, including Chicago. The Institute recently worked in Milwaukee to help create a new citywide education advocacy group.

The Designs for Change staff stress the preparation of Institute graduates as leaders in improving public policies that impact Chicago's young people. Graduates secure critical staff positions in institutions that make up the learning paths of Chicago's children and youth, such as early education centers, elementary and secondary schools, community organizations on public school issues, and youth mentoring programs.

Program descriptions emphasize several features: students as a part of a cohort taking courses together; active learning methods; individually set learning goals; cutting edge technology; internships in exemplary community institutions; and stress on strengthening students' basic skills in reading, writing, and technology use. The Institute plans to award an Associate of Arts degree in Human Services. As the program is new, there are no results to report at the time of this writing.

**What Seems Especially Promising about
Designs for Change?**

1. It uses research as the basis for its advocacy and action.
2. It acts politically to promote legislation such as that
   which established the Local School Councils in 1988.
3. It emphasizes the link between parent and community
   participation and student achievement.
4. It is independent of the school system and free to criticize it publicly, while remaining a staunch advocate for
   public schools, combining advocacy with direct helping
   work in schools.
5. The Learning Path Institute is one of a growing number
   of non-traditional approaches to granting college
   degrees aimed at urban populations often not well
   served by traditional post-secondary education institutions. Such programs meet a clear need for preparing
   informed civic leaders for urban areas.

Kentucky's Pritchard Committee for Academic Excellence

The Pritchard Committee for Academic Excellence is statewide organization with substantial statewide and local impact. The Committee, which
was established in 1983 and has about 100 members and works with
through a large network of local activists and organizations and appears to
have been successful in having good access to the elite political, educational, and corporate leadership of the state. Over the years they have won
support from dozens of national and state foundations and corporations.
The Executive Director is Dr. Robert Sexton.

The Committee led the fight for the passage of the Kentucky Educational Reform Act. The editors of a recent study of the reform assert that
the Pritchard Committees work "symbolizes the important work that parents and other citizens can play in transforming public schools" (Pankratz
& Petrosko, 2000, p. 8).

As an aggressive watchdog of and advocate for the public schools, the
Committee has used a wide variety of methods. These include mass mailings
on the responsibilities of school councils, a toll-free telephone line, many
publications explaining school policies and laws in user friendly language,
newsletters, a monthly column in 200 local newspapers in the state, radio
spots, a network of regional organizers, and extensive parent training.

The Community Accountability Team of Jefferson County (the state's
largest urban district) is an example of a local project spawned by the Prit-

chard Committee and financially supported by it. The Community Accountability Team is an unincorporated group of parents, citizen activists, business people, researchers, and educators, who set out to gather data first hand about the school district's progress in raising student achievement and closing achievement gaps among various groups of middle grades students. The team used the data to educate and mobilize the efforts of parents and the community. The school system responded with a set of actions and policies and a strong commitment to work toward improvement.

In 1997, the Committee launched the Commonwealth Institute for Parent Leadership, cosponsored by the state PTA. This Institute was a response to the findings of studies of the Kentucky Reform Act. These findings revealed that many school site councils were falling short of realizing their potential. Many schools and communities had not recognized the importance of family and community participation in achieving the results of the reform.

The Institute is open to anyone who has or previously had children in the Kentucky public schools and those who work with students. Prospective enrollees submit an application, letters of recommendation, and their reflections on why they want to participate. The enrollees commit themselves to attend three two-day training sessions held regionally around the state, to design and carry out a project in their own community, and participate in a statewide conference. The Institute, which seeks to train about 200 people a year, is free, including lodging, meals, and materials. Participants are trained in leadership and communication skills, using interactive and experiential methods. They are given explanations about the state's educational system, including the state's academic standards and testing programs. Regional staff members of the Pritchard Committee Academic Excellence help participants with their local projects and bring together graduates in regional groups to share knowledge and experience.

A 1999 evaluation report (Corbett & Wilson 2000) concluded the following:

> Institute participants had become both sophisticated learners about school reform in Kentucky and resourceful leaders in making sure that positive changes for students occurred. The Institute has become an effective vehicle for three things: arming parents with information about how schools should and do operate; instilling a confidence in parents as credible and worthy educational individuals; and providing parents with a willingness to act on behalf of all students, not just their own.

Kelly Mazzoli (2000), Institute Director, applauds the idea that they are helping activists to extend the reach of their training and "buck a national trend toward limited parent involvement in school governance." More than 45 of its alumnae have been elected to local school boards or school site councils. Many others are serving on other planning and policymaking groups.

One of the few researchers to focus much attention on independent citizen groups is Susan Fuhrman, who studied external groups in Kentucky and South Carolina. She argued that organizations such as the Pritchard Committee on Academic Excellence could overcome some of the characteristics of the political system that block coherent reform. She concluded "the Pritchard Committee ... provide(s) many lessons about the role of constituency-building groups in building and sustaining support for reform (Sexton, 2000, p. 249).

Bob Sexton (Sexton, 2000, p. 251) believes that the main accomplishments of the Pritchard Committee over the years include creating a sense of urgency about school reform. He continually reminds the public why reforms are needed. In addition, he persuades the public that reform is a long-term change not a quick fix. Sexton represents the public in state policy discussions, assuming an aggressive monitoring role and helping parents become stronger advocates for their children.

What Seems Especially Promising about the Pritchard Committee for Academic Excellence?

1. They have a solid strategy for positive influence, combining grassroots activism with statewide political influence and welding research and political action.
2. Its training arm is well designed and has the potential to provide a continuous supply of informed, motivated citizen leaders in Kentucky.
3. The combination of a statewide organization supported by a regional and local network of activists seems to be a viable model.
4. It uses a collaborative approach to its work.

Principals as Leaders of Cultural Change

The goal of schools embracing the partnership concept should be to move beyond councils, projects, and events toward the time that democratic participation becomes the standard operating procedure, the way the school does business. When this happens, the school has achieved a new culture as a democratic learning community.

I have identified two schools, which can be characterized as having achieved such cultural change: The Patrick O'Hearn School in Boston, and the Ford School in Lynn, Massachusetts. In both cases it was the work and inspiration of a principal, which made the difference. Most of us who have been involved in the family/community/school arena for a long time, know that the principal is almost always the key to success or failure to having the partnership idea take root.

There are scores—perhaps even hundreds—of other schools like the O'Hearn and the Ford and many other outstanding principals, so the descriptions below are representative examples of movement toward cultural change with partnership as a centerpiece.

Skeptics about this approach to partnership argue that to rely on the skill and charisma of extraordinary principals has severe limitations, saying that changes often do not last past the departure of the initiator, and that there is a limited supply of extraordinary leaders in any field. I share these concerns but argue that the skills and dedication of the principals are actually not so rare and are within the reach of hundreds, even thousands, of men and women who will provide school leadership. State and local systems share the responsibility to support and nurture their efforts. The concern about sustainability can be addressed if key aspects of the cultural change are institutionalized in school policy and laws and in the expectations of the community that the school serves.

The Ford Elementary School

The Ford School in Lynn, Massachusetts, serves about 900 children in grades pre-K–12, with a mostly low-income student population about evenly divided among African-Americans, Latinos, and Southeast Asians. About 40% are from families of recently arrived immigrants from at least twenty countries. It is in the poorest area of a small city of 80,000 facing many problems of poverty, inadequate housing, child abuse, crime, drug abuse, and a transient population.

Dr. Clare Crane, a woman with a background in social work, became the principal in 1989, determined to change the school, which was labeled a failure, with its standardized test scores ranked 18th out of 18 schools, low teacher morale, poor attendance, and isolated from its neighborhood. By 2000, Ford's student test scores had risen substantially, moving the school from 18th to 5th place in test scores, near the top of schools serving mostly low-income students, and the school has become a center for adult education, family and social services, recreation, and community development.

Some of the features of the school, which has been widely reported in local and national press, visited by Hillary Rodham Clinton, and honored by a White House Citation, include:

1. An all day kindergarten and outstanding school library, enhanced by a $900,000 DeWitt Wallace Foundation and staffed by a full-time library media specialist;

2. A year-round program of community education, including morning parent; support groups and evening classes for all ages in English as a Second Language, Graduation Equivalent Diploma, citizenship, and computer training;

3. An extensive after school and summer program for children, stressing both enrichment and academics;

4. A year-round program of community education, including morning parent support a collaboration with Salem State College and the Northshore Community College—including programs for children and educational, social, and health programs for families and on-site pre-college prep and college courses at the school;

5. A parent center and resource room in the school, with staffing by parents; and

6. An active school site council with decision making authority and a Leadership Team, which meets daily and includes the principal, teachers, and some parents.

Dr. Crane used community-organizing strategies, an attractive parent education program, and a parent room to lure parents to the school and get them involved in many ways in the school. She took seriously the opportunity presented by the state-mandated school site councils in the Education Reform Act. These councils across the state have the reputation of being largely inactive, with token participation, and dominated by the principal. She made the Ford Council an integral part of planning and decision making in the school, and expanded the membership beyond parents and teachers to include several of the city's civic and business leaders, adding noticeably to its political influence in the city.

Two selected examples of Council activism involve the following:

1. School district officials decided to close the all-day kindergarten, which had been started because of parent requests. The parents organized; nearly 400 of them appeared at a City Council meeting on the budget, and the all-day kindergarten survived; and

2. City officials proposed taking a parcel of land adjacent to the school, which had been set aside for a new Ford school, to use for a sports field. The Council helped to organize parents and others in the neighborhood to protest this action. They succeeded. In the spring of 2001 the plan for building the new school on the adjacent site is underway.

Ford School parents organized an independent organization, the Lynn Family Support Coalition, which works closely with the School Site Council. This Coalition sponsors social events, field trips, community improvement activities, political forums, voter registration, and has raised federal and state money for an after-school program and adult education.

Dr. Crane now points with pride to the Village School Program, which she says is based on the family-community-school partnership concept. Being located in the U.S. Empowerment Zone has helped with funding and technical assistance, as the school has moved to being able to offer school-based social and health services and community education, year round. Dr. Crane's activism and the political successes of the parents have incurred negative reactions from the central administration of the school district, and she has been "recognized" negatively at the time of salary increases.

What Seems Especially Promising about the Ford School?

1. Democratic procedures, respect for diversity, and a culture of partnership characterize this urban school.
2. The initiative and risk-taking of the principal over twelve years have been essential to the progress that the school has made.
3. Parents and other family members are involved in nearly all aspects of life in the school.
4. The principal uses community-organizing techniques and politically savvy advocacy strategies to achieve a school with improved academic achievement along with a wide variety of programs for families, children, and the community.

The Patrick O'Hearn School in Boston

The O'Hearn School is another urban turn around story in which a dynamic and well-prepared principal played the key role. The school, with about 225 students, is located in Dorchester, a racially and economically mixed section of Boston. Since 1989 the school has "a special integration model school," with about 25 per cent of its children in grades pre-k to grade 5 classified as "special needs." Three-fourths of all of the students are African Americans or recent immigrants from Asia, Africa, and the Caribbean.

When he became site principal in 1991, Dr. Bill Henderson inherited what was considered a "failing school." Test scores were low; there were frequent behavior problems; and many parents opted to send their children to other schools under a "controlled choice" plan. He set out to turn the school around by involving the families and communities in a process of "whole school change."

The school's academic performance has improved dramatically, with reading and math test scores climbing from near the bottom to near the top for the city. The school now has a long waiting list. Behavior problems have diminished significantly, and teacher turnover is very low. The O'Hearn has attracted much favorable attention from the press, visiting dignitaries, and benefactors who support special projects. Henderson is in demand as a speaker and panelist in national and regional conferences.

Some of the features of the O'Hearn program include: well-tested home visitor programs in which trained parent volunteers visit the homes of all new and entering students; a good library; a parent center; several business and cultural partnerships; sophisticated technology equipment and instruction in all classrooms; and read-at-home contracts for parents. The school has been chosen to participate in several competitive projects with the Institute for Responsive Education, including the action research project described in an earlier section of this chapter.

Parent participation in decision making is a major priority for the principal, with the focus being on the state-mandated School Site Council. Six parents sit with five teachers and the principal. The council helps hire the school staff, select textbooks, and set spending priorities. A democratic process prevails. In one instance, the council refused to accept the principal's announcement that the school would lose two staff positions because of district-wide cutbacks. After discussion, Council members protested to the central office and had the positions restored.

In another example, the parent members and the principal were interested in encouraging all parents to read regularly to their children at home, but parent and teacher members were not happy with the plan drafted by the principal for a written reading contract for parents. After collaborative discussion and negotiation, the plan and contract were modified. Parents agreed to read with their children at least four days a week for 15 or 20 minutes. The revised contract permitted parents to skip days when there was a crisis and to designate other family members or family friends to be the readers. When an evaluation revealed that the reading contract was only partly successful, a parent committee was formed to plan, revise, and carry out additional ways to promote home reading. By the middle of the 1999–2000 school year, Dr. Henderson reports that 95% of the families now participate in the program.

O'Hearn School is infused with a spirit of democratic participation and a commitment to achieving success for all students. The school certainly has not achieved all its aspirations. Many problems remain, but these problems will be faced by a school community in which a new participatory culture is well entrenched.

What Seems Especially Promising about the O'Hearn School?

1. A school site council with an equal number of parents and educators works in a fruitful and collaborative way, using democratic procedures to negotiate differences and reach compromises when needed.
2. A school that strongly emphasizes instructional and curricular improvement and excellence can also maintain a strong component of family participation in decision-making.
3. The various components of school, family, community partnership—including decision-making and advocacy—are functioning in harmonious and mutually supportive ways.
4. A participatory culture is producing solid student achievement gains.

PARENT TEACHER ASSOCIATIONS AND CHARTER SCHOOLS

Parent Teacher Association [PTA]

Any full discussion of parent or family participation in all aspects of school life must include the National PTA and its thousands of local chapters. But, historically, decision making and advocacy have not been major part of the agenda of many local PTA's. There have always been some exceptions to this rule. Strong, active local PTA's (or PTO's not affiliated with the national organization) that are able to include a good cross section of a school's parent constituency, have promise to contribute as supporters of school improvement, training grounds for civic leadership, and as a means of building public support for the public schools.

In addition, the National PTA has been a strong advocate on parent issues on many occasions since its founding in 1896. Advocacy examples involve lobbying for kindergartens, parent education, and protection and services for children. At local, state, and national levels PTA has been a strong ally of public schools as they sought increased funding and better facilities.

But discussion of these matters is beyond the space allowed for this chapter. I suggest four sources for further information and discussion, both favorable and critical:

1. The National PTA Web Site;
2. William W. Cutler's new book, *Parents and Schools*;
3. The sections about the PTA in Robert Putnam's *Bowling Alone*; and
4. New York Times Education Life section feature by Thomas Toch, "The Plight of the PTA."

Charter Schools

Charter schools often embody the essence of parental decision making and advocacy. Many of the thousands of charter schools that now exist in more than 35 states were created by the initiative of parents. This is clearly an important form of family decision making and advocacy and is a promising option for families in the future.

Discussing this topic further, however, is precluded by space limitations. For readers who want to follow up on this topic, I list a few examples of schools that were largely parent-initiated. Sometimes with the involvement of teachers and other community residents: Academy Charter School, Castle Rock, CO. Linscott Charter School, Watsonville, CA; Marblehead Community Charter Public School, Marblehead, MA; and San Carlos Charter Schools, San Carlos, CA. In some of these schools, as well as in many other charter schools across the country, there is also substantial parent participation in decision making.

CONCLUSION

The main point of this chapter is that family and community participation in school decision making and advocacy will be significant in the years ahead to the extent that such participation can contribute strongly to two goals of great importance to the health of our country. To reframe these goals:

1. Parent participation in decision making and advocacy will contribute strongly to school reform so that all students can achieve academic success with high standards.
2. Parent decision making in school governance will provide community members a forum to acquire and practice democratic practices. These opportunities will contribute to the development of a more civil and democratic society.

The programs and practices described here were selected because they exhibit at least some of the elements that have promise to contribute to such goals. These include:

1. Honoring democratic principles and procedures;
2. Seeking inclusion across lines of race, ethnicity, gender, and social class;
3. Seeking to support and sustain public schools while also pressing them to make difficult changes;
4. Recognizing the need to codify and institutionalize regulations and procedures;
5. Focusing on high standards of student achievement and accountability;
6. Employing a variety of strategies and methods suitable to the setting and the purpose; and
7. Addressing the core issues of decision making: personnel, program, and budget.

Participation with these elements should be seen as an essential component of any comprehensive partnership between schools, families, and communities. Without access to decision making and advocacy, participants are clients not partners.

Sources for additional information:

BPON and IRE
Institute for Responsive Education
50 Nightingale Hall
Northeastern University
Boston, MA 02115
Tel.: 617-373-5922; Fax: 617-373-8924;
Web Site: www.resp-ed.org

Right Question Project
218 Holland Street
Somerville, MA 02144
Tel.: 617-628-4070; Fax: 617-628-8632

The Pritchard Committee for Academic Excellence
P.O. Box 1658
Lexington, KY 40588-1658
Tel.: 800-928-2111; e-mail: admin@pritchardcommittee.org

Parents for Public Schools
1520 North State Street
Jackson, MS 3902-1645
Tel.: 800-880-1222; e-mail: parents4publicschools.com

Designs for Change
6 North Michigan Ave.
Chicago, IL 60602
Tel.: 312-857-9992; Fax: 312-857-9299; e-mail: dfc@aol.com

REFERENCES

Alliance Schools Initiative (February 1, 2001). Unpublished report of dataa from the Alliance Schools. Austin, TX: Southwest Industrial Areas Foundation.

Arnstein, S.R. (1971). Eight rungs on the ladder of citizen participation. In E.S. Cahn & B.A. Passett (Eds.), *Citizen participation: Effecting community change.* New York: Praeger.

Boston Parent Organizing Network. (1999). *Organizing guidelines.* Boston: Author.

Bryk, A.S. et al. (1993). *A view from the elementary schools: The state of reform in Chicago.* Chicago: Consortium on Chicago School Research.

Consortium on Chicago School Research. (1997, December). *Charting reform: LSC's—Local leadership at work.* Chicago: The Consortium.

Corbett, D., & Wilson, B. (2000). *I didn't know I could do that: Parents learning to be leaders through the Commonwealth Institute for Parent Leadership.* Unpublished manuscript, Pritchard Committee for Academic Excellence.

Cortes, E. Jr. (1993). Reweaving the fabric: The iron rule and the IAF strategy for power and politics. In *Interwoven destinies: Cities and the nation* (pp. 295–213).

Cortes, E. Jr. (1995). Making the public the leaderss in education reform. *Education Week,* November 22, p. 34.

Cutler, W.W. III. (2000). *Parents and schools: The 150-year struggle for control of American education.* Chicago: University of Chicago Press.

David, J. (2000). Educators and parents as partners in school governance. In R.S. Pankratz (Ed.), *All children can learn: Lessons from the Kentucky reform experience* (pp. 209–249). San Francisco: Jossey-Bass.

Davies, D. (1988, Spring). Low income parents and the schools: A research report and a plan of action. *Equity and Choice,* pp. 51–59. Davies, D. (1981). *Communities and their schools.* New York: McGraw-Hill.

Davies, D. et al. (1979a). *Sharing the power: A report on the status of school councils in the 1970's.* Boston: Institute for Responsive Education.

Davies, D. et al. (1979b). *Patterns of citizen participation in educational decisionmaking,* Vol. I: *Grassroots perspectives: Diverse forms of participation.* Boston: Institute for Response Education.

Designs for Change. (1998). *What makes these schools stand out: Chicago elementary schools with a seven-year trend of improved reading achievement* Chicago: Author.

Epstein, J.L. (1995, May). School/family/community partnerships: Caring for the children w share. *Phi Delta Kappan*, pp. 701–710.

Epstein, J.L., & Coates, L. (1997). *School, family, and community partnerships: Your handbook for action.* Thousand Oaks, CA: Corwin.

Fruchter, N. et al. (1992). *New directions in parent involvement.* New York: Academy for Educational Development.

Gittell, M. (1979). *Citizen organizations: Citizen participation in educational decisionmaking.* Boston: Institute for Responsive Education.

Industrial Areas Foundation (1994). Engaging the public: One way to organize—a Concept Paper. Washington, DC: National Alliance for Restructuring Education.

Institute for Responsive Education. (2001). *Parent leadership exchange* [Brochure]. Boston: Author.

Katz, M.B. (1995). *Improving poor people: The welfare state, the "underclass," and urban schools as history.* Princeton, NJ: Princeton University.

Kentucky General Assembly. (1999). *Office of Educational Accountability annual report.* Frankfort, KY: Office of Educational Accountability.

Kentucky Institute for Education Research (1997). *School-based decisionmaking: Shared findings and insights of researchers.* Lexington, KY: Kentucky Institute for Education Research.

Learning Path Institute. *Associate of arts program* [Brochure]. Chicago: Designs for Change.

McLaughlin M.W., & Shields, P.M. (1987, October). Involving low-income parents in the schools: A role for policy? *Phi Delta Kappan*, pp. 155–160.

Malen, B., & Ogawa, R.T. (1988). Professional-patron influence on site based councils: A confounding case study. *Educational Evaluation and Policy Analysis, 10*(4), 251–270.

Mauceri, K. et al. (2000, August). *The Impact of the Right Question Educational Project on parents, schools, education reform organizations, communities, and children.* Cambridge, MA: The Right Question Project.

Mazzoli, K. (2000). Practice prepares fellows for participation in the civic process. *Parent Leader, 2*(2), 3.

National Center for Educational Statistics. (1998). *Parent involvement in children's education: Efforts by public elementary schools.* Washington, DC: U.S. Department of Education.

National Parent-Teacher Association. (1997). *National parent and family involvement program standards.* Chicago: National PTA.

Office of Educational Accountability. (1999). *Kentucky General Assembly, Office of Educational accountability annual report.* Frankfort, KY: Office of Educational Accountability.

Office of Educational Research and Improvement. (1997). *Family involvement in children's education: successful local approaches.* Washington, DC: U.S. Department of Education.

Pankratz, R.S., & Petrosko, J. (2000). *All children can learn: Lessons from the Kentucky reform experience.* San Francisco: Jossey-Bass.

Parents for Public Schools. (1998). *Defining a niche: Evaluation of parents for public schools* Unpublished manuscript.

Putnam, R.D. (2000). *Bowling alone: The collapse and revival of American community.* New York: Simon and Schuster.

Pritchard Committee for Academic Excellence. (1999). *Gaining ground: Hard work and high expectations for Kentucky schools.* Lexington, KY: The Committee.

Sexton, R.F. (2000). Engaging parents and citizens in school reform. In R.S. Pankratz & J.M. Petroska (Eds.), *All children can learn.* San Francisco: Jossey-Bass.

Shirley, D. (1997). *Community organizing for urban school reform.* Austin: University of Texas Press.

Smylie, M.A. et al. (1992). Instructional outcomes of school-based participative decision-making. *Educational Evaluation and Policy Analysis, 18,* 181–198.

Sommerfield, M. (1995). Ordinary people: Interview with Ernesto Cortes. *Education Week, 18,* 16–21.

Texas Interfaith Education Fund. (1990). *The Texas vision for public schools: Communities of learners.* Austin: Texas Interfaith Education Fund.

Wilkerson & Associates. (1999). *1999 statewide education reform study: Final report.* Louisville: Kentucky Institute for Educational Research.

Woestehoff, J. (1998). LSC parents have earned support. In *What matters most, web site report of: Catalyst, the voice of Chicago school reform* [on-line]. Available: www.catalyst-chicago.org

CHAPTER 7

PARENT EDUCATION AS AN ESSENTIAL COMPONENT OF PARENT INVOLVEMENT PROGRAMS

Mary P. DiCamillo

It's 6:45 p.m. and the parents have begun to arrive at Sunnybrook Elementary School for the parent education meeting. It is a cool, crisp evening, and the atmosphere in the school is warm and inviting. This evening a local pediatrician will be speaking at the meeting on the topic of child safety. On the way into the meeting, several families stop by the parent information center where they are encouraged by the center's director to pick up some new brochures and parent education pamphlets. In the corner of the parent information center a monitor is playing a video of a parent and child doing homework together highlighting important strategies for developing a nightly routine. The Media Center director is also there this evening demonstrating a new software program on the computer that the children are using to develop language skills. As the lights flicker in the auditorium, it signals that the meeting is starting...

WHAT IS PARENT EDUCATION?

Parent education is identified as specific training and support which is provided to parents by schools and agencies to aid them with parenting skills, and with the developmental, academic, social, and health issues of their children. Parent education includes the creation of and dissemination of parenting information and educational supports for parents and children

153

for enhancing learning at home. Teachers, parents, students, administrators, interagency team members, nurses, physicians, social workers, psychologists, librarians, university professionals, police and fire officials, and community members are some of the groups of people who may participate together in parent education programs. Parent education programs occur at school during school hours and after school at meetings and classes, as well as in the community as provided by service agencies. Parent education may also occur through home visits by parent educators, through parent information/education centers, and through on-line resources such as newsletters and web pages. Quality parent education programs strengthen families and communities by bringing teachers, administrators, parents, students, and community members together; thus enabling school personnel to better meet the needs of students and parents as they support the growth and development of children.

CHARACTERISTICS OF EFFECTIVE PARENT EDUCATION PROGRAMS

Redding (2001) has noted that programs that include both parents and children are more effective than programs that deal with only the parents, and that most of the successful programs offer a combination of parent group learning and private sessions. It is important to respond to the needs of families and to provide curriculums and experiences to match that need (France & Hager, 1993). "Education for parents and future parents should increase knowledge of children's learning in the home and community and of parents' contribution to that learning" (Schaeffer, 1991, p. 244).

A thorough review of the literature has revealed several characteristics that contribute to the success of parent education programs. Effective parent education programs:

1. Complete thorough assessment procedures before program implementation to ascertain parent and student needs (Conner, 2000; Freedman & Montgomery, 1994).
2. Attract parents and keep them involved by continuously reaching out to them (France and Hager, 1993; Freedman & Montgomery, 1994). Involve fathers and help them develop roles of nurturing and care-giving as they may not have had role models for when growing up (Beale, 1999).
3. Demonstrate sensitivity, respect and affirmation of diversity at all times (Freedman & Montgomery, 1994; Hurd, Lerner, & Barton, 1999; National PTA Standards, 2000).

4. Involve parents, teachers, and community members in setting goals and determining the activities of parent education programs (Conner, 2000).
5. Develop on ongoing training programs in which parents, administrators and staff are participants, teachers, and learners (Freedman & Montgomery, 1994).

PARENT EDUCATION AS A COMPONENT OF PARENT INVOLVEMENT

Parent involvement programs are very important to schools, children, and parents because they increased shared responsibility, participation, and decision making. Research demonstrates that quality parent involvement programs such as those previously presented can have significant effects on student social, learning, and achievement outcomes. Freedman and Montgomery (1994) have agreed that parent involvement is key to student success, but it is their view that parent education is essential for effective parent involvement to occur.

Joyce Epstein, the director of the Center on School, Family and Community Partnerships at Johns Hopkins University, also agrees that parent involvement is important to student success. She has identified six important types of cooperation between families, schools, and others community organizations. These are: (a) parenting, (b) communicating, (c) volunteering, (d) learning at home, (e) decision making, and (f) collaboration within the community (*Harvard Education Letter,* 1997).

Parent education, in Epstein's model, is a component of parent involvement based on the first component—parenting. Parents need to provide for the health and safety of children and should maintain a home environment that encourages learning and good behavior in school. Schools can help parents by providing training and information to help them understand their children's development and how to support the changes they undergo. Beneficial programs and services schools can offer to meet this need are: (a) parent education and other courses for parents; (b) family support programs to assist families with health, nutrition, and other services; and (c) home visits at transition points to preschool, elementary, middle and high school (Fairbanks North Star Borough School District, 2001).

Parent education is also a component of Epstein's model based on the fourth type of cooperation—learning at home. Teachers can guide and support family members in supervising and assisting their children at home with homework assignments and other school related activities (Williamson, 1997). Ways schools can help meet this need are: (a) offering information to families on skills required for students in all subjects at each grade, (b) offering information on homework policies and how to monitor and discuss schoolwork at home, and (c) encouraging family participation in setting student goals each year and in planning for college or work (Fairbanks North Star Borough School District, 2001). Redding (2001) also suggest that schools should "make a specific list of what the school wants from parents according to the age group of the child, and then organize parent education around this list" (p. 23).

In order for a parent education program to be a quality program it must be a two-way process. The program should serve the needs of the school to disseminate information to parents as to how they can help their children succeed in school but it should also be focused on the needs of the parents it is serving so they can be supportive of their children. Parents are able to help their children in school more effectively if their educational, cultural, and literacy needs are also being met.

HISTORY OF MAJOR PARENT EDUCATION PROGRAMS

National PTA

National PTA (Parent Teachers Association) is the oldest and the largest volunteer parent/child advocacy organization in the United States. It has been serving parents and children since 1897 (About the PTA Our History, 2001). For the last 100 years, this nonprofit association of parents, educators, students, and other citizens has worked diligently to help people be active in their schools and communities. It is a large organization, widespread throughout the nation. Almost every school in America has an active PTA chapter (Hiatt-Michael, 2001). "PTA has nearly 6.5 million members working in 26,000 local chapters in all 50 states, the District of Columbia, the U.S. Virgin Islands, and the Department of Defense schools in the Pacific and Europe" (Children First, 2001, p. 1).

The threefold mission of the National PTA is to:

1. Support and speak on behalf of children and youth in the schools, in the community, and before governmental bodies and other organizations that make decisions affecting children;
2. Assist parents in developing the skills they need to raise and protect their children; and
3. Encourage parent and public involvement in the public schools of this nation (Children First, 2001, p. 1).

The PTA provides parent education in many forms including workshops, training, meetings, resource kits, videos, and Web sites for parents.

Violence prevention and creating safe nurturing environments for children are current priority issues of the National PTA.

Project Head Start

The first federally funded integrated service agency to provide services to parents and children in the United Stated was Head Start. This federally funded preschool program was founded in 1965 for the purpose of providing child development and support services to families in need. It began as part of President Johnson's program of the war on poverty (Hurd, Lerner, & Barton, 1999).

Head Start programs are family service centers, in which the physical, emotional, cognitive, and family needs of a child are addressed (Hurd, Lerner, & Barton, 1999). This agency is distinguished as a leader in the provision of integrated services for preschool children. The four main components of Head Start are: health, education, social services, and parent involvement. Currently, more than 18 million low-income preschool children and their families have been served. "Head Start has grown from a 6-week summer program with a budget of $96 million to a nine-month school year program with a $5.3 billion allocation in fiscal year 2000" (NHSA-National Head Start Association, 2001, p. 1).

Head Start caseworkers closely monitor the support for each child and her family (Hurd, Lerner, & Barton, 1999). Initially, Head Start began as a half-day program but statistics indicate that the numbers of full-day Head Start programs are on the rise, due to the increasing parent need for full-day care services for children. Another benefit of the Head Start program is that it provides jobs. Parents acquire teaching and parenting skills while working in Head Start programs. Programs have employed more than 60,000 Head Start parents in 1999 (NHSA-National Head Start Association, 2001).

It is evident that Head Start has made a difference in the lives of children and families. Research has shown that Head Start children come to school better prepared to learn and have higher self-esteem and social behavior, than peers who do not attend this program (NHSA-National Head Start Association, 2001). Studies have indicated that Head Start children have shown positive school achievement and motivation past the third grade, have lower grade retention, reduced enrollment in special education, and fewer cases of delinquency. Other positive benefits demonstrated as the result of participating in this program include better health, motor development, nutrition, and dental care.

The Comer School Development Program

Established in 1968, by child psychiatrist Dr. James Comer and his colleagues at Yale Child Study Center, this program also known as the Comer Process, was designed to improve the educational experience of poor minority children and youth. This process focuses on "urban, inner-city schools that are often in the most serious need of support" (Technical Support Consortium Best Practices, 2001, p. 1). The School Development program builds supportive bonds among children, parents, and school staff to promote a positive school climate (Office of Education Research Consumer Guide, 1993). Comer's conclusions are that "children's experiences at home and in school deeply affect their psychosocial development, which in turn shapes their academic achievement" (Office of Education Research Consumer Guide, 1993, p. 1). It is also Comer's theory that poor academic performance is largely based on the failure to bridge the social and cultural gaps between home and school. The Comer School Development program has been implemented in 389 schools (elementary through high schools) through February 2000 (School Development Program, 2001).

Comer's Process aims to create an environment where children feel comfortable, valued, and secure. When children feel safe and secure they form positive emotional bonds with school staff and parents. A positive attitude toward school is created in this process that in turn may have a positive effect on the children's overall development and academic learning. The three guiding principles of the Comer process are: no-fault problem solving, consensus decision making and collaboration (A Brief Summary of SDP Effects, 2001). The primary goal of this program is to "mobilize the entire community of adult caretakers ... to support students' holistic development and to effect academic success" (School Development Program, 2001 p. 1). Three teams: (a) The School Planning and Management Team–which includes administrators, teachers, parents, support staff, and a child developmental specialist; (b) The Student and Staff Support Team—which includes teachers, administrators, psychologists, social workers, and nurses; and (c) The Parent Team—led by parents; are integral to the joint decision-making process and operations of the school. The three main operations of the SDP are (a) the Comprehensive School Plan, (b) the Staff Development Plan, and (c) Monitoring and Assessment (School Development Program, 2001).

Quantitative, qualitative, and theory development research strategies have been used to evaluate the effectiveness of the School Development Program (A Brief Summary of SDP Effects, 2001). Many schools that have adopted the Comer Process have shown great gains in social skills, educational achievement, and attendance levels. It has been found that student achievement improves more at schools where the process is done faithfully

(Technical Support Consortium Best Practices, 2001). Cook, Murphy, and Hunt (2000) in their study of the Comer School Development Program in 10 inner city Chicago schools found that students' and teachers' perceptions of the school's academic climate had improved. The students in Comer schools gained about 3 percentile points more than control group subjects in both reading and math. Results also indicated that students reported less acting out and reported greater ability to control their anger.

MegaSkills

Dr. Dorothy Rich, director of the Home and School Institute in 1972, established the MegaSkills Program. This program, which focuses on building competencies and relationships for learning, has served more than 3400 schools at all grade levels. "MegaSkills is a basic parent involvement model focusing on the educational role of the family with specific curricula for home" (MegaSkills Education Center, 2001, p. 2). The primary goal of this program is "to build high standards, habits, behaviors and attitudes that determine achievement in school and beyond." (MegaSkills Education Center, 2001, p. 1). This program emphasizes teacher training, classroom and parent program curricula, synergy between school and home, linkage to the work world, multi-languages, and educational values to build achievement (Chavkin, Gonzalez, & Rader, 2000).

The primary building blocks of the program are the MegaSkills and they are: confidence, motivation, effort, responsibility, perseverance, caring, initiative, teamwork, problem solving, common sense, and focus. Dorothy Rich calls these the inner engines of learning (Chavkin, Gonzalez, & Rader, 2000). These skills are needed for success in school and in the workplace. The MegaSkills are used in all settings with all grade levels and give all the participants a common language.

Schools who use this program report that students benefit from having their parents become more involved in their education. The program also has an effect on student attitude and self-discipline. Students are more self-disciplined, referrals decrease, there are fewer discipline problems. Students in this program work more cooperatively, and spend more time on homework and less time watching TV. Parents report that their kids spend more time with them.

Improvements in student achievement and student competencies have been seen. In a study of a rural district on the Texas-Mexico border who used the MegaSkills program, it was found that "at one elementary school 75% of the second grade students are now reading at grade level according to the Gates Reading Test, (and) … avgerage math and reading scores on the Iowa Test of Basic Skills have increased 19 and 14 points per grade level, respectively" (Chavkin, Gonzalez, & Rader, 2000, p. 129). At the middle school and high school in this study at least 90% of the students passed the reading and math sections of the TAAS test. It is reported that attendance at parent workshops has doubled at the elementary schools and that parent involvement has increased in the middle school and high school (Chavkin, Gonzalez, & Rader, 2000).

STEP—Systematic Training for Effective Parenting

This program developed by Dr. Don Dinkmeyer and Dr. Gary McKay in 1976, is based in Adlerian Psychology (Clarkson, 1980). It comprises a nine-week parent-training course that teaches a theory of behavior, communication skills, problem solving, and discipline. Parents who have participated in this program have shown differences in parental attitudes, and are more accepting of their children's behavior and feelings, aggressiveness, need for affection, and self-expression (Summerlin & Ward, 1981.) Nystul (1982), in his study of 28 Australian mothers, reported that STEP mothers (as compared to non-STEP mother) were more democratic in their child rearing attitudes, encouraged more verbalization, and were less strict with their children.

Brookline Early Education Program

The Brookline Early Education Program, which began in the late 1970s, is a multi-service preschool early intervention program which was a joint effort of researchers from Harvard University, medical personnel and Brookline, MA public school officials (Hurd, Lerner, & Barton, 1999). It was one of the first programs of its kind to be based in the public school system. The goals of this program are parent empowerment and child social competence. Results of program evaluations indicated that parents saw themselves more as advocates for their children. Benefits to children included that they demonstrated more social competence and had a decreased need for special services (Hurd, Lerner, & Barton, 1999).

FAST—Families and Schools Together

The Families and Schools Together program that was created by Dr. Lynn McDonald, began in 1988 in Madison, Wisconsin (Family and Schools Together, 2001). This program is "a highly successful school-based family support program which helps schools build strong relationships with the families of children aged 6–9 who are experiencing behavioral or academic difficulties" (Hernandez, Hernandez, Lopez, Kreider, & Coffman, 2000, p. 85). It is a comprehensive prevention/intervention program which focuses on family involvement and strengthening interagency collaboration and home-school relationships (Hernandez et al., 2000). The goals of the FAST program are to strengthen families; enhance family, school and community ties; help children succeed at school and at home; reduce drug and alcohol abuse; and reduce stress and isolation (Family and Schools Together, 2001).

The FAST program involves whole families in weekly gatherings for 8 weeks at the school site in specific, fun, research-based activities. These sessions are aimed at empowering parents and building a sense of community among them. A 2-year follow-up program called FASTWORKS maintains the parent network and the home school connections that are established during FAST (Hernandez et al., 2000).

Parents who participate in this program consistently report "improved interactions with children and feeling more appreciative of what teachers and staff need to do to provide a quality education for a child" (Hernandez et al., 2000, p. 87). Results also show improvements in children's classroom and home behaviors, increased self-esteem and family closeness, and increased parent involvement in the school. FAST is now operating in more than 600 schools in 38 states, three Indian nations, and five countries (Family and Schools Together, 2001).

PARENT EDUCATION SERVICE DELIVERY MODELS

There are a number of ways in which parent education may be disseminated. These include: (a) home visits that may be conducted by parent educators, (b) group sessions that may be led by previously trained parents, (c) workshops and courses that may be taught by experts, (d) parent information/education centers, and (e) on-line resources such as newsletters and web pages (France & Meeks, 1988; National PTA Standards, 2000; Redding, 2001).

Home Visits

Benefits of home visit programs according to Redding (2001) are that "they are convenient for parents, they place the educator in the natural setting of the home, and enable the parent educator to focus on one family at a time" (p. 23). Spewock (1988) also noted the value of doing home visits in a home-based parent education program in a rural community to train parents to teach their preschoolers through literature. France and Meeks

(1988) also suggested that reading specialists should visit homes, as parents who cannot read may not feel comfortable coming to school. Redding (2001) states that home visits are "most effective when combined with group meetings with other parents" (p. 22).

Group Sessions Led by Trained Parents

The National PTA actively involves and trains parents to train other parents. Redding (2001) noted that this is a good practice and recommends this strategy. He suggested that schools "use parents to organize, recruit, and lead other parents" (Redding, 2001, p. 23). Redding (2001) indicated that "small group sessions led by previously trained parents are inexpensive, encourage parental attachment to the school, and allow parents to share experiences and assist one another" (p. 23). Parents with special training also become mentors and role models for other parents. It is also good idea to recruit parents and community members with expertise in child development, education, psychology, health, and other related areas to volunteer their time to provide workshops for parents.

Workshops and Courses Taught by Experts

Historically, experts in the field taught many parent education workshops. They were brought in to motivate teachers and parents, bring in a new perspective, and create enthusiasm (D. Hiatt-Michael, personal communication, June 12, 2001). One downside of this approach is that it may be a one-time occasion in which nothing builds upon it. Generally, change does not occur in a school this way. The best way to use experts is to bring them in when the school is in the First Stage of Awareness according to the Concerns Based Adoption Model (CBAM) (Hall & Hord, 1987). After a workshop or course is completed, schools benefit from site-based support to apply the skills and techniques learned as well as facilitate growth and change.

Although bringing in an expert speaker can be motivational, it can also be costly depending on the type of program provided, the length of the program, and the curriculum, materials, and training involved. If funding is available for specialty training programs taught by experts, it is important to get as many parents involved as possible and to sustain their interaction to receive the maximum benefits of the program.

Parent Education/Information Centers/Resource Rooms

Parents need to feel welcome and part of the school. They need a place they can call their own on the school grounds. National PTA recommends that a special area in the school or community should be designated just for parents and family members. The center should be focused on the needs, issues, and concerns of the school and its members. It may be an informal gathering place for parents to share information, and it could be used to provide access to community services. A wide array of family resource and support materials should be offered including videos, brochures, and other publications. Television and videos can be highly effective media through which parents can be shown how to help their children (France & Meeks, 1988). Some centers also offer parenting workshops, have book and toy-lending libraries, or offer ESL classes. Using the school newsletter to highlight what's new at the family center throughout the year helps to increase the center's visibility and effectiveness (National PTA Standards, 2000).

On-line Resources

The Internet has made it increasingly easier for schools to provide information to parents and to provide opportunities for communication. Schools now have lots of wonderful tools at their fingertips to educate parents and disseminate information via the World Wide Web. Parents now have opportunities to learn about school activities and events through school home pages, many of which have e-mail access to teachers and administrators. Some schools use the Internet to provide information to families about homework assignments and the school calendar. Some schools also disseminate parenting advice and education. New technologies are continuing to evolve every day. With the advance of streaming video content, schools could make parent education videos available to be viewed on their Web sites. "By using technology to keep parents informed, the school builds community support for future technological advances" (Connor, 2000, p. 62). The Parents Guide to the Information Superhighway (available on-line) is also an excellent parent education resource available from the National PTA which helps parents use commonsense along with simple, practical tips about the new technology and offers rules and tools to help children and families at home, at school, and in the community (Children First, 2001; Lazarus & Lipper, 1998).

Conner (2000) suggested that schools should design parent education workshops to extend parents' computer knowledge so they can explore Web sites with their children. Families can apply this knowledge for use at

home and in the classroom setting. Parents and children could be introduced to new educational software the school is using. It is also a good idea
to have this software available to be checked out in the parent resource
room. Benefits of these strategies include: enhanced learning at home and
improvement of parents' computer knowledge and skills. These factors
may help parents to get better jobs in the communities and may also provide a better educational climate for children at home.

THE BENEFITS OF PARENT EDUCATION

Family Benefits

Children benefit greatly from parent education programs because these
programs often involve children and parents together so they the children
are spending more time with their parents. It is ideal when families are
able to develop a love of learning together, which creates an optimal lifelong learning pattern. Children learn to communicate with their parents
better and family bonds are enhanced through more family time activities.
Beale (1999) has noted that parent education activities can: (a) help parents develop added knowledge and understanding, (b) cause them to evaluate their ways of thinking, and (c) help them to develop more effective
ways of dealing with their children.

The ways that schools present parent education can have a big impact
on the benefits families receive from participating. Cultural sensitivity on
the part of schools, teachers, and program administrators can have a key
influence on parents' perceptions. In an evaluation study by Norwood,
Atkinson, Tellez, and Saldana (1997) of a culturally responsive parent edu-
cation/parent involvement program they found that urban minority parents who participated in the program responded positively to the program
when parenting or schooling information was presented in a warm, supportive, and nonjudgmental environment. They also stated that these families were more likely to internalize and use the tools they were provided
when information was presented in this way. The parents in this study indicated that they had more knowledge and a higher level of confidence,
which enabled them to interact more effectively with their children's teachers and the children themselves.

Jacobson, Huffman, and Rositas de Cantu (1998) also noted that culture
and language was important in working with Hispanic parents. They stated
that Spanish is a key element to successful participation by Hispanics families and that some parents do not attend parent-training sessions because
of the language barrier. They also suggested that schools should encourage
parents to spend time with their children. Additionally, schools should

offer classes that specifically address parents' needs, increase their skills, and develop their talents.

There are many parent education programs taught in Spanish by Hispanics that address cultural issues of parenting and interacting with the teachers and school staff. One notable program, The Parent Institute for Quality Education (PIQE) has been providing parent education to the community since 1987. It has had great success and is well attended by both mothers and fathers. This program "supports the belief that parents respond well to the chance to participate in the education of their children. The results are a better educational environment for the students, and a greater opportunity for their future academic success" (Parent Institute for Quality Education, 2001, p. 1).

The Effects of Parent Education on Student Achievement

Research consistently demonstrates that children whose parents are involved in parent education programs perform better on academic tasks, than children whose parents are not involved in parent education (Bangs, 1994; Jordan, Snow, & Porche, 2000; Starkey & Klein 2000; Wang, Wildman, & Calhoun, 1996). "Parents knowledge and skills of (child) rearing and relationships as well as reading, writing, and arithmetic contribute to the academic competence of their children" (Schaeffer, 1991, p. 245.). In Norwood et al.'s (1997) study the children of the parents who participated in the parent education program scored better in math and reading on standardized tests than students whose parents did not participate in the program. Freedman and Montgomery (1994) have found in their research that California schools in which parents are involved consistently rate at the top one-half of the district's ranking in terms of achievement levels. Bangs (1994) reported that the percentage of children at grade-level reading rose from 7 to 30% during two years of a parent education project, and significant improvements in school-wide basal reading were also observed. The results of many studies indicate that parents have an impact on their children's learning.

Benefits of Teachers, Administrators, and Schools

Parent education programs increase relationships between schools and parents and can help them to get to know each other on a more personal level. This opportunity affords teachers the ability to customize family learning programs and support based on need when and if time allows. Teachers who work more closely with families through parent education programs are better able to meet their needs (Chavkin et al., 2000). School climate is often improved when parents are involved in parent education programs, thus making the jobs of teachers and administrators easier and more enjoyable. Teachers and administrators feel personal success when students achieve. Research has shown when families are involved in parent education programs they are more involved with their children. This involvement in turn leads to higher self-esteem and fewer disruptions at school. Teachers and administrators can do their jobs more effectively when there are fewer discipline problems. Teachers and principals at schools where quality parent education programs are implemented, report increased parent volunteerism, better teacher-parent communication, improved child behavior and attendance (Covarrubia, 2000).

RECENT PARENT EDUCATION PROGRAMS

Pre- and Peri-Natal Parent Education Programs

There definitely is a need for more emphasis, research, and program development in the area of parent education programs for parents of infants and toddlers (Mahoney, Kaiser, & Girolametto, 1999). Parents can learn valuable skills that dramatically affect their relationship with their child at birth and even prior to birth. Babies are capable of bonding and learning in utero (Sallenbach, 1998). It is crucial for parents and infants to bond during the first days of life outside the womb. Experts believe that the bonding and healthy attachment of babies and parents in the period before and around birth will have lifelong importance and major psychological implications for the developing child. "Fifteen percent of U.S. children enter life without such an attachment, feel no intimate, safe and loving connection with anyone, posing high risk of violent behavior" (Birth and the Origins of Violence, 1998, p. 1). There is a great need for more programs that foster attachment and bonding in early development.

All parents should be encouraged to participate in parenting and birth preparation classes prior to the birth of their child. Verny and Weintraub (1991) offer a program for expectant parents called Nurturing the Unborn Child: A Nine-Month Program for Soothing, Stimulating, and Communicating with your Unborn Baby. Two other programs that use music during pregnancy and birth to enhance bonding family development are the Sound Birthing Program, (DiCamillo, 2000) and the Center for Prenatal Music (Whitwell, 1999).

According to Involving Parents (1998) there continues to be a need for more education in parenting and related skills, and there is a definite need for more information on services especially for teenage mothers. We need to direct teens to resources for parent education and support groups at local hospitals and community centers and involve them in school-based programs where they are available. Frequently courses on new baby care, breastfeeding, and parenting are offered. The La Leche League is also a great free parent support group for breastfeeding mothers. Another notable parent education program for parents of infants is the Feeding Support Program for Infants and Young Children (Pridham, 1998). This program, developed by the University of Wisconsin-Madison School of Nursing in 1992 provides support for caregivers with the goal of preventing feeding problems. Nurse mentors come to the homes to do in-depth assessments and develop a plan of action. They also provide nutrition education and how to address behavioral issues related to eating. This program is extremely valuable for children with special needs or teen parents who may need extra support.

Postnatal follow-up is critical to linking at-risk families of special needs children with support services such as WIC (Women, Infants and Children Supplemental Foods Program), Healthy Families (Insurance), Cal Optima, and Medicaid. In California, a registered nurse provides in-home assessments and a social worker through the Bridges Program to ensure the family has insurance, food (WIC), and parent education. Parents also need training on car seat safety, poisons, Infant CPR, and general safety in the home. Classes such as these are frequently offered by local hospitals and fire departments.

Infant massage programs can also be extremely beneficial for all parents and children, but especially for special needs babies and teen parents (Oleson, 2000). Massage promotes well-being and calmness in babies. When babies are well and calm they are easier to care for, be with, and love. A simple program such as this can help parents get through the day in a less stressful way. These factors can significantly affect the parents' ability to bond with and care for their newborn. It can make parenting easier, especially for new, young parents. Another benefit is that massage provides babies the touch they need for bonding and psychological development. Instruction on infant massage is available for parents of well babies and special needs children. There are books available in children's stores on this topic and classes available in the community. There is also a Healthy Touch infant massage video available for teen parents (Lombardo, 1998) that demonstrates the techniques and explains the benefits of this parenting skill. The purpose of this video is to help parents bond more deeply with their babies.

Another quality comprehensive parent education program that provides of a variety of parent education services in a number of different settings is The Missouri Parents As Teachers Program (Winter & Rouse, 1990). This program provides the following services to families:

1. Information and guidance that help expectant parents prepare for the adjustment of having a new baby in the home.
2. Personalized home visits by specially trained parent educators who offer timely information on child development, practical ways to foster growth and learning, and effective ways to deal with difficult situations.
3. Group meetings where parents can share experiences, common concerns, frustrations, and successes.
4. Ongoing monitoring and periodic screening that ensures against youngsters reaching age 3 with an undetected developmental delay or handicapping condition.
5. A referral network that helps parents link with any needed special services that are beyond the scope of the program (p. 384).

Literacy Programs

It is very important to begin reading to children at an early age (even in the womb.) All children need literacy skills to be successful in school, work, and life. One must be competent in reading because most other subjects of study are based on the ability to read. There has been a big surge in intergenerational literacy programs throughout the nation in recent years to promote parent and child literacy development and as an attempt to break the cycle of underachievement and poverty in urban areas.

Schools have a responsibility to address the needs of parents who cannot read and those who have great difficulties in helping their children succeed in school. France and Meeks (1988) suggested that teachers should call parents if necessary to arrange conferences and have stated, "teachers can increase the amount of parent involvement, even among parents who have little education" (p. 46). One suggestion by France and Meeks (1998) is to develop a Reading Club or a program designed to help parents tutor their children. The skills of both parent and child can be enhanced in programs like this.

Parents of infants and toddlers also need to be encouraged to read to their children and need to be informed of the benefits of reading at this age, in promoting literacy and a lifelong love of learning. The Queens Borough Public Library in New York County offers a formal program that encourages parents to read to their infants and toddlers (Cerny, 2000). The library requires parents to attend programs with their children and conducts parent education lectures within the children's department. They also have parenting collections available as resources in the children's reading room. The responses from the parents who have participated in this program have been excellent. As a result a toddler-learning center has developed and parent and child playgroups have been created.

Baby's First Library Media Card Program

Another great early literacy program for parents of infants and toddlers is the Baby's First Library Media Card Program (Tichenor, Bock, & Sumnner, 1999). This program is an excellent example of how multiple agencies can collaborate to address the literacy needs of an at-risk group. The purpose of this program is to get teen parents excited about reading to their children. The importance of teen parents reading to their children is especially crucial because they are already at-risk. Eighty teens, aged 13–20, and their babies aged 3 weeks to 2 years, participated in a research study to evaluate the effectiveness of this teen parent dropout prevention program. Several members of an interagency team participated in this project including: a high school media specialist, a high school language arts/dropout prevention teacher, the school's technology coordinator, university faculty, university students majoring in elementary education, and a public librarian. This project was also funded through a grant from the Corporation for Public Broadcasting. Project activities included visits to the public library, writing of books by the parents for their children, instruction on how to choose books and read to their children, storytelling techniques, use of flannel boards and music shared info on parenting, book talks, technology lessons in the school media center, and a book sharing festival (Tichenor, Bock, & Sumnner, 1999). Results of this study indicated notable progress in the teen mothers, and there was more opening up to the teachers by the students and great enthusiasm for the project. This program is a great example of how multiple agencies can collaborate with each other to enhance literacy of an at-risk group. When schools collaborate with other institutions and agencies, it opens up new possibilities (Dunlap & Alva, 1999).

Project PRIMER

Cronan and Walen (1995) reported on the results of a study that evaluated the effectiveness of Project PRIMER (Producing Infant/Mother Ethnic Readers) a community-based literacy project. One hundred forty-seven low-income families participated. The curriculum for this program emphasized exposing children to reading in an interesting and positive way, teaching mothers how to develop emergent literacy skills, and teaching and encouraging mothers to act as positive role models in the reading process (Cronan & Walen, 1995). Results of this study indicated that parents did demonstrate the skills taught during the parent classes and that children in the high intervention program demonstrated improvements in their cognitive development.

Programs for Parents of Preschoolers, Kindergartners, and School-Aged Children

There have also been several successful literacy development programs developed and evaluated for parents of preschoolers and older children. It has been reported that teaching specific instructional skills for parents to use at home with their children can have significant benefits (Warren & Fitzgerald, 1997). The Parent Readers Program, which included young and school aged children was aimed at "increasing the literacy status of community college students who are parents and of their children" (Handel & Goldsmith, 1988, p. 250). In a study of this program the community college students' motivation as parents was effectively used to support gains in reading for themselves and their children.

Project EASE—Early Access to Success in Education

Jordan, Snow, and Porche (2000) reported the results of the effects of this family literacy project on kindergarten students' early literacy skills. This year-long project involved 248 kindergarten students and their families in an experimental program that included parent education sessions, at-school parent/child activities, and at-home book activities (Jordan, Snow, & Porche, 2000). This program was designed to increase language interactions through reading activities and to provide parents with information about how to support their children's developing literacy abilities. Results indicated that children whose families engaged in the at-school and at-home activities made significantly greater gains in language scores on standardized measures. Parents who participated in the training generally showed high levels of involvement during training, and they reported that they enjoyed the program. This program illustrates the impact that parent education programs can have on children's language and literacy development when provided with a rich, structured, parent-supported environment.

Project SPARKLE

This program, Project SPARKLE, or Supporting Parents as Readers with Kindergarten Literacy Experiences, which was provided by teachers at Juan Seguin Elementary in Seguin, TX, introduced children's classics to parents in an effort to get them to read aloud to their kids (Put SPARKLE, 1996). The main goals of this parent education program were to: (a) train parents in ways to use books effectively at home and in school, (b) assist parents in starting a library at home of appropriate children's books, (c) promote reading aloud together as a family, and (d) involve parents classroom guest reading experiences (Put SPARKLE, 1996). The curriculum included weekly two-hour training sessions for parents over six weeks. Kids and parents participated in book talks and "make it and take it" craft activities relating to the book that was read. At the end of each session, parents received two books to take home begin developing a family library. The benefits of reading aloud were covered and parents were instructed on ways to use books to help kids discover and experience the world around them. Parents were also prepared for classroom involvement as guest readers and were provided with ways to encourage writing development in their children. This program also included an orientation session at the local public library.

Project FIEL

This project, the Family Initiative for English Literacy (FIEL), is an intergenerational, bilingual project in which parents and their young children work as teams to explore events and ideas and to read and write about them (Quintero & Velarde, 1990). This program began in the early 1990s in El Paso TX—and emphasized the development of bilingual Spanish and English skills. This parent education program used multicultural themes and a holistic methodology. Five steps in curriculum included: an initial inquiry, learning activities, Language Experience Approach activities, storybook demonstrations, and home activity choices. Participation in this program had significant effects on reading skills and literacy behaviors of the parents and children during the project. Quintero and Velarde (1990) concluded "both children and adults grow into literacy when their experiences and interests are made central. Cultural diversity is not a barrier when each learner's culture is the learner's text and context" (p. 13).

Toyota Families in Schools Program

Schools can expand their programs to accommodate parents with varying literacy needs and offer special parent tutoring programs (France & Meeks, 1988). Another interesting new national parent education model is the Toyota Families in Schools Program (Covarriubia, 2000). This program effectively creates a learning community among the children, parents, and community members. In this program parents actually attend school with their children on a daily basis. Parents, teachers, children, and administrators work together to implement this comprehensive family literacy program. Parents attend independent classes on the school campus during school hours. They also have Parent and Child together time—where they sit beside their children and learn with them. There is no stigma to the children, as one might imagine but rather the other children want to bring their parents to school too. There is also discussion time for parents during the day when they can talk about what was learned that day, issues with their children's lessons, progress, etc. Information on parenting skills may also be presented at this time. The parents also have an opportunity to engage in Vocational Time where they spend time in various parts of the school learning computer and job-related skills. The parents conclude their day by having lunch in the classroom as a group and discussing the day. The benefits of this program have been many so far. The parent group has become a cohesive unit, fear about interacting with school personnel has been decreased, and the parents have become successful partners in their children's education.

Parent Education Programs for Mathematics

Parent education programs that focus specifically on mathematics can be especially beneficial for parents and children. Starkey and Klein (2000) have found that mother-child dyads can be effective in enhancing children's mathematical knowledge. Training parents how to help their children with their math homework may have positive effects on students' math performance. Programs that teach math skills to parents may also help ease fears and anxieties about math and build skills and confidence. Many parents have math fears or poor problem solving techniques based on the rote memorization strategies of math instruction used in the past. Morse and Wagner (1998) have indicated that it is crucial to appreciate the role that parents' mathematics histories and abilities play in their perception of mathematics and mathematics learning. If the parents are unable to do the math, how will they ever help their children do their math homework, or stimulate creative problem solving abilities? If the parents have fearful, negative connotations about math, how can they impart positive, active problem solving strategies to their children?

Greene (1996) has stated that "proficiency in mathematics is widely accepted in our society as an important preparation for life and work in an increasingly technological world" (p. 693). We need to do everything we can to ensure that children are getting the help they need at home in order to master mathematical content and develop problem solving strategies. Parents can help their kids do better in math and should be encouraged to sit down with their kids and support them when needed. Regular homework routines, and family policies are recommended. Even in busy families, in which both parents work, children can still benefit from parent-child interaction during homework time. Balli, Wedman, and Demo (1997) in their study of 74 sixth-grade students found that the quality of family involvement with homework was as important as the quantity of involvement.

Results of Wang, Wildman, and Calhoun's (1996) study of middle school mathematics indicated that there was a strong relationship between student achievement in math and parent education and encouragement. They also recommended parent strategies for helping middle school students succeed in math such as: (a) expressing confidence in their children's abilities, (b) encouraging the children to do their homework independently, (c) promoting their children's natural interest in math, and (d) developing logic skills through extracurricular activities.

Math for Moms and Dads

Morse and Wagner (1998) have also stated math content also plays an important role in parents' participation and engagement in math experiences with their children. Whiteford (1998) has stated that "parents who have a conceptual understanding of elementary school mathematics will be stronger advocates for effective teaching strategies and more active teaching partners in their children's education" (p. 66). Whiteford's Math for Moms and Dads, workshop that was conducted at Richmond Elementary School in Richmond, Vermont during 1997, was a parent education workshop designed to help parents develop a better understanding of their children's math skills. Seven, hour-long workshops were offered every two weeks throughout the semester. Topics focused on the language of math and new problem solving techniques. Parents and children practiced the content of the workshop by doing real world tasks together such as use the decimal point at the ATM machine. At the end of the project, parents expressed that they felt more confident in helping their children. Many parents requested that the series be repeated the following year with emphasis on other topics such as measurement and geometry, and algebra.

Jose Valdes' Summer Math Institute

Perhaps one of the most effective math programs of all times for underachieving students is the Jose Valdes' Summer Math Institute (Greene, 1996). This 7-week course, which began in 1988, has helped more than 4800 students. This program was originally designed specifically to increase the number of students entering ninth grade Algebra I (college preparatory math) classes. Specially trained teachers and speakers teach summer classes. The institute also offers field trips to industrial sites and tours of the local college campus. There is a strong parent education component of this program. Parents are required to attend an orientation program prior to the institute. They are also encouraged to attend workshops on parenting skills and are trained in techniques for working with their children academically. Some of the parent education sessions are conducted in Spanish. Another benefit is that counseling and tutoring is provided throughout the year. So far this program has been highly effective. Between 1989 and 1994 the number of students who had taken Algebra I or a higher-level math course during their four years at Andrew Hill High School rose from 49% to 74%. This school that once had a poor academic reputation, now has the highest grade-point average in the district. Daily attendance has risen from 75% to 90%. Additionally, increased communication and collaboration between the elementary schools and the high schools in the district has been noted.

PARENT EDUCATION PROGRAMS FOCUSING ON SOCIAL SKILLS, ISSUES, AND VIOLENCE PREVENTION

Parents have a huge responsibility in imparting social guidance as part of child rearing. Unfortunately, due to current societal and family conditions, it is not always possible to provide children with the guidance they need as situations are occurring. Families can definitely benefit from parent education experiences that offer curriculum and strategies for developing social skills and pro-social behavior. Parents also need assistance in talking with their children about social and preventive health issues.

Teaching Children to Be Pro-Social

Elksnin and Elksnin (2000) have suggested that involving parents in the social skills instructional process can help promote social skills generalization to different aspects of everyday life. There are several ways in which teachers can teach parents to support their children's pro-social behavior. Parents can be shown how to be emotional coaches and how to assist their children in understanding and dealing with their emotions. Teachers can show parents how to capitalize on teachable moments and have them model, prompt, and reinforce the use of pro-social skills at home. Parents who participate in the Australian PATCH program (Parents as Teachers of Children), an outstanding family intervention and support program are taught how to use active listening skills; the pause, prompt and praise method of responding; and to introduce to children natural and logical consequences (Williamson, 1997). Parents can also be taught to discuss the outcomes of using (or failing to use) a social skill. They can also help their children become better problem solvers.

Anger Management

Training in anger management can be helpful for both children and parents. Families who are educated about healthy ways to direct their angry feelings have fewer negative outcomes. These types of programs are generally available through community service agencies and outreach programs. One such notable program is the Colorado RETHINK Parenting and Anger Management Program. Fetsch, Schulz, and Wahler (1999) reported on the results of an evaluation study of this program. Results indicated that parents who participated in a six-week series of skill-enhancing workshops showed an improvement in anger control levels and a decrease in family conflict levels. Results also showed that the parents had a decrease in their overall anger levels, their violence levels, and their verbal aggression levels. It was also revealed that there was a decline in their partners' violence levels, their verbal aggression levels, and their physical aggression levels. Participants reported increased knowledge levels, improved attitudes, improved behaviors, and decreased unrealistic expectations concerning their children. It was concluded that participation in a six-week course of skill building with trained professionals can lead to positive changes in anger management and parenting (Fetsch, Schulz, & Wahler, 1999).

Gun Court

The incidence of children and teens having access to and carrying weapons is skyrocketing. More family educational programs need to be developed which address the need for gun safety and deterrence of teen weapon use. According to Braun (2001), there is a program in Birmingham, Alabama that is currently addressing this situation through a joint effort of the town's criminal justice agencies. This program has a "Gun Court" model, which was proposed by Judge Sandra Ross Storm, and has stiff consequences for violent behavior. This program also has an education component that includes parent education to change that behavior.

Teen offenders enter this program by pleading guilty to gun possession. Then they are sent to a month-long boot camp in Montgomery, Alabama. After boot camp they are kept under virtual house arrest during a probation period that can last as long as six months. During the probation there are frequent drug tests. Teen offenders and their parents take 10 weeks of classes on family issues and gun safety. Families are instructed about the need to lock away firearms and enforce gun safety. Initially most parents and teens don't want to be there, but eventually they come around. They also take the teens on a field trip to the county morgue. Parents are required to attend the classes so they understand that lack of parental responsibility is part of the problem. The goal of this program is to educate parents and their kids about what their responsibilities are. Judge Storm reported that the reason why this program is so effective is because all of the criminal justice agencies in town are working together to make it successful.

Drug and Alcohol Abuse

Teen alcohol abuse is also a major cause for concern on high school campus throughout the country. Adolescent drinking can lead to poor health, experimentation with other dangerous drugs, and is a large component of teen automobile accidents. The Mothers Against Drunk Drivers group is one organization that actively educates the community about the dangers of drinking and driving. There are also programs that are geared especially for educating youths and their families. Perry, Williams, and Komro (2000) have reported on their community action intervention program to reduce adolescent alcohol use. This program uses multiple interventions and includes a parent education and involvement program. Other components include: community-based methods to encourage citizens to reduce underage access to alcohol, youth action teams, print media to decrease underage drinking, and a classroom-based curriculum for students in the 11th grade. Another notable drug and alcohol prevention resource is a Web site available for PTA leaders and parents on how to raise alcohol and drug-free children called "Common Sense: Strategies for Raising Alcohol and Drug Free Children (Children First, 2001).

HIV/STD

With the health risks and consequences in existence today related to unprotected sex, parents and teens need more support and health education than ever. Often it is difficult for parents to discuss these issues with their children and schools and community agencies can play a large part in helping adolescents develop healthy attitudes about making safe, responsible choices. Coyle, Kirby, Parcel, Basen-Engquist, Banspach, Rugg, and Weil (1996) have designed an HIV/STD and pregnancy prevention program called "Safer Choices: A Multicomponent School-Based Program for Adolescents." This program has a strong parent education component as family members play a key role in influencing their children's behavior. The purpose of the parent education component of this program is to help parents provide accurate information to their children, and to reinforce the norm that adolescents should avoid unprotected intercourse. Parents receive project newsletters 3 times each year on various topics that include tips on talking with teens about these issues. Quotes from parents who have discussed these issues with their children are also provided to serve as role models for other parents. Two homework activities for parents and students to do together are also assigned at each grade level.

CREATING PARTNERSHIP EDUCATION

The Benefits of Integrated Services

The benefits of parent education programs can increase many-fold when different organization work together and provide their expertise in putting together quality parent education programs. We have seen, as demonstrated by research, that programs such as Head Start and those based on the Comer model of community supported schools, those that link early childhood settings with universities, and those facilitated by child care resource and referral agencies are very effective in providing quality comprehensive services for families (Hurd, Lerner, & Barton, 1999). Families have a great need for social, emotional, educational supports and care. Hurd, Lerner, and Barton (1999) have stated that "teaching, nurturing, and caring for children is a community process. When most effective, many constituents—parents, teachers, extended family, neighborhoods, agencies and community partners—are engaged" (p. 75).

Integrated services agencies are perhaps best equipped to meet parent education needs because they draw on the expertise and resources of a variety of educational and health professionals. Hurd, Lerner, and Barton (1999) have stated that the most effective programs give intensive and individualized attention to program participants and are responsive to the individual needs of the people most at risk. Training for teachers and administrators on this type of service provision is very important. Hurd, Lerner, and Barton (1999) have suggested that in order to serve children better teachers need to realize that they (a) are called upon to provide a variety of resources for children, (b) must address the complex needs of children and their families, and (c) must recognize the contextual nature of teaching children and supporting families.

Overcoming Barriers to Partnership Education

Dunlap and Alva (1999) have noted several barriers that must be overcome in establishing successful school partnerships. One common barrier is that some minority parents and families may feel alienated from the school due to a lack of knowledge about school operations. These parents may feel inadequate or unwelcome due to a difference of income, education, or ethnicity as compared to school personnel. This difference may result in the parent's perception that the school is indifferent to these feelings. When parents have these feelings, they withdraw from the school environment. As a result, school personnel then has the tendency to assume that the parents are uninterested in school involvement. Another factor noted by Dunlap and Alva (1999) that widens the gap between school personnel and the families is when teachers and administrators do not see themselves or the school as a part of the surrounding community.

Dunlap and Alva (1999) have stated that school-family-community partnerships can only grow when they are based on mutual trust and respect for other's values, perspectives and experiences. These barriers can be addressed by reaching out to families and providing them the individualized attention, education programs, and services they need to become active participants and stakeholders in the school. They need to work together with families as equal partners to make the school a central, learning institution for the entire community. Schools need to let parents know that diversity of culture and values is respected. Sielo, Sileo, and Prater (1996) have stated that parent education programs should be focused on increasing parents' influence on their children's education. They stated that such programs are effective when teachers and administrators: (a) involve parents as equal partners in problem-solving dialogues (b) observe and participate in community activities; (c) develop mutual understandings and shared personal needs, hopes, and concerns by listening to parents and talking with them, and (d) informing parents of their rights and responsibilities with regard to how to improve the educational environment.

Brand (1996) has indicated that training for teachers and administrators in helping them to develop partnerships with parents is very important. She emphasized that they need to make a concerted effort to show parents that their input and collaborative relationship matters and is valued. Whiteford (1998) has noted that as public schools work toward enhancing their partnerships, informed and knowledgeable parents and community members become important allies. For example, in Project Interconnecting Teachers, Children, and Homes (PITCH), support and training for partnership education is provided (Brand, 1996). Issues related to overcoming communication barriers, keeping parents informed, strategies for how to validate parents, and how to validate school personnel are addressed.

There are also resources on building partnerships that are available from the National PTA. Building Successful Partnerships is a multifaceted program which focuses on increasing awareness and implementation of the National Standard for Parent /Family Involvement Programs. Additionally, on January 31, 2000 the book "Building Successful Partnerships: A Guide for Developing Parent and Family Involvement Programs," written by National PTA, and was published by National Educational Service. The book provides a comprehensive program implementation guide based on the National Standards for Parent Involvement (Children First, 2001.)

Government officials need to be reminded of the need for more home-school partnerships. Further research and development of new programs can only occur through funding from federal, state, and local government and organizations. Fortunately, in the last couple of years parent involvement and education is receiving more attention and support by the government, specifically in the state of California. According to Sandham (1999) during October 1999, a bill on parent involvement was signed into law by Governor Gray Davis providing $15 million in grants to pay teachers to visit their students' homes after school and on weekends. Part of this initiative also included a training program for parents who wish to become more actively involved in schools. It is hoped that through further research and government and corporate funding that our children and families will continue to benefit from quality parent education programs which are based in partnership education. It may be further concluded that integrated services agencies that actively involve and educate parents as well as promote collaborative processes among families, schools, universities, health professionals, and community agencies are excellent models by which partnership education can be created and established.

REFERENCES

About the PTA Our History. (2001). *PTA milestones along the way.* [On-line document] Retrieved 3/11/01 from the World Wide Web: http://www.pta.org/apta/mile1890.htm

A Brief Summary of SDP Effects. (2001). *Yale Child Study Center School Development Program.* [On-line document]. Retrieved 3/15/01 from the World Wide Web: http://info.med.yale.edu/comer/effects.html.

Balli, S.J., Wedman, J.F., & Deom, D.H. (1997). Family involvement with middle-grades homework: Effects of differential prompting. *The Journal of Experimental Education, 66*(1), 31–48.

Bangs, S.E. (1994). Parents, Harrisburg Area Community College and the Melrose Elementary School: working together for children's achievement. *Equity and Excellence in Education, 27,* 32–35.

Beale, A.V. (1999). Involving fathers in parent education: the counselor's challenge. *Professional School Counseling, 3*(1), 5–12.

Birth and the Origins of Violence. (1998). *Quick facts on violence.* [On-line document]. Retrieved 5/16/98 from the World Wide Web: http://www.birthpsychology.com/violence/quick.html

Brand, S.F. (1996). Making parent involvement a reality: helping teachers develop partnerships with parents. *Young Children, 51,* 76–81.

Braun, S. (2001, January 16). The young guns of Alabama. *LA Times,* pp. A1, A11.

Cerny, R. (2000). Family literacy programs: Joint projects of the programs and services departments. *Journal of Youth Services in Libraries, 13*(2), 27–29.

Chavkin, N.F. Gonzalez, J., & Rader, R. (2000). A home-school program in a Texas-Mexico Border school: Voices from parents, students, and school staff. *The School Community Journal, 10*(2), 127–137.

Children First. (2001). *National PTA fast facts*. [On-line document]. Retrieved 3/11/01 from the World Wide Web: http://www.pta.org/apta/fastfcts.htm

Clarkson, P.J. (1980) *Effects of parent training and group counseling on children's functioning in elementary school*. Paper presented at the Annual Meeting of the American Personnel and Guidance Association, Atlanta, GA.

Conner, C. (2000). Rebuilding a parent program with technology. *Principal, 80*(1), 61–2.

Cook, T.D., Murphy, R.F., & Hunt, D.H. (2000). Comer's School Development Program in Chicago: A theory based evaluation. *American Educational Research Journal, 37*(2), 535–597.

Covarrubia, J. (2000). Family literacy: Sharing classrooms with parents. *Principal, 80*(1), 44–45.

Coyle, K., Kirby, D., Parcel, G., Basen-Engquist, K., Banspach, S. Rugg, D., & Weil, M. (1996). Safer choices: A multicomponent school-based HIV/STD and pregnancy prevention program for adolescents. *The Journal of School Health, 66*, 89–94.

Cronan, T.A., & Walen, H.R. (1995). The development of Project PRIMER: A community-based literacy program. *Reading Research and Instruction, 35*, 37–47.

DiCamillo, M. (2000). *The Sound Birthing program manual: Family birth preparation and labor support services*. Rancho Santa Margarita, CA.

Disney, J. (2000, March 10). PINpoints: Parent Information Network. *The Times Educational Supplement*, no. 4637 [on-line], p. 36.

Dunlap. C.Z., & Alva, S.A. (1999). Redefining school and community relations: Teachers' perceptions of parents as participants and stakeholders. *Teacher Education Quarterly, 26*(4), 123–133.

Elksnin, L.K., & Elksnin, N. (2000). Teaching parents to teach their children to be prosocial. *Intervention in School and Clinic, 36*(1), 27–35.

Fairbanks North Star Borough School District. (2001). *Epstein's six types of parent involvement*. [On-line document]. Retrieved 2/23/01 from the World Wide Web: http:// www.northstar.k12.ak.us/parent/pacifour.html

Family and Schools Together. (2001). *Fast building relationships...Family & Schools Together*. [On-line document]. Retrieved 3/13/01 from the World Wide Web: http://www.wcer.wisc.edu/fast/

Fetsch, R.J., Schulz, C.J., & Wahler, J.J. (1999). A preliminary evaluation of the Colorado RETHINK parenting and anger management program. *Child Abuse and Neglect, 23*(4), 353–360.

France, M.G., & Hager, J.M. (1993). Recruit, respect, respond: a model for working with low-income families and their preschoolers. *The Reading Teacher, 46*, 568–572.

France, M.G., & Meeks, J.W. (1988). Parents who can't read, what school can do. *The Educational Digest, 53*, 46–49.

Freedman, E., & Montgomery, J.F. (1994). Parent education and student achievement. *Thrust for Educational Leadership, 24*, 40–44.

Greene, L.C. (1996). Jose Valdes' Summer Math Institute. *Phi Delta Kappan, 77*, 692–693.

Hall, G., & Hord, S. (Eds.). (1987). *Change in schools facilitating the process*. Albany: State University of New York Press.

Handel, R.D., & Goldsmith, E. (1988). Intergenerational literacy: A community college program. *Journal of Reading, 32,* 250–256.

Harvard Education Letter Research Online. (1997). *Six types of school-family-community involvement.* [On-line document]. Retrieved 2/23/01 from the World Wide Web: http://www.edletter.org/past issues/1997-so/sixtypes.shtml.

Hernandez, L.P., Hernandez, A. Lopez. M.E., Kreider, H., & Coffman, J. (2000). Local and national implementation of the Families and Schools Together (FAST) program. *The School Community Journal, 10*(1), 85–110.

Hiatt-Michael, D. (2001). Parent involvement in American public schools: A historical perspective 1642–2000. In S. Redding & L.G. Thomas (Eds.), *The community of the school* (pp. 247–259). Lincoln, IL: Academic Development Institute.

Hurd, T., L., Lerner, R.M., & Barton, C.D. (1999). Integrated services: Expanding partnerships to meet the needs of today's children and families. *Young Children, 54*(2),74–80.

Involving parents, educating parents. (1998). *The Delta Kappa Gamma Bulletin, 65*(1), 9–61.

Jacobson, A.L., Huffman, J.B., & Rositas de Cantu, M.C. (1998). Parent involvement training with Hispanic parents. *The Delta Kappa Gamma Bulletin, 65*(1), 30–37.

Jordan, G.E., Snow, C.E., & Porche, M.V. (2000). Project EASE: The effects of a family literacy project on kindergarten students' early literacy skills. *Reading Research Quarterly, 35*(4), 524–546.

Lazarus, W., & Lipper, L. (1998). *The parents' guide to the information superhighway. The Children's Partnership.* [On-line document]. Retrieved 3/11/01 from the World Wide Web: http://www.childrenspartnership.org/ pub/pbpg98/pg98.pdf

Lombardo, C. (1998). Healthy touch: Infant massage for teenage parents. *School Library Journal, 44*(6), 82.

Mahoney, G., Kaiser, A.P., & Girolametto, L.E. (1999). Parent education in early intervention: A call for a renewed focus. *Topics in Early Childhood Special Education, 19*(3), 131–140.

MegaSkills Education Center. (2001). *MegaSkills and school reform.* [On-line document]. Retrieved 3/11/01 from the World Wide Web: http://www.megaskillshsi.org/intromegaskills/schoolreforl.htm

Morse, A.B., & Wagner, P. (1998). Learning to listen: Lessons from a mathematics seminar for parents. *Teaching Children Mathematics, 4,* 360–4.

NHSA-National Head Start Association. (2001). *Head Start quality, performance, and outcome: The real story.* [On-line document]. Retrieved 2/23/01 from the World Wide Web: http://www.nhsa.org/research/The Real Story.htm.

National PTA Standards. (2000). *Parenting.* [On-line document]. Retrieved 3/11/01 from the World Wide Web: http://www.pta. org/programs/pfistand.htm#Standard2

Norwood, P.M., Atkinson, S.E., Tellez, K., & Saldana, D.C. (1997). Contextualizing parent education programs in urban schools: The impact on minority parents and students. *Urban Education, 32,* 411–432.

Nystul, M. (1982). The effects of Systematic Training for Effective Parenting on parental attitudes. *Journal of Psychology, 112,* 63–66.

Office of Education Research Consumer Guide. (1993). *The Comer School Development Program.* [On-line document]. Retrieved 2/23/01 from the World Wide Web: http://www.ed.gov/pubs/OR/ConsumerGuides/comer.html

Oleson, C. (2000). Infant massage. *Child Care Information Exchange, 131,* 46.

Perry, C.L., Williams, C.L., & Komro, K.A. (2000). Project Northland High School interventions: Community action to reduce adolescent alcohol use. *Health Education and Behavior, 27*(1), 29–49.

Parent Institute for Quality Education. (2001). *PIQE mission and philosophy.* [On-line document] Retrieved 6/12/01 from the World Wide Web: http://www.brekke.oxnardsd.org/School% 20Activities/Parent%20Education/PIQE.htm

Pridham, K. (1998). Feeding support for infants and young children. *The Exceptional Parent, 28*(8), 76.

Put SPARKLE in parent-child reading efforts. (1996). *Curriculum Review, 35,* 10.

Quinter, E., & Velarde, M.C. (1990). Intergenerational literacy: A developmental bilingual approach. *Young Children, 45,* 10–15.

Redding, S. (2001). Parents and learning. *International Academy of Education Educational Practices,* Series-2. [On-line document]. Retrieved 2/23/01 from the World Wide Web: http://www.ibe.unesco.org.

Sallenbach, W.B. (1998). Claire: A case study in prenatal learning. *The Pre and Perinatal Psychology Journal.* [On-line document]. Retrieved 5/16/98 from the World Wide Web: http://www.birthpsychology.com/journal/sallenbach.html.

Sandham, J.L. (1999). Davis signs law on parent involvement; vetoes pesticide bill. *Education Week, 19*(8), 18.

Schaefer, E.S. (1991). Goals for Parent and future-parent education: Research on parental beliefs and behavior. *The Elementary School Journal, 91*(3), 239–247.

School Development Program. (2001). *Yale Child Study Center School Development Program.* [On-line document]. Retrieved 3/15/01 from the World Wide Web: http:// info.med.yale.edu/comer/quicklook.html.

Sileo, T.W., Sileo, A.P., & Prater, M.A. (1996). Parent and professional partnerships in special education: Multicultural considerations. *Intervention in School and Clinic, 31,* 145–153.

Spewock, T.S. (1988). Training parents to teach their preschools through literature. *The Reading Teacher, 41,* 648–652.

Starkey, P., & Klein, A. (2000). Fostering parental support for children's mathematical development: An intervention with Head Start Families. *Early Education and Development, 11*(5), 659–680.

Summerlin M.L., & Ward, G.R. (1981). The effect of parent group participation on attitudes. *Elementary School Guidance Counseling,* pp. 133–136.

Technical Support Consortium Best Practices. (2001). *Comer School Development Program.* [On-line document] Retrieved 2/23/01 from the World Wide Web: http://www.coe.wayne.edu/TSC/sdp.html

Tichenor, M.S., Bock, A.M., & Sumner, M.A. (1999). Enhancing literacy of an at-risk group: A reading incentive program for teen parents and their babies. *Reading Improvement, 36*(3), 132–142.

Verny, T., & Weintraub, P. (1991). *Nurturing the unborn child: A nine-month program for soothing, stimulating, and communicating with your unborn baby.* New York: Delacorte Press.

Warren, L., & Fitzgerald, J. (1997). Helping parents to read expository literature to their children: Promoting main-idea and detail understanding. *Reading Research and Instruction, 36,* 341–360.

Wang, J., Wildman, L., & Calhoun, G. (1996). The relationships between parental influence and student achievement in seventh grade mathematics. *School Science and Mathematics, 96,* 395–399.

Winter, M., & Rouse, J. (1990). Fostering intergenerational literacy: The Missouri Parents as Teachers program. *The Reading Teacher, 43,* 382–386.

Whiteford, T. (1998). Math for Moms and Dads. *Educational Leadership, 8,* 64–66.

Whitwell, G. (1999). *Center for prenatal music; program literature.* Granada Hills, CA.

Williamson, L.L (1997). Parents as teachers of children program (PATCH). *Professional School Counseling, 1,* 7–12.

CHAPTER 8

EDUCATING PROFESSIONALS FOR SCHOOL, FAMILY AND COMMUNITY PARTNERSHIPS

Howard Kirschenbaum

"If there is one thing I wish my teachers had learned in college or graduate school, it's how to work with parents. Most of the problems that have escalated to the point of needing my attention could have been solved at the classroom level, or wouldn't have occurred in the first place, if the teacher knew how to communicate with parents."
—Middle School Principal

THE NEED FOR PROFESSIONAL TRAINING IN PARTNERSHIPS

As school, family, and community partnerships have risen high on the national agenda, the profession and the public have come to recognize the need to train teachers, administrators, and other school personnel in school-family-community collaboration. The American Federation of Teachers (1996) writes that *"professional development can make a powerful difference in the depth, breadth and quality of programs that involve parents and families in their children's learning, whatever the children's ages"* (emphasis in original). The U.S. Department of Education (1994b) recommends that states encourage families and schools to work together by providing support for teacher training in family involvement.

In promulgating national standards for parent/family involvement programs, the National PTA (1997) states:

> One of the most significant challenges to conducting an effective program is the lack of instruction on parent and family involvement that educators and administrators receive in their professional training ... Even with the preponderance of research establishing the connection between effective parent involvement and student achievement, few teachers receive substantive preparation in how to partner with parents. (pp. 9, 23)

A Communitarian Network position paper (Kirschenbaum, 1999a) argues that teachers and administrators need pre-service and in-service training that prepares them to communicate with parents frequently and effectively, to become parent educators, to involve parents in their children's homework, to work with parents and community members on decision-making committees, and to resolve conflicts with parents as they arise so they don't escalate out of control.

Recognizing that professional development is a necessary condition for the implementation of effective school, family, and community partnerships, a number of states have begun to mandate pre-service training and ongoing professional development in parent involvement and school-family-community partnerships. The State Education Department in New York (1999), for example, requires that by 2004, all teachers receiving certification will have training that includes:

- The impact of ... factors in the home, school, and community on students' readiness to learn (p. 14);
- The importance of productive relationships and interactions among the school, home, and community for enhancing student learning—and skill in fostering effective relationships and interactions to support student growth and learning... (p. 16);
- Experiences practicing skills for interacting with parents or caregivers (p. 18);
- Participating in collaborative partnerships for the benefit of students with disabilities, including family strengthening partnerships (p. 41); and
- Communicating assessment results to parents, caregivers, and school personnel (p. 61).

California first drafted detailed standards for preparing teachers to work in partnership with families in 1991 (Shartrand et al., 1997). A few years later, in response to a legislative initiative, a task force within the California Commission on Teacher Credentialing (1996) recommended the adoption of such standards and requirements. The following year the California Commission on Teacher Credentialing (1997) formally adopted these standards. As a result, all teacher credential programs in California must now assure that:

Each candidate learns about the full range of ways family-school partnerships can enhance good teaching and support student learning and well-being. Each candidate gains an in-depth knowledge of families, communities and self, and is able to foster respectful and productive relationships with families in diverse home and community environments.

As the California experience suggests, it often takes state legislatures and education departments a long time to act. A survey of 1992 state certification materials (Shartrand et al., 1997) showed that only 22 states mentioned family involvement in their teacher certification requirements.

However, Gray (2001) reported a significant increase during late 1990s in the number of states that had some administrative or credential statement requiring that teachers should possess some knowledge and skills related to parent and community involvement. These state-credentialing bodies added a parent and community involvement component into teacher education standards or adopted National Council for the Accreditation of Teacher Education (NCATE) standards that include such standards for working with parents and the community. The increase may be attributed to state governments being lobbied to include teacher preparation for partnerships in their teacher preparation standards. This is similar to earlier lobbying at the federal level by the National PTA and others which caused the federal government to make parent involvement a priority and to expand the National Education Goals in 1994 to include:

Goal 8: Every school will promote partnerships that will increase parental involvement and participation in promoting the social, emotional and academic growth of children. (U.S. Department of Education, 1994a; White, 1997)

In addition to state legislatures and state and national education departments, various national accreditation bodies have recognized that professional preparation and development should include school, family and community partnerships. The National Council for Accreditation of Teacher Education (NCATE) (2000) has built school-family-community partnerships into a number of its standards for teacher education. Under its "Standard 1: Knowledge, Skills and Dispositions," NCATE mandates that as a result of their professional training, teachers should:

1. Consider school, family, and community contexts in connecting concepts to students' prior experiences (p. 6);
2. Work with students, families, and communities (p. 6);
3. Foster relationships with school colleagues, parents/families, and agencies in the wider community to support students' learning and well being (p. 8);

4. Understand ... diversity of student populations, families, and communities (p. 9); and

5. [be] assessed along with other performances in [their] work with students, families and communities (p. 9).

In their field experiences and clinical practice (Standard 3), teacher candidates should demonstrate "skills for working with colleagues, parents/families and communities" (p. 17). For "Standard 4: Diversity," teacher preparation programs should "provide opportunities for candidates to reflect on their observations and practices in schools and communities with students and families from diverse ethnic, racial, and socioeconomic groups" (p. 20).

Aside from these standards for *all* teachers and school professionals, NCATE delegates to the various specialties—elementary teachers, English teachers, science teachers, etc.—the responsibility for delineating "program standards" for those specialties. Thus the addenda to the NCATE 2000 standards which focus on early childhood education, elementary education, special education, and middle school education—developed by the national associations for each of these areas—all identify parent, school, and community collaboration as an important area of professional preparation. For example, the NCATE's Elementary Education Task Force (NCATE, 2000), representing many national organizations, identifies "Opportunities to develop understanding and skills in the dynamics of interactions with parents, community members, professional colleges, and other school personnel" as one of its standards (p. 68).

In the same document, none of the national associations for English, social studies, mathematics or science education includes a special standard for family-school collaboration or for school-community collaboration, with the exception of the science educators who say that schools should utilize the science resources of the community. Perhaps the implicit message is that it is up to preschool, elementary and special education teachers and to elementary and middle schools, as institutions—all of whom deal with the "whole child"—to work in partnership with families and communities. However, when the focus is on secondary school academics, working in partnership with students' families and community support systems is no longer important. If this interpretation is correct, apparently not everyone in education has recognized the importance of partnerships.

In any case, with few exceptions, there appears to be a growing recognition at the highest levels of the education establishment of the importance of training educators in school-family-community collaboration. Simultaneously, there is an equivalent realization that *in practice* such training is not happening as widely or quickly as necessary. A publication of the American Association of School Administrators (Decker, Gregg, & Decker, 1994) points out that "Most administrators and teachers have not had pre-service training in parent involvement, so in-service training is necessary . . . " (p. 63). Similarly, Ammon (1999) concludes, "Yet, for the most part, institutions of higher education have been slow to invest time, effort and imagination in the preparation of teachers for partnerships with the families of their prospective students" (p. 1).

RESEARCH ON TRAINING PROFESSIONALS FOR PARTNERSHIPS

Conclusions about the insufficient preparation of professionals to form effective partnerships with families and communities are not merely the result of informal observation and anecdotal evidence. As the need for professional training for partnerships has become widely recognized, research has begun to identify the types and extent of training being offered. The most common form of research has been the survey. Initial studies demonstrated the lack of preparation in family involvement. Shartrand et al. (1997) report that,

> ...research has shown that pre-service teacher education programs often do not adequately prepare teachers to involve parents (Chavkin, 1991). In a study by Houston and Williamson (1990), beginning elementary teachers related that during their pre-service education they had received little or no training in conducting parent conferences or in communicating with or building relations with parents. Other surveys have also shown that teachers feel that they need more instruction in how to work with parents (Bartell, 1992; McAfee, 1987). A recent report by the U.S. Department of Education (1997) found that 48 percent of principals in Title I schools also believe that lack of staff training in how to work with families poses a barrier to family involvement. (p. 9)

Given the data from practitioners documenting their *lack of* training in building partnerships, other researchers have attempted to document the extent of partnership training that *does* exist in professional preparation programs. Epstein, Sanders, and Clark (1999) report on a number of studies from the 1980s and early 1990s documenting a paucity of partnership training in colleges and universities (Chavkin & Williams, 1988; McBride, 1990; Hinz, Clarke, & Nathan, 1992).

A well-publicized study on preparing teachers for family involvement was conducted by Angela Shartrand and her colleagues at the Harvard Graduate School of Education (Shartrand et al., 1997). They surveyed 60 teacher preparation programs in the 22 states that in 1992 had mentioned family involvement in their teacher certification requirements. Examining types of parent involvement addressed in these courses, the researchers found, for example, that while 88% of programs addressed parent-teacher conferences and 67% addressed parents as class volunteers, only 23% addressed communicating with parents and 21% addressed understanding parents and families. Teaching methods were primarily discussion (92%), required readings (90%), lecture (86%) and class assignments (73%). Those programs that utilized direct work with parents, guest speakers, and role play constituted 23%, 21%, and 10% respectively. The authors concluded that "Family involvement training was often traditional in definition, teaching methods, and delivery" (p. 12).

Joyce Epstein and her colleagues at Johns Hopkins and Howard Universities conducted a more recent and extensive study of schools, colleges, and departments of education (collectively termed colleges hereafter) in the United States regarding preparing educators in school, family and community partnerships (Epstein, Sanders, & Clark, 1999). Representing a good cross-section of the field, 161 colleges responded to the survey. The researchers discovered that "most [colleges] offer at least one course and some coverage of topics on partnerships, but not enough to prepare all teachers, counselors, and administrators to effectively conduct practices and programs of school, family and community partnerships" (p. ix). As previous studies showed, early childhood and special education courses received a disproportionate amount of the partnership attention.

In examining the types of partnership practices that colleges incorporate in their courses, the majority of the colleges include traditional forms of parent involvement. A smaller percentage include more complex forms of partnership such as utilizing interactive homework with parents (48.7%), conducting parent workshops (48.6%), designing and producing class or school newsletters (46.2%) and planning a concerted, year-long program of partnerships (24.1%).

Another recent study by Hiatt-Michael (2000) surveyed how California's teacher training institutions were implementing the new state mandate to include three types of family involvement practices in teacher education programs. These types of practices are skills for communicating with families, involving parents in learning activities with their children at home, and ways to connect the family culture to learning at school. Fifty-three out of 66 universities that train California teachers responded to the survey. Hiatt-Michael found that 87% of the respondents reported that they incorporated a concept or skill related to parent involvement in at least one of their courses, with a range of one to eleven courses, and a mode of five. The most common courses in which parent involvement training occurred were language arts and reading methods (62% of respondents), cultural diversity (59%), and second language acquisition (55%). The types of par-

ent involvement activities most utilized in the courses were parent conferencing (64%), dealing with parent concerns (51%), home reading (47%),
and parent interviews (42%). If anything, her findings were even stronger
than Epstein, Sanders, and Clark (1999) in indicating that teacher preparation programs tended to emphasize the more traditional forms of family
involvement.

Hiatt-Michael also found that the most frequently used instructional
methods in California were the following: case studies (59%), research
studies (40%), role-playing (38%), conflict resolution (34%), project creation (34%), and home surveys (25%)—a somewhat different pattern than
found in the Shartrand study. Although Hiatt-Michael acknowledges that
"Teacher preparation programs have a long way to go" to prepare teachers
to implement comprehensive school-family-community partnerships, she
takes a more optimistic tone than Epstein, Sanders, and Clark. She notes
that the vast majority of California's teacher training institutions (87% in
this study) have at least begun to incorporate parent involvement training
in teacher preparation.

To determine the extent of parent involvement issues in K-12 teacher
education programs in the nation, a still more recent survey of 147 representative universities with teacher education programs tapped department
chairs or deans of private and public institutions in each of the 50 states
(Hiatt-Michael, 2001). The survey raised questions on number of courses,
types of courses, topics, and class instructional methods. Of the 96 who
responded to the survey, 7 indicated that parent involvement issues were
not included in any course. Twenty-two replied that the school offered a
course devoted to parent involvement, but this course was not required for
K-12 teacher education students. Such courses were developed for special
education or early childhood teachers or offered as an elective course.

Ninety-three percent of the respondents reported that parent involvement issues were woven into existing teacher education courses, such as
special education, reading methods, instructional methods, and early
childhood education in that rank order. In states with major portions of
the population coming from diverse cultures, parent involvement is
included in cultural diversity and teaching English-as-a-Second-Language
courses. Universities in Hawaii and California, locales with a high proportion of diverse ethnic groups, reported the greatest number of courses that
included parent involvement issues.

Respondents replied that the most popular topic is parent conferencing. This finding is important because parent conferences are the most
pervasive home-school practice in schools after the ubiquitous report card.
Other topics, in rank order, included parent concerns, parent newsletters,
and working within the community.

Forty-nine respondents reported that students utilized case studies in one or more courses. Other instructional methods were research studies (40%), role-playing (40%), conflict resolution (32%), project creation (24%), and home surveys (15%).

Her findings are similar to those reported by Epstein (2001). Hiatt-Michael and Epstein determined that early childhood and special education receive a disproportionate amount of parent involvement attention within university preparation and in school practice.

When these surveys of college partnership practices spanning a 20-year period are taken together, it appears that an increasing proportion of professional training institutions are incorporating an increasing number of partnership practices in their training of educators. At the same time, only a minority of colleges provide a concerted or comprehensive program in school-family-community relations that gives educators a thorough grounding in the theory, research and practice of partnerships. Epstein, Sanders, and Clarke conclude that their national survey "reveals a dramatic gap at most schools, colleges, and Departments of Eduction between leaders' strong beliefs about the importance for educators to conduct effective partnerships with all families and communities, and their reports of low preparedness of graduates to work effectively on partnerships" (p. 29).

In addition to surveys, case studies on training for partnerships have also begun. Following California's adoption of professional development standards, Ammon (1999) and her colleagues documented a number of that state's institutions that were experimenting with different models for teacher preparation for partnerships. These models include a program that uses role-plays and simulations to help teachers understand families from diverse backgrounds, a program that has students collect data about the families and communities they are serving, and another program that has pre-service professionals each work in depth throughout the semester with a family in need.

Similarly, Shartrand et al. (1997) present many, brief vignettes of colleges that offer different types of preparation in family involvement. First they outline seven different areas in which preparation is needed: General family involvement, general family knowledge, home-school communication, family involvement in learning activities, families supporting schools, schools supporting families, and families as change agents. For each of these areas they outline the knowledge, attitudes, and skills educators need, organized under four approaches to training: functional approach, parent empowerment, cultural competence, and social capital. Finally, for each of the seven areas of preparation, the authors describe one or more colleges which are engaged in professional preparation addressing that area.

Less common are outcome studies on partnership training. Laurie Katz and Jerold Bauch (2001) reported on one such study, assessing how teachers who received training in family involvement felt more prepared and subsequently engaged in a greater number of family involvement practices than teachers who received no training. This was a pilot study and statistical significance was not reported.

No doubt additional research will be forthcoming—documenting the proliferation and variety of training for partnerships; qualitatively examining the dynamics and difficulties of professional preparation in this area; and studying the results of professional preparation programs on educators' subsequent partnership practices.

PROMISING PRACTICES

While research proceeds, professional preparation for partnerships continues and expands at colleges and through in-service professional development across the United States and beyond. There appears to be little or no research available to specifically say that one model of training for partnerships is better than another or that any particular model is proven effective. Nevertheless there has been a great deal of experience with training professionals in partnerships that has produced a body of experience, opinion, and anecdotal evidence regarding promising practices. The remainder of this chapter, first, explores two issues related to the actual practice of preparing educators to work in partnership with family and community and, second, presents some of the models and methods that appear promising toward this end.

Separate or Infused

One of the biggest issues regarding professional training for partnerships in schools, colleges and departments of education is whether to offer this preparation in a separate course or infused throughout the curriculum. Institutions do it both ways. Epstein, Sanders, and Clarke (1999) report that over half the colleges in their study offer a full course on parent involvement or school, family and community partnerships (p. 9). About two thirds of these are required, at least for some students. More than 90% report they have at least one course, not necessarily required, that has a few sessions on the topic. About a third report they have two required courses in which parent involvement topics are covered for at least part of the course. Hiatt-Michael's (2001) nationwide survey reported a much smaller proportion of teacher training institutions that have a full course on parent involvement—22 institutions (23%) of those responding to that survey question. Within her California survey (2000), only five (9%) had a course devoted to family involvement issues. In that survey's report, Hiatt-Michael remarked, "Teacher education institutions primarily incorporated the standard regarding parent involvement within existing courses in their program" (p. 10).

Whether to offer a required course or infuse the content throughout the curriculum is a dilemma not unique to partnership preparation. Colleges also debate whether multi-cultural issues, working with exceptional children, classroom management, character education, and a host of other things educators should know about are best dealt with in a separate course or infused throughout the program—or *both*.

On the one hand, to treat the subject separately is to isolate it from its connection to all other facets of the curriculum. Teaching methods courses can benefit immensely by training in family and community partnerships. Field experiences, student teaching, and internships can be enhanced by having students work with families and communities. Theory and foundations courses are incomplete without considering the school's relationship to families and community. Even the four special areas mentioned above— multi-cultural issues, classroom management, working with exceptional children, character education—are essentially tied to working with families and communities. For all these reasons and more, it would be hard to argue that partnership preparation *should not* be infused throughout the curriculum. Hence, Shartrand et al. (1997) offer this recommendation: "Integrate training throughout [the] teacher preparation curriculum rather than treating it as an isolated component" (p. 58). Indeed, all other arguments aside, given the mandates of state certification and the marketplace, there simply may not be room in the program for any additional courses.

On the other hand, while infusion may be ideal, it rarely occurs in practice. Not all professors are equally committed to or prepared to work in this area. There are many competing priorities. To decide to infuse it throughout the curriculum means all too often that it doesn't happen, or it happens too briefly or perfunctorily, or it occurs in a disjointed fashion or with undue duplication across courses. While it looks good on paper, and may satisfy state evaluation teams looking to see if the new partnership requirement is satisfied, teachers, administrators, and counselors still graduate insufficiently prepared to work effectively with parents and communities.

Therefore, this author would argue that, unless colleges are seriously committed to integrating partnerships throughout the curriculum in a thoughtful, concerted manner, a required course should be offered if at all possible. If this is not possible, then an optional course should be available for those faculty and students who see partnerships as a priority in professional preparation.

Stated a bit differently, colleges should best handle partnerships in the following order of preference:

1. To actually and effectively infuse partnerships in all or most courses;
2. To offer a separate, required course; or
3. To attempt to infuse it in all courses, but to fail to do so or to do so in a cursory or superficial way..

Pre-service, In-service, and Other Forms of Professional Development

Not all professional development in partnership practices—or in any other area of professional practice—takes place in professional training institutions. One can teach and learn only so much in college or graduate school. As former students often point out, they learn a lot more on the job than in the classroom. No matter how good a job is done of preparing teachers, counselors and administrators to work with families and communities, there will be much more to learn and relearn when they are employed in their field. Aside from unplanned, on-the-job experience, professional development frequently occurs in structured in-service training and professional development workshops.

The National PTA (1997) states that "Effective training is essential. The best models for training are those that provide staff with several opportunities to interact with the issues, work together, and monitor and evaluate progress" (p. 25). The U.S. Department of Education began offering professional development workshops on building school-family partnerships for learning for urban educators in the early 1990s (Moles & D'Angelo, 1993). The American Federation for Teachers (1996) and National Education Association (Rich, 1987) have also developed publications and workshops to help their constituents learn to work in partnership with families.

The National Network of Partnership Schools, based at Johns Hopkins University, coordinates the most widespread effort to help teachers and administrators at the school level learn to work with families and communities, and they provide a well-known, research-based model for doing this (Epstein et al., 1997). This "Partnership Schools" model includes six types of parent involvement (parenting, communicating, volunteering, learning at home, school decision making, and linking with community resources); a representative "action team" in each school to plan, coordinate and implement partnership activities; and a variety of useful planning tools, training materials, evaluation methods and district support structures to enhance success. The model is consistent with the viewpoint that staff development is most effective when it is not done in isolated in-service experiences but integrated into ongoing, systemic reform efforts. Teachers and administrators learn to work in partnership with families and communities as they actually form partnerships. Aside from being employed in schools, the National Network model also is widely used and taught in universities within professional preparation programs.

Components of Professional Preparation

What do teachers, counselors, administrators and other school staff need to know and be able to do when it comes to working with and building partnerships with families and communities? The following chart outlines the knowledge, attitudes and skills that are helpful, and in many cases essential, to professionals who wish to have meaningful partnerships. The chart is a composite of factors highlighted in the various surveys and case studies described above, as well as derived from the wide body of literature on school-family-community relations. The combined weight of this evidence argues that it is not enough for professionals simply *to know* what it means to work in partnerships and why doing so is important. They also need *to want* to do so. And even if they want to do it, they need *to feel* comfortable doing it and *to believe* that they can be successful in their efforts. But even a desire and a sense of efficacy is not enough. Unless one has *the skills* to succeed, that sense of efficacy will not last long. So comprehensive preparation for partnerships must involve a cognitive, affective and behavioral component if it is ultimately to be effective.

This list is by no means complete. Rather the list is meant to be suggestive of the variety of areas that might compose a meaningful preparation for developing partnerships. One might easily modify the list by editing, adding or deleting items. The important thing is that educators seeking to prepare professionals to work in partnerships not only have a list of relevant objectives, but appreciate the wide variety of knowledge areas, attitudes and skills that are useful and often necessary for forming effective partnerships.

Knowledge—understandings and perspectives

- Theoretical understanding of school-family-community relations (knowing one or more theories).
- Paradigm shift in the role of the school professional vis-à-vis the family and community.

- Importance of parent and family involvement.
- Diverse families and the effects of class and culture on parenting practices and home-school relations.
- Understandings that counter stereotypes about families.
- Types of parent and community involvement.
- Research on parent involvement—e.g., parent involvement and student achievement; the effect of school parent involvement practices on parent involvement.
- Implementation models—e.g., the National Network of Partnership Schools model, the "Comer model," etc.

Attitudes

- From receptivity to excitement about working in partnership.
- Comfort with diverse populations.
- Self-knowledge—e.g., how one handles conflict, how one feels about one's own background, how one feels about people from different backgrounds.
- Sense of efficacy in family/community relations.

Skills—how to:

- Establish two-way communication with families--via newsletters, notes, phone calls, surveys, new technology, etc.
- Deal with parents' concerns ["parents" refers to parents and other family members who provide care to children].
- Conduct parent-teacher conferences.
- Solve problems and resolve conflicts with parents.
- Communicate across barriers of language, class and culture.
- Involve parents in their children's learning outside the school—e.g., at home in general, with interactive homework, in the community.
- Enlist parents as volunteers.
- Work with parents on shared decision-making teams.
- Involve community resources in supporting children's education.
- Conduct home visits.
- Help parents develop their parenting skills in support of their child's education.

Knowledge, attitudes, and skills are not discrete categories but have significant overlap. For example, teachers or administrators will be more likely to want to work in partnership with families if they believe they can be effective in doing so. Where does this sense of efficacy come from? It comes in part from a knowledge of the field, including the research that demonstrates that what teachers and schools do to invite parents to become involved really works, that persistent efforts indeed pay off. Efficacy also comes from being comfortable with parents in general and parents of diverse backgrounds in particular. That, in part, comes from knowing and being comfortable with oneself. A sense of efficacy also comes from having the practical skills to work effectively with parents. And at the end of the day, the greatest sense of efficacy comes from actually doing it—from having successful experiences in working with families, when one's knowledge, attitudes and skills all work together to produce satisfying results.

Teaching Methods

How do professional preparation programs go about conveying these many different forms of knowledge, attitudes and skills to teachers, counselors and administrators? The literature describes a wide variety of methods and examples of their use. Again, the inventory below is not intended to be an exhaustive listing, but is meant to suggest the variety of methods that have been found to be helpful in preparing professionals to work in partnership with families and communities. Implicit in this inventory of methods is the idea that, for such training to be effective, it is necessary to go beyond the conventional methods of readings, lectures, discussions and case studies, to hands-on activities and field experiences in self-reflection, cultural diversity, and skill development. To conduct instruction solely on the cognitive level may achieve the knowledge objectives of partnership preparation, but fails to instill the attitudes and skills necessary for success in developing real partnerships.

The teaching methods and assignments listed below can be used in academic courses, but many can also be used in student teaching and internships. These occasions provide excellent opportunities for students to write newsletters to parents, interview parents, visit students' homes, and the like. Indeed, *not to* include such experiences as part of student teaching and interning may suggest to students that building partnerships is not really part of their job as professionals, but just something we talk about in the classroom.

Many of these methods can also be used in in-service training and ongoing professional development. For example, one of the field experiences below involves the students (teachers, administrators or counselors in training) visiting community agencies and institutions. The same activity can be and has been done as part of staff development, with the whole school staff being taken on a bus tour of the community before the school year begins. Parents and community members play a leading role in conducting the tour.

Classroom Methods

- Lectures
- Discussions and debates. Epstein (2001) provides numerous class discussion questions for exploring issues related to partnerships.
- Case studies; case method.
- Role-playing—to develop empathy and build parent conferencing and conflict resolution skills.
- Guest speakers—e.g., parents, teachers and administrators who represent excellent partnership practices; parents who describe their experiences, successful and unsuccessful, in dealing with teachers and schools; home-school coordinators, etc. Guests may speak individually or as panel members.
- Practice—hands-on activities learning to create interactive homework assignments, write newsletters, notes and other forms of communication, etc.
- Student reports—students presenting on partnership-related topics assigned to or chosen by them; students presenting on their field assignments and experiences (see below).

Assignments at Home

- Read required or optional texts.
- Write books reports, reaction statements, or other assignments on the readings.
- Autobiographical Work—understanding one's own family's involvement practices and their cultural context.
- Practice writing class newsletters, notes, and other forms of communication, such as designing a classroom Web site for parents.
- Design a program, project or other intervention to foster positive home-school or school-community collaboration in their current setting. Relate the plan to current

knowledge in the field of school, family and community partnerships.
- Develop a plan for how one will incorporate school, family and community partnerships in one's future teaching, administering, or counseling.
- Develop a school, school district, or state policy on partnerships. Revise, update or improve the current policy in their school or district.
- Other planning and writing assignments associated with field experiences below.

(Assignments can be done as individuals or in groups and teams)

Some of the field experiences and field assignments below are designed to sensitize future teachers, administrators and counselors to the communities and diverse populations with whom they will work. Appreciating the range of family diversity includes understanding various family configurations (single parent, blended, gay and lesbian families, etc.) and the diversity of family ethnic, national and cultural backgrounds. Experiences such as these should be well planned and supervised to insure good learning experiences that lead to greater empathy and understanding rather than simply reinforcing initial stereotypes. Giving students specific questions to ask and things to observe can help improve the experience for all.

Field Experiences and Assignments

- Interview parents from diverse backgrounds.
- Home visits—including visits to homes of students with diverse backgrounds.
- Community visits--as individuals or as a group, students visit community institutions such as community centers, churches, clinics, businesses, etc.
- Community service; working in a community agency.
- Observe shared decision-making teams; interviewing parents and other members on the team.
- Work intensively with one family–students get to know a family in depth, interview children and parents, provide tutoring, help family get needed services, write reports, support the parents, help the child's teacher(s) work more effectively with the child.

- School case study—students study and describe a school in terms of its family-school-community partnership practices or lack thereof.
- Attend, observe or visit--at PTA meetings, school board meetings, parent centers, parent education classes, and other school-related settings where parents are present or where parents and professionals interact.
- Shadow a teacher, counselor, administrator or parent who represents excellent partnership practices; shadow a parent liaison.
- Conduct a parent education class or workshop.
- Do something in their own work setting to foster better school-family relations and evaluate the results. Write up the "experiment" in the form of a research report— background, goals, methodology, results/findings, discussion, etc.
- Observe and describe the school's parking, entrances, signage, hallways, etc. in terms of welcoming, family-friendly qualities, clarity of directions, informativeness, etc.
- Help a teacher or school use voice messaging or Web site technology to communicate with parents or the wider community.
- Design one or more interactive homework assignments. Use the assignment(s) themselves (if teaching) or get a teacher to use them. Describe the results.
- Videotape themselves conducting a teacher-parent conference, parent education class, training session for community volunteers, or other intervention involving school-family or school-community collaboration
- Research family-oriented policies of area employers. Make recommendations for employment policies and practices that encourage school-family-community partnerships.
- Conduct research on partnerships. Perhaps work with the professor/instructor on his or her research.

Additional classroom methods, assignments, and field experiences for preparing professionals to understand and implement school, family and community partnerships may be found in Shartrand et al. (1997) and Epstein (2001).

Sample Courses

In order to offer a more three-dimensional view of many of the ideas and approaches mentioned in this chapter, in this section two courses focusing on school, family and community relations are described in some detail. Epstein, Sanders, and Clark's (1999) survey demonstrated that many such courses are being offered in schools, colleges and departments of education around the United States, although not all may be as comprehensive as these. Several courses have been described elsewhere (e.g., Allexsaht-Snider, Phtiaka, & Gonzalez, 1996; Bermudez & Padron, 1988; Evans-Shilling, 1999). Shartrand and her colleagues (1997) provide many examples of strategies for preparing teachers in family involvement taken from different courses around the country.

Bank Street College of Education

Rena Rice (1998) has pointed out that Bank Street College of Education in New York City has offered a course in school-family relations at least since the 1950s. For example, their 1952–53 catalogue included this course description:

> Parent-Teacher Relations: Designed to help teachers cooperate effectively with parents in the education of children. Special emphasis is placed upon developing better understanding of the dynamics of the parent-teacher relationship. Parent conferences, formation of parent study groups, programming for parent groups, interpretation of community resources and agencies are among topics discussed. Open to parents and teachers.

Today Rice's course at Bank Street continues and builds upon this tradition. It is a required course for all early childhood and elementary teacher education students. Its goal is "to help teachers develop competency in working with families and communities." As in the outline above, competency is defined as tri-partite, including "content knowledge; attitudes/dispositions, and practice/performance skills." Because even experienced teachers often feel apprehension about working with parents, "changing attitudes toward families through developing empathy and establishing rapport, while maintaining appropriate boundaries, is the prime focus of the course, and a thread that runs throughout the content."

To achieve these goals and objectives, Rice uses a variety of teaching strategies: reading; reviewing research on school-family-community collaboration; learning about families of diverse backgrounds; ample use of role-playing to develop empathy and understanding; self-reflection; modeling the kinds of communication skills and respect that should be part of school-family relations; interactive learning methods. One student assignment includes writing an autobiographical essay in which they reflect on their own family's involvement in their and their siblings education and on their own out-of-school educational experiences. Another assignment has students "analyze and critique the family involvement policies, practices (written and unwritten) and attitudes of the settings in which they teach or student teach, and offer rationales and suggestions for changes." In a third assignment, they "design a work plan for family and community collaboration and involvement which they can implement during the coming school year."

University of Rochester

My own course, "Improving School, Family and Community Partnerships," at the Warner Graduate School of Education, University of Rochester, New York, devotes roughly equal time to school-family and school-community partnerships. Students in the school's teaching, counseling, and school administration programs register for this course. The objectives of the course are to help students develop:

1. An *understanding* of the field of school, family and community partnerships—its theories, research and methods;
2. The *beliefs* that (a) establishing partnerships is worth doing and (b) they can succeed in creating such partnerships;
3. The *ability* to implement partnerships; and
4. The *intention* to implement family partnerships in their practice.

Class sessions on school-family partnerships more or less follow the first five of Epstein's (1993) six types of parent involvement: parent education, communicating with parents, parents as volunteers, involving parents in homework; and parent empowerment. I also do a class on parents' rights and other controversial issues. The portion on school-community partnerships devotes class sessions to: school-linked health and social services, community curriculum enrichment, mentoring and tutoring programs, alternative forms of community support and school-business partnerships, school-to work programs, community service learning, and controversial issues in school-community relations. Theory, research, practical methods, attitude exploration, skill development and discussion of required readings on these subjects are woven throughout the sessions.

Because I work closely with the Rochester City School District on implementation and research projects involving parent involvement (e.g., Kirschenbaum, 1999b, 2000), I am able to bring my experience into the classroom. For example, I share our work in developing a strategic plan for parent involvement for the district, implementing the National Network of Partnership Schools model in district schools, studying the effect of parent liaison activity on the attendance of low-attending students, implementing a comprehensive plan for parent education, studying 57 collaborative projects between the university and the city school district (Kirschenbaum & Reagan, 2001).

I also invite resource people into the classroom and take the class on field trips into the community. In the semester just concluding, there were five such events. The class attended the Superintendent of School's "Annual Report" to the community (a major public relations event in which school-family-community partnerships are emphasized) and visited an inner-city elementary school where we met with a teacher who is a master at working with parents and who invited several of her students' parents to join and speak with us that evening. Three other resource persons visited the class: a school principal who has been inspired in gaining community support to develop at his site a Montessori preschool, a school health clinic, a school orchestra, a myriad of parent and community volunteers, and now a major lead-abatement program in the school's neighborhood (Freedman, 1998); the coordinator of volunteer tutoring and mentoring programs for the city school district; and one of the district's most active parent volunteers who also has worked as a "school-parent liaison."

Two of my assignments are similar to Rena Rice's at Bank Street—an autobiographical essay on their own family's involvement in their education and a school-case study. I have my students select a school they are not familiar with; interview a parent, teacher, and administrator in the school to get a range of information and perspectives on school, family and community relations at that school; and write a report which synthesizes the data from their interviews, observations, and any documentary evidence they collected. The case study should address the various types of school-home and school-community partnerships we have studied throughout the course. For a third assignment, I give them a variety of "field experiences" to choose from, such as attending a school board meeting, observing parent-professional interactions on a share decision making team, assisting on one of my research projects, reading an additional book of their choice on school, family, community relations, and others such as those listed in the previous section. Each experience includes a written report or a class presentation.

Although this course will have been taught for five years by the time this chapter is published, ironically, its future is uncertain. It is currently an elective course. As accreditation requirements in our teaching, counseling, and school administration programs place increasing demands on the curriculum, students have less room for electives in their program of study. Some programs now have no electives at all. If this trend continues, there may not be enough students to make the course viable. The dilemma of whether to offer separate courses or infuse partnerships throughout the curriculum may be solved by market forces.

SUMMARY

We may think of the school-family-community partnership "movement" in the United States as having three phases. The first is *research and development.* Beginning in the early 1980s, this phase involved developing the case for partnerships through theory building, research, and the development of practical strategies and models for implementation. This phase will continue for the foreseeable future, because there is much more to be learned about partnerships, including how they work with different populations in different settings, how different forms of partnership produce different outcomes, and how to implement partnerships effectively. Nevertheless, twenty or more years of research and development have succeeded in making the case for family and community involvement in education and demonstrating its feasibility through practical example.

The second phase may be thought of as *policy and initial implementation.* Once research and development had sufficiently demonstrated the importance and feasibility of school, family and community partnerships, two things began to happen simultaneously. New partnership programs began to be implemented widely around the country, and local districts, the federal government, states, and accrediting bodies began to implement policies in support of school, family and community partnerships. Inevitably, as many thousands of schools have developed and implemented partnership programs, some of the implementation has been superficial while other programs have been comprehensive and effective. Similarly, as districts and states write policies to address family and community partnerships in education, some policies are comprehensive and backed by the funding and infrastructure to support partnerships practices, while others policies are good for public relations but are not backed by a serious commitment to implementation.

We are well into the second phase. A widespread national consensus has developed on the importance of family involvement and school, family and community partnerships. Policies and programs have proliferated on a scale barely dreamed of by partnership proponents a decade or more earlier. New programs and policies are coming on line continuously. Yet the question remains: have all these policies and all this initial implementation activity truly made a difference in the *quantity and quality* of school, family and community partnerships across American education? Research is needed to chart the movement's progress, but history reminds us that educational movements often get to the point of widespread acceptance and initial implementation, then a few years later begin to fade from prominence. The crucial test of a movement's longevity and significance is whether the second phase can proceed to the last phase—that of *integration.*

For school, family and community partnerships to become integrated into the fabric of educational and family practice, partnerships must become a significant part of how education does its business. In part, this means implementing the subject of this chapter, that is, a thorough preparation in school, family and community partnerships must become integrated in how professionals are trained in pre-service settings and in ongoing professional development. However, reforming professional education to include partnership preparation, while necessary, is not in itself sufficient. Districts must also develop the funding and infrastructure to support partnership practices. Professional evaluation must meaningfully address teachers' and administrators' partnership practices. And, most important, unions and district administrators must find common ground in supporting partnership practices. This requires agreeing on the proposition that being a teacher no longer means simply teaching students in a classroom. It also means working with families. Only when large numbers of teachers can comfortably and proudly say, "I'm a teacher. I work with students and their families" will partnerships have become integrated in education. And only then will they succeed.

REFERENCES

Allexsaht-Snider, M., Phtiaka, H., & Gonzalez, R. (1996). *International perspectives: Preparing teachers for partnership.* Paper presented at the Education is Partnership Conference, Copenhagen, Denmark, November, Royal Danish School of Education.

American Federation of Teachers. (1996). *Parent and family involvement* [Manual]. Washington, DC: Educational Research and Dissemination Program/Author.

Ammon, M. S. (1999). Introduction: Many hands, multiple voices. In M. S. Ammon (Ed.), *Joining hands: Preparing teachers to make meaningful home-school connections.* Sacramento: California Department of Education and California Commission on Teacher Credentialing.

Bermudez, A., & Padron, Y. (1988). University-school collaboration that increases minority parent involvement. *Educational Horizons, 66,* 83–86.

California Commission on Teacher Credentialing. (1996, June). *Preparing educators for partnerships with families: Report of the advisory task force on educator preparation for parent involvement.* Sacramento, CA: Author.

California Commission on Teacher Credentialing and the California Department of Education. (1997, January). *California standards for the teaching profession.* Sacramento, CA: Author.

Chavkin, N.F. (1991). Uniting families and schools: social workers helping teachers through inservice training. *School Social Work Journal, 15,* 1–10.

Chavkin, N.F., & Williams, D.L. (1988). Critical issues in teacher training for parent involvement. *Educational Horizons, 66,* 87–89.

Decker, L.E., Gregg, G., & Decker, V.A. (1994). *Getting parents involved in their children's education.* Arlington, VA: American Association of School Administrators.

Epstein, J. (1995). School, family and community partnerships: Caring for the children we share. *Phi Delta Kappan, 77*(9), 701–712.

Epstein, J. (2001). *School, family and community partnerships: Preparing educators and improving schools.* Boulder, CO: Westview Press.

Epstein, J., Coates, K., Salinas, M., Sanders, M., & Simon, B. (1997). *School, family and community partnerships: Your handbook for action.* Thousand Oaks, CA: Corwin Press.

Epstein, J., Sanders, M.G., & Clark, L.A. (1999, February). *Preparing educators for school-family-community partnerships: Results of a national survey of colleges and universities* [Report No. 34]. Baltimore, MD: Center for Research on the Education of Students Placed At Risk/Johns Hopkins University.

Evans-Schilling, D. (1999). Preparing educational leaders to work effectively with families: The parent power project. In M.S. Ammon (Ed.), *Joining hands: Preparing teachers to make meaningful home-school connections.* Sacramento: California Department of Education and California Commission on Teacher Credentialing.

Freedman, M. (1998). The power of partnerships in a primary school. *Contemporary Pediatrics, 15*(11), 164–176.

Gray, S.F. (2001). *A compilation of state mandates for home school partnership education in pre-service teacher training programs.* Unpublished manuscript, Pepperdine University.

Hiatt-Michael, D. (2000, April). *Parent involvement as a component of teacher education programs in California.* Paper presented at American Educational Research Association Annual Meeting, New Orleans, LA.

Hiatt-Michael, D. (2001, April). *Preparing pre-service teachers for home-school partnerships across the United States.* Paper presented at American Educational Research Association Annual Meeting, Seattle, WA.

Hinz, L., Clarke, J., & Nathan, J. (1992). *A survey of parent involvement course offerings in Minnesota's undergraduate preparation programs.* Minneapolis: Center for School Change, Humphrey Institute of Public Affairs, University of Minnesota.

Houston, W.R., & Williamson, J.L. (1990). *Perceptions of their preparation by 42 Texas elementary school teachers compared with their responses as student teachers.* Houston: Texas Association of Colleges for Teacher Education.

Katz, L., & Bauch, J.P. (2001). Preparing pre-service teachers for family involvement: A model for higher education. In S. Redding, & L. G. Thomas (Eds.), *The community of the school* (pp. 185–204). Lincoln, IL: The Academic Development Institute.

Kirschenbaum, H. (1999a). *From public relations to partnerships.* Washington, DC: The Communitarian Network.

Kirschenbaum, H. (1999b). Night and day: Parent involvement at School 43. *Principal, 78*(3), 20–23.

Kirschenbaum, H. (2000, January). The principal's view [of parent involvement]. *High School Magazine, 7*(5), 26–29.

Kirschenbaum, H., & Reagan, C. (2001, September). University-school partnerships: An analysis of 57 collaborations between a mid-sized university and an urban school district. *Urban Education*, 36(4), 479–504.

McAfee, O. (1987). Improving home-school relations: Implications for staff development. *Education and Urban Society, 19*(2).

McBride, B. (1990). *Preservice teachers' attitudes toward parental involvement* [mimeo]. Athens, GA: University of Georgia.

Moles, O., & D'Angelo, D. (Eds.). (1993). *Building school-family partnerships for learning: Workshops for urban educators.* Washington, DC: Office of Educational Research and Improvement, U.S. Department of Education.

National Council for Accreditation of Teacher Education. (2000, March 31). *NCATE 2000 Standards Adopted by the Unit Accreditation Board.* Washington,DC: Author.

National PTA. (1997). *National standards for parent/family involvement programs.* Chicago: Author.

New York State. (1999). *Registration of programs leading to classroom teaching certificates.* Albany: State Education Department, University of the State of New York.

Rice, R. (1998, Winter). Preparing teachers to work with families and communities. *Family, School, Community Partnerships*, pp. 3–4.

Rich, D. (1987). *Teachers and parents: An adult-to-adult approach.* Washington, DC: National Education Association.

Shartrand, A.M., Weiss, H.B., Kreider, H.M, & Lopez, M.E. (1997). *New skills for new schools: Preparing teachers in family involvement.* Cambridge, MA: Harvard Family Research Project, Harvard School of Education.

U.S. Department of Education. (1994a). *Goals 2000: National education goals.* Washington, DC: Author.

U.S. Department of Education. (1994b). *Strong families, strong schools: Building community partnerships for learning.* Washington, DC: Author

U.S. Department of Education. (1997). *Overcoming barriers to family involvement in Title I schools.* Washington, DC: Author.

White, L.J. (1997). Preface. In A. Shartrand, H. Weiss, H. Kreider, & M. Lopez (Eds.), *New skills for new schools: Preparing teachers in family involvement.* Cambridge, MA: Harvard Family Research Project, Harvard School of Education.